Aldous Huxley
(courtesy of Mrs Laura Huxley, Los Angeles)

"Human Potentialities"

Studien zu Aldous Huxley & zeitgenössischer Kultur
Studies in Aldous Huxley & Contemporary Culture

herausgegeben von

Prof. Dr. Bernfried Nugel
(Englisches Seminar der
Westfälischen Wilhelms-Universität Münster)

und

Dr. Gerhard Wagner
(Englisches Seminar der
Westfälischen Wilhelms-Universität Münster)

Band 13

LIT

Jerome Meckier

Aldous Huxley and Utopia

LIT

Cover Picture: Erwin J. Löhr

This book is printed on acid-free paper.

Bibliographic information published by the Deutsche Nationalbibliothek
The Deutsche Nationalbibliothek lists this publication in the Deutsche Nationalbibliografie; detailed bibliographic data are available on the Internet at http://dnb.dnb.de.

ISBN 978-3-643-91521-4 (pb)
ISBN 978-3-643-96521-9 (PDF)

A catalogue record for this book is available from the British Library.

Contact:
Fresnostr. 2 D-48159 Münster
Tel. +49 (0) 2 51-62 03 20 Fax +49 (0) 2 51-23 19 72
e-Mail: lit@lit-verlag.de https://www.lit-verlag.de

Distribution:

In the UK: Global Book Marketing, e-mail: mo@centralbooks.com
In North America: Independent Publishers Group, e-mail: orders@ipgbook.com

“HUMAN POTENTIALITIES”:
STUDIEN ZU ALDOUS HUXLEY & ZEITGENÖSSISCHER KULTUR /
STUDIES IN ALDOUS HUXLEY & CONTEMPORARY CULTURE

is a series focused on the writings of Aldous Huxley, his ideas and their cultural context. Throughout his works he confronts us with the limits and possibilities of man’s development. It is particularly in his later writings that the term “human potentialities” assumes a key-position. The individual, he maintains, should actualize his potential in relation to society and culture. Huxley’s spectrum of ideas is culled from a wide range of different fields. He draws on the natural sciences and comparative religion, on economics and philosophy, art, politics, psychology, ecology, history, sociology, not to mention mysticism and critique of utopian thought. Hence the series is not confined to monographs on the literary significance of Aldous Huxley, but also presents a forum that aims to establish a dialogue between literary scholarship and other disciplines. The term “contemporary culture” refers not only to Huxley’s standpoint but also to the views of the present-day reader.

We welcome dissertations, *Habilitationsschriften* and other monographs in German or English. As to their layout, they should follow the *MLA Handbook for Writers of Research Papers* (5th ed., New York, 1997). A special style sheet is available on request. Please send all inquiries to: Prof. Dr. Bernfried Nugel, Westfälische Wilhelms-Universität, Englisches Seminar, Centre for Aldous Huxley Studies, Johannisstr. 12–20, 48143 Münster, Germany; phone +49-251-83-24828; fax +49-251-83-24827, or e-mail: <nugel@uni-muenster.de>.

Die Reihe "HUMAN POTENTIALITIES": STUDIEN ZU ALDOUS HUXLEY & ZEITGENÖSSISCHER KULTUR / STUDIES IN ALDOUS HUXLEY & CONTEMPORARY CULTURE umfasst Arbeiten über den Schriftsteller und Denker Aldous Huxley und sein kulturelles Umfeld. In seinem gesamten Oeuvre hat Huxley durchgängig die Frage nach den Entfaltungsmöglichkeiten des Menschen aufgeworfen und mit dem Begriff „human potentialities" vor allem in seinem Spätwerk Überlegungen verbunden, die die Fähigkeit des Menschen betreffen, sein eigenes Potential besser auszuschöpfen und es als Individuum und gesellschaftliches Wesen kulturschaffend einzusetzen. Hierbei bezog Huxley prinzipiell Erkenntnisse und Vorstellungsweisen aus einem breiten Spektrum unterschiedlicher Gebiete ein, so aus Naturwissenschaft und Religion, aus Wirtschaft und Philosophie, aus Kunst, Politik, Psychologie, Geschichte, Soziologie, Mystik, Utopiekritik u. a. m. In diesem Sinne nimmt die Reihe nicht nur literaturwissenschaftliche Studien zu Huxley und seinem literarhistorischen Kontext auf, sondern steht als Forum auch solchen Arbeiten offen, die einen Dialog zwischen Literaturwissenschaft und anderen Disziplinen anstreben. Der Begriff „zeitgenössische Kultur" bezieht sich dabei sowohl auf Huxleys eigene Position als auch auf die des heutigen Lesers.

Willkommen sind Dissertationen, Habilitationsschriften und andere Monographien in deutscher oder englischer Sprache. Für die formale Gestaltung sei auf das *MLA Handbook for Writers of Research Papers* (5th ed., New York, 1997) verwiesen. Auf Wunsch wird ein besonderes *style sheet* zugesandt. Alle Anfragen bitte an: Prof. Dr. Bernfried Nugel, Westfälische Wilhelms-Universität, Englisches Seminar, Aldous-Huxley-Forschungsstelle, Johannisstr. 12-20, 48143 Münster; Telefon +49-251-83-24828; Fax +49-251-83-24827, oder E-mail: <nugel@uni-muenster.de>.

General Editor's Notice

After the deeply mourned death of co-editor Lothar Fietz (see the In memoriam in *AHA*, 19 [2019]), to whose expertise the series "Human Potentialities" had been indebted for more than twenty years, a change has become necessary on the editorial board: Dr. Gerhard Wagner has kindly agreed to take Lothar Fietz' place, and I gratefully welcome him as new co-editor.

Bernfried Nugel

For Helen Brozyniak
(1914–2002)

Contents

Introduction and Acknowledgements 1

Chapter One
Erewhon to *Island* 5

Chapter Two
Cure Scenes 99

Chapter Three
Golf in *Brave New World* 123

Chapter Four
Four Notes on *Brave New World* 133

Chapter Five
"My Hypothetical Islanders": The Role of Islands in *Brave New World* and *Island* 149

Chapter Six
Enemies of Utopia: Young Krishnamurti and Madame Blavatsky in *Island* 171

Chapter Seven
Thanatopsis / Thanatology in *Brave New World* and *Island* 187

Chapter Eight
Fabre, Wheeler, and the Mantises in *Island* 201

Works Consulted 207

Index of Names and Titles (*compiled by Uwe Rasch*) 223

Introduction and Acknowledgements

The argument: within the utopian Tradition that begins with Plato and starts over again with Sir Thomas More, a modern British Cycle exists. It runs for nearly a century from Samuel Butler's *Erewhon* (1872) to Aldous Huxley's *Island* (1962). Within this cycle of positive and negative futures, the golden age for the utopian novel,[1] Competition is paramount; utopists compete to produce the most persuasive picture of what the future might, or should, be like. It is tempting to condense discussion to "The Two Futures: A. F. 632 and 1984," i.e., Huxley and Orwell (Firchow, *End*, 117–28); but between *Erewhon* and *Island* lie numerous futures, each, whether optimistic or pessimistic, allegedly authoritative. The modern literary utopia establishes its vision of things to come while refuting the notions of one or more of its rivals, thus becoming statement and counterstatement simultaneously.

"What else is satire," asks one commentator, "but a way of redescribing things in order to make them look bad?" (Greenberg, 9) "Redescribing" is the important word; it connotes revaluing. As practiced by modern utopists, revaluation is a form of satire in which the "things" being redescribed, i.e., 'made to look bad,' are rival versions of the future. Huxley substitutes the World State for H. G. Wells's World-state, which Yevgeny Zamiatin previously replaced with the One State. World State, World-state, One State—each claims to describe the future but the future cannot validate all three. George Orwell's Oceania contradicts the brave new world and tries to outdo Zamiatin's novel simultaneously. Always the revalued utopia is found to be ridiculous or undesirable, often both. *Brave New World* tries to make Wells's *A Modern Utopia* seem preposterous. Pala, in *Island*, is the brave new world redone positively. Huxley in effect reaffirms his earlier novel as a travesty of perfection. If Pala is the brave new world done right, then the brave new world is even more clearly the perfect place done all wrong. The creation of Pala reveals the brave new world's glaring imperfections more clearly. *Island* redescribes things to make the World State look worse in 1962 than it did thirty years earlier. In every case, a rival utopia is targeted and seen in its true nature thanks to its counterstatement, which the revaluator presents as the truth, usually a deflation of another so-called perfect place or, sometimes, an improvement upon it.

A salient feature of the major interactive utopias published between *Erewhon* and *Island* is the struggle between Hypothesis and Prediction: which should a utopian novel be? Is it an entertaining possibility to discuss, an actual recommendation, or an urgent warning? Jokingly, Samuel Butler's

Erewhon inaugurated a fateful shift from hypothesis to prediction. Ninety years later, attempting to restore a balance, Huxley's *Island* moves the literary utopia back towards the hypothetical.

Tradition, Cycle, Competition, Hypothesis, Prediction—these are the key terms. Krishan Kumar found "no one pattern or theme in the revival of utopia" that he agrees took place after 1870 (Kumar, 65), but here are no fewer than five of its preoccupations. Aldous Huxley proves exceptionally useful in studying them; before bringing the cycle to a close, he made three significant contributions to the modern British utopian tradition at roughly fifteen-year intervals. Collectively, *Brave New World* (1932), *Ape and Essence* (1948), and *Island* (1962) certify him as a major voice in the twentieth-century debate concerning the nature, uses, and justification of utopian speculation, i.e., its form and function. Of twentieth-century novelists who spend much of their careers as utopists coming to terms with the change of direction from hypothesis to prediction that Butler originated, none scrutinizes it more intensely, or with graver reservations, than Aldous Huxley.

Chapter one expands material from "Aldous Huxley and Utopia: Five Assertions," which appeared in *Aldous Huxley: East-West Centenary Essays*, ed. A. K. Tripathy (New Delhi: Creative Books, 2008), 193–200, and "What the Books Were Always Saying," a review essay on *The Dystopian Impulse in Modern Literature*, *ANQ*, 9 (Spring, 1996), 39–48. Chapter two, which first came out as "Aldous Huxley and the Cure Scene in Modern Literary Utopias," *AHA*, 19 (2019), 243–66, traces the development of the cure scene from its humble beginnings in *Erewhon* to its nearly novel-length deployment in *Island*. A succession of protagonists struggle to avoid being converted or exterminated by a series of dystopian societies ironically less healthy than they are. Only in *Island* do the Palanese achieve a genuine cure when they nurture Will Farnaby back from despondency to the brink of enlightenment. Chapter three, "Golf in *Brave New World*," appeared in *The Perennial Satirist: Essays in Honour of Bernfried Nugel*, ed. Hermann J. Real and Peter E. Firchow (Münster: Lit Verlag, 2005), 235–43. Huxley capitalized upon the growing preoccupation with golf in the 1920s, finding it the perfectly mindless game with which to pacify brave new worlders from the end of their workday until bedtime. The four interconnecting "Notes" in chapter four come from *AHA*, 17/18 (2017/2018), 209–24. Why does Huxley withhold the surnames of the Savage's parents and never name the author of "A New Theory of Biology"?

Is Bernard Marx actually sent off to Iceland? "'My Hypothetical Islanders': The Role of Islands in *Brave New World* and *Island*" (chapter five) is reprinted from *AHA*, 12/13 (2012/2013), 319–40. In *Brave New World*, while exile to an island is punishment, it also seems at times a reward. With Pala, Huxley returns to More's ideal of utopia as an island that is perfect place and no place; Pala's attractive society proves unsustainable and becomes more of a hypothesis than a prescription. An earlier version of "Enemies of Utopia: Young Krishnamurti and Madame Blavatsky in *Island*" (chapter six) was originally published in *AHA*, 10/11 (2010/2011), 299–315. Huxley drew upon Krishnamurti's early years under the influence of Madame Blavatsky and theosophy to create Murugan and his mother, the Rani, the two principal internal conspirators responsible for Pala's demise. Chapter seven, "Thanatopsis/Thanatology in *Brave New World* and *Island*," first came out in *AHA*, 16 (2016), 237–50. The brave new world does everything possible to distract its citizens from an awareness of their mortality. It also conditions them not to take anyone's death, including their own, seriously. However, the Palanese raise thanatology, the art of dying, to a science. Huxley's perfect place is one that best prepares its inhabitants for leaving it. "Fabre, Wheeler, and the Mantises in *Island*" (chapter eight) appeared in *Notes and Queries*, 55 (December 2008), 515–18. The work of Fabre and Wheeler inspired the grisly scene in which a female mantis devours her mate much as Rendang swallows Pala.

I have tried to minimize the reuse of comments from my previous studies of Aldous Huxley unless the material is recycled for new purposes. However, some repetition has proven unavoidable inasmuch as there are many overlapping concerns. Readers of this volume will benefit from prior knowledge, or a subsequent reading, of *Aldous Huxley: Satire and Structure* (London: Chatto & Windus, 1969), especially 175–84, 196–202, and *Aldous Huxley: Modern Satirical Novelist of Ideas* (Münster: Lit Verlag, 2006), chapters 8–13, 15–17.[2] For encouragement, I am especially grateful to Professor Dr. Bernfried Nugel, with whom I co-edit the *Aldous Huxley Annual*, and to the late Professor Peter Firchow, a fellow Huxley scholar and long-term friend. Alison Johnson typed the manuscript. Tirelessly, Gerhard Wagner edited it. Uwe Rasch formatted it and compiled the index.

---

[1] According to Merlin Coverley, the Golden Age of Utopia was 1790–1920, after which faith in utopias, which he calls "impossible dreams," died (Coverley, 163).

[2] Also pertinent are Jerome Meckier, *Aldous Huxley, from Poet to Mystic* (Münster: Lit Verlag, 2011), and the essays in Jerome Meckier (ed.), *Critical Essays on Aldous Huxley* (New York: G. K. Hall, 1996).

Chapter One

EREWHON TO *ISLAND*

Each of Aldous Huxley's three utopias corrects a predecessor. According to his own classifications, one should consider the first two "negative," the last one "positive."[1] Like Samuel Butler's, Huxley's interest in the genre started as a joke but in his case soon became a life-long preoccupation, culminating with his last completed novel the year before he died. Butler wrote *Erewhon* to poke fun at Darwin. Huxley began *Brave New World* (1932) to spite H. G. Wells. *Ape and Essence* (1948) he wrote to remedy omissions from his first utopia. In *Island* (1962), he created a positive alternative to the brave new world by enlarging upon hints in his first and second negative utopias.

Brave New World was conceived as a satirical reply to H. G. Wells. Huxley claimed that his younger self—presumably "the amused Pyrrhonic aesthete" identified as "the author of the fable" (*BNW*, vii)[2]—was "allergic" to the older writer's overly optimistic pronouncements. In particular, Huxley writes,

> the reading of *Men Like Gods* evoked in me an almost pathological reaction in the direction of cynical anti-idealism. So much so that, before I finished the book, I had resolved to write a derisive parody of this most optimistic of Wells's Utopias. But when I addressed myself to the problem of creating a negative Nowhere, a utopia in reverse, I found the subject so fascinatingly pregnant with so many kinds of literary and psychological possibilities that I quite forgot *Men Like Gods* and addressed myself in all seriousness to the task of writing the book that was later to be known as *Brave New World*. ("Utopias," 1)

Huxley describes perfectly the revaluation process. Competitions within the modern British utopian tradition crystalize when a utopist resolves to "reverse" (i.e., contradict) an existing work and the reversal, in Huxley's case a "derisive parody," takes on a life of its own without ceasing to be any less revaluative. In effect, Huxley wrote two books at one sitting. *Brave New World* is his vision of the future that, not coincidentally, happens to rewrite and refute H. G. Wells. Or it is a repudiation of Wells that also puts forth Huxley's unsettling vision of things to come. One can study *Brave New World* as either in turn or as both at once.

Huxley gave a similar account of the novel's inception on two other occasions. In a 1958 lecture about "A Second Visit to a Future World,"[3] he recalled how Wells had "irritated" him to the point where he resolved to write "something comical against [his] ideas" ("Second," 23). He told interviewers from *The Paris Review* that *Brave New World* "started out as a parody of H. G. Wells's *Men Like Gods*, but gradually it got out of hand and turned into something quite different" (W/F, 198). Actually, *Brave New World* can still be read as an inspired parody of Wells's positive forecasts generally, not just of *Men Like Gods* (1923). As preservers of "Stability" (*BNW*, 1), Huxley's deceptively benevolent World Controllers, for example, are a negative reworking of Wells's *samurai* in *A Modern Utopia* (1905); these impossibly selfless technocrats administer a technologically advanced society that is scientifically organized and constantly improving. Huxley's World State is H. G. Wells's World-state reconfigured as the static, authoritarian regime he thought it would become. Reusing many of Wells's criteria for a perfect place, Huxley obtains very different results. Despite an abundance of drugs and sex and a populace conditioned to consider itself happy at all times, every brave new worlder's development has been arrested at a predetermined point far short of humanity's evolutionary potential.[4]

As did Wells, Huxley recognized the utopia as a forum for intellectual discussion, hence an extension of the novel of ideas. Whether the ideas should be offered as actual predictions—i.e., proposals, recommendations, indeed, veritable blueprints—was a vexing question that Huxley struggled with for the next thirty years. *Brave New World* he fashions into a modern satirical novel of ideas in which to ridicule the intellectual qualifications of Wells, Freud, Pavlov, Sir Alfred Mond, and Henry Ford (among others). Their ideas, as synthesized in the World State, pose a threat to human nature, thanks to a mechanistic, anti-humanist bias Huxley believed they all share.[5] By contrast, *Island* bristles with ideas that he found attractive and eagerly combined. But they are presented as interlocking hypotheses for joint consideration, not as a recipe for perfection that Huxley expected to see enacted. On the contrary, he doubted a society such as Pala could survive even if it came into existence.

Dubbing *Brave New World* "a negative Nowhere, a Utopia in reverse" ("Utopias," 1), Huxley defined a brand-new category: a utopia that simultaneously revaluates the genre that Sir Thomas More's *Utopia* devised while also subverting more recent partisan proclamations such as Wells's. Positive utopia, Huxley concludes in 1927, is just a "compensatory dream" (*PS*, x) from escapists who create alternative worlds because they cannot cope with a depressing reality. Wells's dreams, among the rosiest, Huxley deemed risible. Cynical, anti-idealistic, *Brave New World* may be classified as any of the following: negative utopia (adverse view of the future), parodic utopia (irreverent response to Wells), and ultimately, anti-utopia (dismissal of positive utopian writing in toto).[6]

When the first atomic bomb exploded at Alamogordo, New Mexico, on 16 July 1945, Huxley realized he had overlooked a grim possibility: long before the World State arrives in A. F. 632, civilization might destroy itself. *Ape and Essence* opens in "February 2108," one hundred and sixty years into the future from its publication in 1948.[7] It is "more than a century" since the Third World War; "the danger" from radioactivity is "finally over" (*AE*, 28). Huxley's post-nuclear-war society, located in the vicinity of Los Angeles, still has more than four hundred years to recover from virtual self-annihilation and turn into the pleasure-laden brave new world. But *Ape and Essence* does not make sense as a prequel. All traces of Henry Ford and Sir Alfred Mond, for instance, have been obliterated. There can be no Our Ford, no Mustapha Mond as "Resident Controller of Western Europe" (*BNW*, 26). All of Western Europe has been blown to bits. Only isolated New Zealand, which sends a search party to southern California to look for survivors, has escaped the nuclear holocaust intact. Neither prequel nor sequel, *Ape and Essence* amounts to an alternative hypothesis to *Brave New World* and, by coincidence, to Orwell's *Nineteen Eighty-Four*, which was published the following year. Abominations such as Big Brother, double-think, face crime and Oceania (part prisoner-of-war compound, part extermination camp, part gulag) are all equally unnecessary in a postapocalyptic society that Huxley doubtless considered worse than any of the above.

That "*Brave New World* contains no reference to nuclear fission," Huxley admitted, is "one vast and obvious failure of foresight," especially since he concedes that "atomic energy" had been a hot topic "in the late twenties" (*BNW*, x).[8] This "oversight may not be excusable," Huxley thinks, but "it can be easily explained" (*BNW*, x). In *Brave New World*, he claims, the "advancement of science," the "triumphs of physics, chemistry and engineering are tacitly taken for granted" so that the novel can deal with "the application to human beings" of future discoveries "in biology, physiology and psychology"; these will bring about "the really revolutionary revolution," undesirable changes in human nature itself (*BNW*, x).

But the revised society in post-nuclear-war California is the awful result of perversions of "the sciences of matter," as opposed to "the sciences of life," from which Huxley, in 1932, apprehended the greater danger (*BNW*, x). When the baboon-like armies square off in the war that ends in nuclear devastation, each side flaunts its own Einstein "on a leash" (*AE*, 28–9). "Baboon technicians" on both sides release "aerosols" and "two streams of yellow fog start toward one another" (*AE*, 32). Biologists, pathologists, and physiologists rush to produce cannisters of even "deadlier" germs. If scientists become subservient to political squabbles, Huxley warns, World

War III will amount to "the death, by suicide, of twentieth-century science" (*AE*, 40).

There are no *samurai* in twenty-second-century America, no Alphas, just degenerates worse than Wells's ape-like Morlocks in *The Time Machine*. They make "the sign of the horns" instead of "the sign of the T" used by brave new worlders to commemorate Henry Ford's automotive achievements. Brave new worlders are much scarier than *Ape and Essence*'s devil worshippers, however, in that they rejoice in their own degradation. From the "Foreword" to *Brave New World*, written prior to *Ape and Essence* but not published in England until two years after it, one senses that Huxley, though clearly apologetic concerning his failure to foresee the atomic bomb, nevertheless greatly prefers his first negative utopia to his second, which critics, too, find less impressive.

Recognizing a second omission, Huxley regrets not having offered the Savage "a third alternative" to the brave new world, on the one hand, and a primitive Indian village on the other. He felt he ought to have included "a community of exiles and refugees from the Brave New World, living within the borders of the Reservation" (*BNW*, ix). Like Huxley by 1946, this community would be centered on "man's Final End," the achievement of "unitive knowledge" with "the transcendent Godhead or Brahman," the first principle of existence (*BNW*, ix). The Savage, Huxley decides, should be given a chance to pursue "the immanent Tao or Logos," the Atman or Godhead within him that is identical with Brahman, the Godhead without (*BNW*, ix). Such a redemptive conclusion, unfortunately, would compromise the major counterpoint in the novel: Fordian London versus a parodically Lawrentian Malpais, each of which rests on a set of beliefs that Huxley repudiated as a way of life. It would have watered down the idea that life consists of impossible choices, pointless contradictions, an idea that the cynical thirty-eight-year-old satirical novelist of ideas, the Pyrrhonic aesthete, had brought to "philosophical completeness" in 1932 (*BNW*, ix), even though the fifty-two-year-old author of the "Foreword" now thought his novel lacked this quality.

Towards the conclusion of *Ape and Essence*, Huxley provides Alfred Poole and Loola the option he denied John Savage. "'[R]unaways from Southern California,'" the "two fugitives" hope to find refuge "'up north'" near Fresno[9] in a Lawrentian community of "'Hots'" (*AE*, 152, 103), people who enjoy having sex year round instead of during the annual five-week mating period rigidly observed in the south. Here is the "community of exiles and refugees" Huxley regretted leaving out of *Brave New World*. It also serves as the prototype for Pala, the positive utopian society in *Island*.

Open-minded about sex, the Palanese practice the "'yoga of love'"; contraceptives are distributed monthly to every household.[10] They also adhere to Vedanta, the so-called perennial philosophy, predicated on the belief that "'thou are That,'" namely, that, as Huxley puts it in *The Perennial Philosophy* (1946), "the Atman, or immanent eternal Self, is one with Brahman, the Absolute Principle of all existence" (*I*, 74; *PP*, 8). As yet, Poole and Loola are merely year-round lovers; but they have begun to seek "an understanding" of "the wordless doctrine of the Pure in Heart" (*AE*, 149). On Pala, Huxley's perfect place, their search comes to fruition: D. H. Lawrence and the Buddha, sexual emancipation and spiritual enlightenment, go hand in hand.

Huxley described *Island* to the *Paris Review* as a "fantasy," "a kind of reverse *Brave New World*, about a society in which real efforts are made to realize human potentialities" (W/F, 198). Thus *Island* is a reversal of a "Utopia in reverse" ("Utopias," 1). Huxley confessed that "the general notion" for his positive utopia was "already in the back of [his] mind" when he wrote the 1946 "Foreword" to *Brave New World* (W/F, 198). Huxley's first utopia was a rebuttal of Wells and his third a conscientious reversal of his first—not an apology to Wells but a positive reworking of Huxley's own negative material. Nearly everything brave new worlders do wrong the Palanese get right, be it sexual behavior, drug use, modification of family life, or approaches to education; in short, as the consummate reviser, Huxley pits his third utopia against his first, point counter point.[11]

Moksha medicine in place of *soma*, Mutual Adoption Clubs instead of dissolving the family—major corrections of the brave new world's enormities abound in Pala. But several of Huxley's lesser redoings from negatives to positives are worth mentioning. For example, the Central London Hatchery and Conditioning Centre contains the Social Predestination Room wherein each bottle-baby, having been transferred from its test-tube and properly labeled, is "'predestined in detail'" (*BNW*, 6–7). That is, it is assigned its caste and given its job or occupation. Predestinators stay busy "'making people like their inescapable social destiny'" (*BNW*, 12). We "'predestine and condition,'" Mr. Foster explains. "'We decant our babies as socialized human beings, as Alphas or Epsilons, as future sewage workers or future'" World Controllers (*BNW*, 9–10). Pala, Susila MacPhail tells Will, emphasizes "'Self-Determination. Alias Destiny Control'" (*I*, 95). Only a part of one's destiny is controllable, Susila concedes, but in elementary school, Palanese children are taught "'how to press [their] own buttons,'" i.e., to visualize what they want to happen and move forwards, whether the goal is some facet of personality development or progress towards a desired career. The Palanese "'"systematically teach DC,'" destiny control or self-conditioning.

Examples like the above suggest that just as Huxley examined Wells's novels for incidents to parody, he also carefully reviewed *Brave New World* in search of policies and practices to redo affirmatively. Instead of a "caste system" that produces an air-tight "'"Class Consciousness,'" Palanese children are classified by physique and temperament, but only to assist the "'"actualization'" of every boy and girl into "'"full-blown human beings'" (*BNW*, 38, 39; *I*, 207).

"'"Short cuts to memorizing'" (*I*, 210) worthwhile facts and figures replace sleep-teaching. Conditioning, contraceptives dispensed by the state, eugenics, population control—all are common to both Pala and the World State; sometimes the means in both places seem similar, sometimes the ends, but in the brave new world, one (or both) is usually ignoble, formulated without concern for the individual's "Final End" (*BNW*, ix).

Island also reversed, or at least arrested, the modern trend towards prediction in British utopian writing. Making it "an imaginary island" (W/F, 198) like Sir Thomas More's in *Utopia*, Huxley ceased to be an anti-utopian, a foe of the genre as a whole. Instead, he restored the idea of the perfect place as a Nowhere, a purely hypothetical society whose merits are meant to be discussed in comparison with other utopian suggestions and, of course, in light of the status quo. "I'm afraid it must end with paradise lost—if one is to be realistic," he told interviewers (W/F, 198). Sadly, Pala does not survive the novel. By the time Will Farnaby, an uninvited guest, learns fully to appreciate it, Pala's fate has been sealed: neighboring Rendang overruns the island. Paradoxically, Huxley insists that his "fantasy" conclude realistically, i.e., with a return to harsh reality. The reverse of a negative Nowhere, Pala is a fantastic place that must inevitably come to grief when the perennial Pyrrhonic aesthete, a persona Huxley never completely discarded, reasserts himself, interrupting and overruling the compensatory dreamer.

Huxley's determination to have the last word with Orwell about the future is evident throughout his threefold response to *Nineteen Eighty-Four*: 1) the 1946 "Foreword" to *Brave New World*; 2) the curious fan letter to Orwell for 21 October 1949; 3) the opening pages of *Brave New World Revisited* (1958). *Island*, though not aimed directly at Orwell, is a fourth, this time positive, alternative to both Huxley's World State and the latter's Oceania.[12]

The "Foreword" to the 1950 volume of *Brave New World* in "the Collected Edition" is dated 1946, written just after World War II but a couple of years before either *Ape and Essence* or *Nineteen Eighty-Four* appeared. Huxley had to explain that the recent conflict was not an obstacle to the establishment of a World State. "What has happened in the painful interlude [i.e., between 1932 and 1946] to confirm or invalidate the forecasts of 1931?" he asks (*BNW*, ix). "A book about the future," he concedes, "can interest us only if its prophecies look as though they might conceivably come true" (*BNW*, ix). This is a startling admission for a novelist whose dystopia can be said to parody the idea of forecasting per se, not just H. G. Wells.

Huxley's strategy seems disingenuous. He dismisses the period from 1931 to 1946 as "a painful interlude," no more than a short pause; then he goes on to justify the omission from *Brave New World* of any references to "nuclear fission" (*BNW*, x). *Ape and Essence* was completed in February 1948 (see *L*, 17). By 1950, Huxley had already issued it to deal with the possibility that we might "blow ourselves to bits and so put an end to history" (*BNW*, x), which would make all prediction irrelevant.[13] Having brushed aside a world war and the atomic bomb, Huxley felt free to remind readers of the "Foreword" that *Brave New World* was not the result of "triumphs" in physics, chemistry, and engineering, the sciences of matter pre-eminent in making war and nuclear bombs; the World State results from advances in "biology, physiology and psychology," the so-called "sciences of life" that "modify the natural forms and expressions of life itself" (*BNW*, x), that change, in other words, what it means to be human.

The "Foreword" deplores "the tendency toward statism" but insists "the new totalitarianisms" will not "resemble the old," as does Orwell's (*BNW*, xii–xiii).[14] "Government by clubs and firing squads [...] is not merely inhumane," future dictators will decide; it is also inefficient. "A really efficient totalitarian state," Huxley opines, "would be one in which the all-powerful executive of political bosses and their army of managers control a population of slaves who do not have to be coerced, because they love their servitude" (*BNW*, xiii), unlike citizens of Oceania, who must be coerced constantly. Having dismissed Orwell, Huxley goes on to explain how *soma*, hypnopaedia, and a "scientific caste system" will "facilitate the task of the managers."

The 1949 letter to Orwell begins by thanking him for sending along a copy of *Nineteen Eighty-Four*; it praises the book profusely but quickly turns in Huxley's direction:

> I believe that the world's rulers will discover that infant conditioning and narco-hypnosis are more efficient, as instruments of government, than clubs and prisons, and that the lust for power can be just as completely satisfied by suggesting people into loving their servitude as by flogging and kicking them into obedience. In

> other words, I feel that the nightmare of *Nineteen Eighty-Four* is destined to modulate into the nightmare of a world having more resemblance to that which I imagined in *Brave New World*. (*L*, 605)[15]

Before Huxley sent this letter, he surely must have reread the pertinent paragraphs from his 1946 "Foreword." That he consulted this letter nearly a decade later when Orwell was already dead and he was beginning *Brave New World Revisited*, seems even more likely considering the similar concerns and phrasings in both (see *BNWR*, 1–3).

Nineteen Eighty-Four has been called "a brave new world stood on its head." Huxley's novel allegedly provided "one of the original inspirations for *Nineteen Eighty-Four*," states Peter Firchow: Orwell's "reply" to *Brave New World*, it "conducts a kind of dialogue between the lines with Huxley's novel"—a steady, pervasive reconsideration (Firchow, *End*, 122, 121, 125). Instead of joy and pleasure to keep everyone in line, Oceania uses fear, pain, and sexual frustration. There are shortages and hardship in place of leisure and play. The World State frees the libido but Oceania represses the sex drive; it lusts for power instead. Rather than the feelies and Orgy-porgy at a Solidarity Service, O'Brien takes Winston Smith to Room 101. He tells Winston to "'imagine a boot stomping on a human face—forever'" (O, 220). In his letter, Huxley expresses doubt that "the policy of the boot-on-the-face can go on indefinitely" (*L*, 604) because there are "less arduous and wasteful ways of governing," he tells Orwell.

Martin Green objects to the "transparency" of Orwell's influence on *Brave New World Revisited* (*BNWR*, xii); such obviousness, such retaliation on Huxley's part, albeit acknowledged, allegedly "weakens" his argument that the ultimate revolution lies beyond politics and economics, twin preoccupations in *Nineteen Eighty-Four*. The ultimate revolution strives totally to subvert the individual's psychology and physiology, Huxley repeatedly insists. Contra Green, Peter Firchow, impressed by the many "references" to Orwell in *Brave New World Revisited*, calls Huxley's essays "almost [...] a justification of *Brave New World* in terms of *Nineteen Eighty-Four*" (*End*, 120). One can go further than "almost" and suggest that Huxley was actually encouraging readers to re-examine *Brave New World* as a *de facto* parody of Orwell's novel. He would not write a full-scale response to *Nineteen Eighty-Four* because he had already done so even though it appeared before Orwell's dystopia.

In short, *Brave New World* reverses *Men Like Gods* but *Nineteen Eighty-Four* stands Huxley's novel on its head. Then *Brave New World Revisited* justifies *Brave New World* by enumerating Huxley's reservations about *Nineteen Eighty-Four*, and *Island* reverses Huxley's first reversal, resolving matters handled badly by the society in *Brave New World*. Such are the internecine contests between modern British utopias. No matter how ambivalent Huxley sometimes seems about prophets and prophecies, he refuses to be outprophecied, not by Wells and not by Orwell. First the "Foreword," then the letter, and finally the opening pages of *Brave New World Revisited*—Huxley wanted to make triply certain that the path from 1932 to A. F. 632 remained open; it was not obstructed by World War II, Hiroshima, or *Nineteen Eighty-Four*.

"Towards the end of the nineteenth century," observes Krishan Kumar, "the literary utopia revived." With a few exceptions, "it had been conspicuously absent in the first half of the century […]. After 1870 a spate of utopias poured forth." They "re-established the literary utopia as a fit vehicle for satire and social criticism" (Kumar, 65). The alpha and omega of this outpouring are Butler's *Erewhon* and Huxley's *Island*; Wells's *A Modern Utopia*, Zamiatin's *We*, and Orwell's *Nineteen Eighty-Four* stand out as highpoints in the cycle between them.

In 1905, H. G. Wells gave himself credit for writing the first modern utopia, one fundamentally different "from the Nowheres" utopists produced "before Darwin quickened the thought of the world" (*AMU*, 5).[16] Wells expressed contempt for depictions of imaginary societies, i.e., "Nowheres," as opposed to his own utopic proposals which were meant to be implemented everywhere, world-wide. Nevertheless, 1870, Kumar's date, is accurate. So-called "modern utopianism"[17] begins not with Wells but with Samuel Butler, whose *Erewhon* transformed utopian writing for the next century. Butler first recognized the importance of Darwin for utopian speculation and it was Butler again who initiated the directional shift in modern utopian fictions from hypothesis to prediction.

On or about 29 March 1872, the nature of British utopian writing changed dramatically when Samuel Butler published *Erewhon*.[18] The anonymous narrator, subsequently christened Higgs in *Erewhon Revisited*, revealed the Erewhonians' fears that rapidly evolving machines were about to usurp control of society, an anxiety no less perturbing nearly one hundred and fifty years later.[19] With an elaborate joke at Darwin's expense, Butler shifted utopian speculation from an intellectual exercise into the realm of scientific accountability. Once Darwin's theory of evolution was acknowledged as a mandatory touchstone, nothing not in accord with it was allowable. There could be no more Houyhnhms, for example, nothing blatantly "'unscientific'" to use Butler's term (*E*, 185). This is his major prohibition, no matter how shaky and contrived the proofs Higgs offers for machinery's intellectual advances. After Butler, the question for utopists no longer was whether some hypothetical form of social reorganization might (or might not) be preferable to the *status quo*, but to what extent certain developments—seemingly imminent in the author's opinion—should be welcomed or, more likely, resisted.[20]

If "'consciousness'" has evolved, reasons the unidentified author of *The Book of the Machines*, excerpts from which occupy chapters 23–25 of *Erewhon*, perhaps "'the higher machines'" may be able to develop minds and souls (*E*, 172, 173). Artificial intelligence becomes a distinct possibility. Given the "'extraordinary advance'" machines have made in "'the last few hundred years,'" Butler's alarmed author fears that "'far greater development'" is bound to come (*E*, 173, 177), until human beings, evolving more slowly, are no longer the dominant species. "'[A]ssuming the theory of evolution'" to be incontrovertible, the author of *The Book of the Machines* urged his fellow Erewhonians to "'destroy'" as many machines as possible before they developed far enough to "'tyrannize'" over everyone (*E*, 180). Erewhonians complied. They put a "'stop'" to all further improvements and destroyed those made in the last three hundred years (*E*, 195). Whether this extreme course of action was wiser than Victorian England's rampant industrialization, its growing dependence on machines in manufacturing and for transportation, Butler leaves readers to decide, but one senses that Higgs issues his translation as a warning.

While exploring Erewhon in the hinterlands of New Zealand, Butler's narrator-protagonist comes across *The Book of the Machines*. This polemic, by one of themselves, alerted Erewhonians to the menace from their improving machinery. Unfortunately, its unnamed author seems mentally unstable, indeed, paranoid. Doubts also arise about Higgs's competence as translator. Forced to flee Erewhon after becoming *persona non grata*, Higgs saves his translation but is "obliged to sacrifice the original work" (*E*, 187), which is written in Erewhonian, a language he admits he understands imperfectly. This comic undermining looks back all the way to Sir Thomas More; his descriptions of Utopia come from Raphael Hythloday, a sailor whom More regrets has disappeared without divulging the exact whereabouts of the island utopia he visited. Hythloday's reticence is embarrassing but Butler's unnamed author's claim in *The Book of the Machines* that the future is foreseeable, indeed, predictable, is truly unsettling. If a writer can predict the future and the prognosis is not good, as in the case of Erewhon's evolving machinery, then there is something more worrisome than More's failure to supply latitude and longitude—something for readers actually to lose sleep over. That was never the case with the classical utopias of Plato and More, which merely gave them something to mull over.

Thanks to Butler, prediction, usually in the form of a caveat, becomes one of the modern British literary utopia's predominant characteristics. Suddenly, the utopist was no longer a harmless daydreamer, a wishful thinker; nor was he merely a clever player of intellectual games who compared his society to imaginary alternatives without actually taking sides. For the most part, Higgs compares Erewhonians and Englishmen the way More compares the latter to Utopians and lets the reader decide which party, if either, is more rational. But the author of *The Book of the Machines* quickly turns into a semi-hysterical Cassandra, a hyperbolic progenitor of the modern utopist's persona. Consequently, literary utopias in the cycle from *Erewhon* to *Island* tend to be negative or else conclude negatively so as to become virtually synonymous with dystopia.

One surmises that the anonymous author of *The Book of the Machines* may be speaking for both Higgs and Butler when he asserts his belief in "'the fixity of the future'" (*E*, 190), i.e., its predictability, a concept not to be found in classical utopia. Because one realizes where machines have come from, how far and how fast, one can estimate the extent and rate of speed of their "'further mechanical progress'" (*E*, 195). No matter how much Butler was kidding, he realized that prediction and evolution go hand in hand, the latter making the former increasingly possible. This is one way that Darwin quickened the world's thought process. "'[T]he more the past and present are known,'" the author of *The Book of the Machines* pontificates, "'the more the future can be predicted'" (*E*, 189), thanks to evolution. Absent this premise, and most utopias written during the first half of the twentieth century have no foundation, no *raison d'être*.

Originally, Wells questioned the long-term efficacy of evolution. In the world of "'Eight Hundred and Two Thousand Seven Hundred and One A. D.,'" his Time Traveller discovers "'humanity upon the wane'": in *The Time Machine*, all the evolutionary energy necessary for "'ameliorating the conditions of life'" has been spent (*TM*, 42, 45). The Eloi or upper class are listless and effete. Though they tend society's machines and keep things going, the "'ape-like'" subterranean Morlocks, drudges cut off from all sweetness and light, have degenerated into scarcely human cannibals who feed on the Eloi. They constitute a step backwards for evolution. But after a change of heart, Wells bases his modern utopia squarely on evolutionary assumptions. It must be a "World-state," "[n]o less than a planet" (*AMU*, 12), Wells decrees in *A Modern Utopia* because one part of the globe—one city, state, or country—surely cannot evolve by itself if evolution is a natural law. To be valid, Darwin's theory must apply universally. A modern utopia is "not static but kinetic," says Wells; it never evolves into "a permanent state" but steadily improves through "a long ascent of stages" (*AMU*, 5).[21] It must remain forever open-ended, becoming more and more perfect through "a comprehensive onward development" (*AMU*, 6) that Butler's Erewhonians foolishly deny themselves. The Morlocks, machine-tending monsters, may be seen as Wells's idea of what will befall society if its Eloi (elite) fail to superintend its technology.

Huxley disagreed with both of Wells's positions on evolution. In *Brave New World*, he questioned Wells's confidence that a world-wide, scientific utopia can remain progressive and benevolent. Huxley's World State is static not kinetic, totalitarian not open-ended, "Stability" being the climactic ideal in its three-word "motto" (*BNW*, 1). "'The world's stable now,'" boasts Mustapha Mond (*BNW*, 180), which is essential for "'happiness.'" He tells Bernard Marx and Helmholtz Watson that brave new worlders "'don't want to change. Every change is a menace to stability'" (*BNW*, 184). Consequently, he continues, science must be kept "'carefully chained and muzzled.'" This crackdown is more ruthless than the Erewhonians' suppression of new machinery—which Wells in effect deplored, and it will be unavoidable in a world state, Huxley claims.

On the other hand, *Brave New World* also disputes Wells's earlier contention that evolution has limits. A burgeoning poet and mystic, Helmholtz Watson is an Alpha plus who seems poised to experience an "intensification and refining of consciousness," an "enlargement of knowledge" such as the biology paper that Mond censors posits as "the purpose of life" (*BNW*, 145). To Bernard Marx, Watson describes a "'power I feel I've got inside me—that extra, latent power'" (*BNW*, 149). He uses it to write a poem about contemplation that is in itself an act of it. This "'extra, latent power'" is surely a reservoir of unused evolutionary energy that will carry Watson and humanity forward.[22]

The next evolutionary step for mankind, Huxley speculates, will not be a "comprehensive development" world-wide à la Wells (*AMU*, 6), but the gifted individual's psychological—indeed, spiritual—breakthrough. Nothing short of enlightenment, this advance, as gifted individuals continue to appear and it becomes more and more accessible, will far surpass any increase of material comfort, i.e., "the maintenance of well-being" (*BNW*, 145), which is Huxley's parody of the *summum bonum* in Wells's modern utopia. Beginning with Watson, a wave of Huxley's proto-mystical protagonists—Anthony Beavis, Alfred Poole, Sebastian Barnack, and Will Farnaby—seem headed, in varying ways, towards "the Sovereign Good," a "goal" that, according to the proscribed biology paper, lies "somewhere outside the present human sphere" (*BNW*, 145).

Wells denigrated pre-Darwinian "Nowheres" (*AMU*, 5) but prescribed a modernized utopia that Huxley feared would turn out badly. In effect, Wells disarms More's famous pun, whereas Huxley not only reinstates but also complicates it. In Greek, *eu*topos means good place while *ou*topos means no place. Which does More mean? Perhaps he implies that utopia must remain hypothetical, the good place that exists no place, a possibility, not a prediction. Wells sacrifices half the pun: utopia only designates the perfect place as described by him. As early as 1932, Huxley, at the same time that he satirizes Wells, begins to flirt with the idea of utopia not as a physical place at all but as a blissful state of mind—or perhaps the sort of place most conducive to the development of such a mental state. Paradoxically, his nowhere is also "somewhere" (*BNW*, 145): it lies "outside the present human sphere," awaiting additional breakthroughs like Helmholtz Watson's. The "Sovereign Good" is still the best place even if it cannot be found on the map. Instead of stopping with More's good place that exists nowhere, Huxley posits a *summum bonum* that is internal rather than external, inside the individual yet "outside" or beyond material reality. On "Nowheres" Huxley claims to be the expert, not Wells.

Butler applies Darwin's theory to machinery; in the brave new world, "the principle of mass production [is] at last applied to biology" (*BNW*, 5). Huxley's jest at Henry Ford's expense is essentially Butlerian, a case of grotesque misapplication, the result being thinking machines in one case, manufactured bottle babies in another. But Huxley's fear of what "the sciences of life" (biology, physiology, psychology), if wrongly applied, can do to "the natural forms and expressions of life itself" (*BNW*, x) goes well beyond Butler's unnamed author's one-dimensional dread of an evolving machine. Just as Helmholtz Watson is a superb physical specimen, vastly superior to both Eloi and Morlocks, his potentiality for additional mental and spiritual growth greatly exceeds that of Butler's "'higher machines'" (*E*, 176). For the paranoid fear of evolution in *The Book of the Machines*, the Palanese of *Island* substitute a "'Darwinism raised to the level of compassion and spiritual insight'" (*I*, 199). Instead of propounding a "'biological theory'" that views life as a perpetual "'cockfight,'" the enlightened Palanese have learned to view all living things, even poisonous snakes, not as participants in countless struggles for existence, but as manifestations of "'the Clear Light'" (*I*, 199).

The penchant of post-Butlerian utopists for *prediction* over *hypothesis* reached crisis proportions in H. G. Wells. No longer the mind-game or mental tease that More invented and even Butler emulated outside of chapters 23–25 of

Erewhon, modern utopian thinking became a matter of agendas and manifestos. No one wrote more of these than Wells. New systems were not offered as theoretical constructs meant for contrast and comparison with an existing society but as prognostications, if not blueprints. Butler never claims that machine-smashing Erewhonians behave more wisely than Victorians who promote the industrial revolution, and More does not insinuate that Utopian customs are always superior to his countrymen's. But in *A Modern Utopia*, Wells tries to banish the last vestiges of playful ambiguity from twentieth-century utopian thinking, a banishment process Butler began.

Wells's alter ego, his imaginary "Utopian self" who dreams up a modern utopia, brazenly rewrites Butler when he declares that "there appears no limit to the invasion of life by the machine" (*AMU*, 247, 98). Butler's Higgs had observed that "'there seem no limits to the results of accumulated improvements'" by machines (*E*, 186). The difference is that the speaker's approval of this prospect is unmistakable in Wells: a prediction made enthusiastically. More's plan to the contrary, post-Darwinian utopias will be neither no place nor best place.[23] Utopia will be everywhere, possible rather than hypothetical, world-wide and contemporary rather than peripheral or remote in space and time. Material comforts consequent from technological progress will render it increasingly superior to its antecedents, a society never quite perfect but always more and more so as time goes on.

Strictly speaking, confidence in a fixed, i.e., predictable, future stems not from Wells but from the unnamed author of *The Book of the Machines*. One feels Butler is ultimately responsible for this idea and its impact on subsequent utopists, Wells and Huxley especially. It sounds more like Butler's idea than any one of Hythloday's is More's. Wells has Butler in mind again when he credits "the last three hundred years" for making machinery's limitless invasion of life clearly discernible (*AMU*, 98). Erewhonians, one remembers, destroyed all improvements to machines in "'the last three hundred years'" (*E*, 195), a move Wells finds ill-advised. In the brave new world, Wells's sanguine outlook is made to seem ridiculous in turn: machines have invaded life to the point where they actually produce it, which is worse than anything *The Book of the Machines* imagined. "[T]he modern fertilizing process" turns out however many new citizens the World State requires to maintain a stable population (*BNW*, 2). As hundreds of bottle babies in the Fertilizing Room travel "[t]wo thousand one hundred and thirty-six metres" towards decanting, they do so on "fifteen racks" occupying three floors; "the hum and rattle of machinery," Huxley writes, "faintly stirred the air" (*BNW*, 4, 8).[24]

Huxley's initial reaction to the growing modernist predilection for prediction was to satirize it ruthlessly. Funny and frightening, prophecies in *Brave New World* constitute an oblique variation on Butler's joke against Darwin: the brave new world conforms to several of Wells's criteria for a modern utopia but with dreadful consequences, just as Erewhonian machinery obeys Darwin's precepts but evolves contrary to humanity's best interests. To test the twentieth century's redefinition of utopia as a prophetic prediction, Huxley subverts the plausibility of Butler's confidence in a predictable, hence controllable future, one in which undesirable forms of scientific evolution can be reversed. By deriving un-Wellsian (and unpalatable) results from some of Wells's specifications, he satirizes the idea of prediction itself. Just as Butler used Darwin's theory to suggest that humans might not be evolution's pinnacle, an idea that never bothered Darwin, Huxley made the global, technologically proficient brave new world a humanist's nightmare, something Wells never intended.

The brave new world's state-imposed consumerism, "'the conscription of consumption'" (*BNW*, 40), is a perverse religion, an insult to Wells's exuberant materialism, of which it is allegedly the outcome.[25] The World State's application of "the principle of mass production [...] to biology" (*BNW*, 5) delivers a fatal blow to individuality: "standard Gammas, unvarying Deltas, uniform Epsilons. Millions of identical twins."[26] The adjectives "standard," "unvarying," "uniform," and "identical" are complimentary from a production standpoint but deadly otherwise. Instead of Wells's "classes of mind" (Poietic, Kinetic, Dull, Base) (*AMU*, 265), Huxley predicts a rigid caste system with each member of each caste conditioned to think his or her lot, that is, the point at which development has been arrested, the happiest. In Wells's modern utopia, motherhood is an honorable profession, "a service to the state" (*AMU*, 187–88); mothers get paid. A mother is an anachronism in the brave new world, a "smutty word" in fact (*BNW*, 28). Huxley mocks Wells's glorification of science and commerce by having the former take charge of procreation, which has truly become commercialized, a process of reproduction with science, in effect, serving as everyone's mother and father.

To keep utopia hypothetical, Huxley attacked presumptuous paradigms. He caricatured their proponents, Wells and Henry Ford in particular. This pair he rendered even more ridiculous by saddling their designs with additional components—insidious aberrations, in his opinion, such as Pavlovian behaviorism and Freudian psychology, in which, as in Wells and Ford, he detected an anti-humanist, mechanistic bias. Although Huxley's essays from the 1920s and 30s are crammed with demands for a better, more rational world, he was deeply ambivalent about the possibilities: his sterner self always mistrusted utopian projections as a form of escapism—compensatory dreaming by the perpetually maladjusted. Ironically, he entered the lists, so to speak, only when this conception of utopia as compensation was threatened—i.e., when day dreaming, unobjectionable per se, began to impinge upon reality. Even more ironically, Huxley managed to alarm himself with his own negative prognoses. When he later described *Brave New World* as a parody of Wells's *Men Like Gods* that "got out of hand" (W/F, 198), he revealed how his jest had backfired. Suffusing the satire lavished on sanguine forecasters such as Wells and Ford is Huxley's steadily growing conviction that he actually sees in them the obnoxious future. In other words, Huxley's anti-utopia started as an obligatory parody, a useful deflationary tool, but surprised its author by taking on a life of its own as a sociological possibility. Huxley began by laughing at predictions, then scared himself with his own. A satire on predictability, Wells's in particular, *Brave New World*, Huxley feared, was proving surprisingly predictive.

Given the eccentricity of most thinkers in what Huxley considered a centerless world of seemingly irresolvable counterpoints, definitions of perfection, he realized in 1932, were bound to be lop-sided, if not one-pointed, emphasizing happiness, for example, at the cost of freedom, or embracing technology to the exclusion of poetry. Without a formative mind for the age, a thinker sufficiently well-rounded to guide the fragmented post-war world towards a new consensus, utopian speculation was doomed to fail. Indeed, Huxley concluded that an era less qualified than the modern to configure utopia was more difficult to imagine than utopia itself.

Yet thanks to Butler, Wells, and their ilk, the modern period was pursuing erroneous concepts of perfection with unprecedented urgency—limited, in fact, distorted concepts that an enabling technology was making dangerously realizable, each a veritable Procrustean bed into which human beings would be forced to fit.

Brave New World was conceived not just to prevent a certain kind of utopia but also to discourage the kind of utopian thinking that made the act of prevention necessary. Huxley's first four novels display an unrivaled talent for bringing conflicting ideas and their expounders into mutually discrediting discussions. But if the utopian novel should be a forum for the free play of ideas and not, strictly speaking, a partisan vehicle for their advocacy or stoppage, the paradox is that Huxley was compelled to resort to the latter usage (i.e., obstruction in *Brave New World*, recommendation in *Island*) in order to preserve some semblance of the former. On the one hand, Huxley is an odd modernist: skeptical of the modernization of utopian thinking begun in Butler and amplified by Wells. On the other hand, he remains a modern in good standing because the new idea of utopian speculation becomes prominent among the ideas that are treated irreverently in his novels of ideas.

Brave New World Revisited deals a follow-up blow to the predictive school of utopian thinking: Huxley contends that the "amused, Pyrrhonic aesthete" who authored *Brave New World* on a lark was nevertheless superior as a predictor to Butler and Wells—as well as to George Orwell eventually. The third paragraph of *Brave New World Revisited* delivers a lengthy critique of *1984* as a book that once "seemed dreadfully convincing" but that developments since 1948 "have robbed [...] of its gruesome verisimilitude" (*BNWR*, 2). Its style of dictatorship has become "old fashioned," whereas *Brave New World*, though it came first, presents "a more up-to-date form of tyranny" (*BNWR,* 3) that makes Hitler, Mussolini, and Stalin seem crude and heavy-handed. Yet neither *Ape and Essence* nor *Brave New World Revisited* marks the last chapter in Huxley's investigation of modern utopian endeavor. That distinction belongs to *Island.* Published the year before Huxley died, it is his final retort to Wells, a complete depiction of what he thinks a modern positive utopia should look like.

Island is not just a book of wisdom disguised as a novel, not just a synthesis of Eastern spirituality and Western know-how, although these are surely not trivial accomplishments. Nor is Huxley's last completed novel merely the climax of a lifetime spent in opposition to Wells's ideas while trying to make peace with D. H. Lawrence's. (In *Brave New World*, Huxley savaged Lawrence's primitivism as thoroughly as he demolished the other half of the novel's main counterpoint: Wells's scientific materialism. The Palanese practice enlightened forms of both). Lastly, *Island* is not simply Huxley's strongest effort to become the mind of his age, its beacon-like sage, its intellectual and spiritual guide. One should also read *Island* as an attempt at genre repair; Huxley strives to bridge the split between hypothesis and prediction that Butler initiated. Through the formation of Pala, Huxley tries to have things both ways: he tenders a positive recommendation full-fledged enough to resemble a blueprint but ultimately more of a hypothesis than an actual prediction. In *Erewhon*, which is "nowhere" almost spelled backwards, Victorian England and the novel's eponymous society prove to be mirror images of each other. Similarly, Pala, Huxley's maximum working hypothesis, is the brave new world done correctly by the Palanese. The brave new world and Pala are mirror images in that everything handled badly by the former is redone wisely by the latter, be it sex, behavioral conditioning, or drug use. But we have also come full circle in another and equally important sense: back to the concept of the perfect place as no place, the notion that Butler began to break down by allowing the author of *The Book of the Machines* to predict the future of machinery. Ironically, the more willingly Will Farnaby and the reader enter into the spirit of Pala, the more clearly Huxley suggests that its days are numbered and the closer his fabulous isle is brought to seemingly unavoidable destruction. This contrapuntal strategy in which what is being given is simultaneously being taken away is Huxley's approximation, admittedly somewhat grim, of Sir Thomas More's playful ambivalence. Simultaneous presentation and retraction serves as an equivalent for the give and take, the self-conscious undermining of one's own credibility, that used to characterize imaginary trips to alternative societies, journeys seemingly as different from each other as Raphael Hythloday's to the Utopians and Lemuel Gulliver's to the land of the Houyhnhnms.

In Huxley's opinion, utopian thinking runs counter to the nature of things, which, regrettably, generally goes from bad to worse. When militaristic Rendang annexes pacific Pala, utopia becomes no place again. *Island* validates utopia's tantalizing function as a purely imaginary ideal and certifies Huxley's view of the actual human situation, in which breakdown is more probable than synthesis, collapse more believable than apotheosis. *Brave New World* parodied Wells's criteria for a modern utopia; *Island* also rescinds some of them. Pala is not world-wide, nor is it simply several notches above existing social arrangements; its spiritual dimension, something totally absent in Wells, makes it the apex for utopia, possibly the best place ever, because it facilitates the individual's pursuit of enlightenment, man's Final End over material ends. But since such perfection is not likely, *Island* is both open-ended and closed, i.e., doomed, its terminus steadily approaching chapter by chapter. As Huxley enumerates the island's virtues, their fragility is exposed. That explains why, in Huxley's opinion, a society so marvelous could not long survive even if this ideal community were to come into existence. When Wells declares that a modern utopia must be "conceivably possible" (*AMU*, 6), he means "doable," imperatively so, whereas for Huxley a possible utopia is simply a thinkable one. Of Wells's four criteria for a modern utopia—it must be better than the present, possible, worldwide, kinetic not static (see *AMU*, 5–6, 11)—the brave new world meets the second and third but violates the first and fourth; Pala meets the first and fourth but not the second and third. Together, they overrule all four (see *AMU*, 5–6, 11).

Viewed in the cyclical context from *Erewhon* to *Island*, Huxley's goals as a utopist stand forth threefold: 1. Always the personification of a clearing house for ideas, Huxley appointed himself the policeman of twentieth-century utopian thinking. Early and late, he took on the job of determining which current ideas—not necessarily full-scale utopian proposals—were conducive to the advancement of the race. *Brave New World* is an anthology of bad ideas, *Island* a compendium of good ones. Huxley combined utopia with satire and the novel of ideas. As these proved increasingly interrelated, Huxley posed a triple threat unmatched among modern utopists. 2. Huxley sought to regain artistic control of the theory of evolution. An intellectual heirloom of the Huxley clan, Darwin's theory is arguably the most important idea in English fiction, utopian or otherwise, from the 1850s onward. Butler's spokesperson, the author of *The Book of the Machines*, thinks evolution can be reversed; in *The Time Machine*, Wells feared it might slow down, then stop; D. H. Lawrence denied the phenomenon altogether. To contradict these misconceptions of evolutionary (i.e., utopian) energy, Huxley became the only modern utopian novelist to incorporate elements of the *bildungsroman* into all three of his contributions to the genre. Not just on Pala but no matter how miserable the circumstances in Fordian London or post-World War III California, someone in each of Huxley's alternative societies figures out how to come of age spiritually and intellectually, even if this prelude to full-blown enlightenment happens belatedly, which it does for Helmholtz Watson (*BNW*), Alfred Poole (*AE*), Sebastian Barnack (*TMHS*), and especially Will Farnaby (*I*). The coming of age is presented as a step forwards, setting up a pattern or pathway for others to follow. 3. Ultimately, it was insufficient entirely to revert to the idea of utopia as an intellectual exercise, a hypothesis for discussion rather than a prophecy or warning. Huxley hoped to fashion in *Island* a hybrid, a mutation better suited for survival as a form than Pala is as a place. For this reason and not just because Pala is geographically remote though not distant from us in time, *Island* has as much in common with More's *Utopia* and Plato's *Republic* as it has against *Erewhon* and *A Modern Utopia*.

The later Huxley raises the stakes. If there must be compensatory dreaming, he argued, it should be done by profounder thinkers than business magnates such as Henry Ford or Sir Alfred Mond or technocrats calling themselves modern *samurai*. The effective utopist must be triphibian: poet/philosopher/scientist.[27] Only such a gifted individual can comprehend man's Final End and imagine the sort of society most apt to induce its inhabitants towards full-blown physical and spiritual fulfilment. Economists and scientists, political or otherwise, no longer need apply because, Huxley contended, their grasp of psycho-spiritual evolutionary possibilities was certain to be inadequate. Insisting on a loftier conception of utopia while implying that the idea of utopia should continue to connote unattainable perfection—these are not inconsistent attitudes. One focuses on the idea of utopia as the *best* place, the other on the likelihood of its always being *no* place; each sustains the other.

Not that Huxley's utopias are devoid of predictions. But whenever he feels compelled to make some, particularly in *Brave New World* or in essays leading up to it from the twenties and thirties, he either talks almost exclusively about negative developments that he dreads describing or refutes a rival's predictions, ideas he considers ludicrous—or both.[28] Writers like Butler's author of *The Book of the Machines*, the unnamed narrator whose "Voice" enunciates Wells's position in *A Modern Utopia*, and the Orwell who anatomizes Oceania deliver their predictions more willingly than Huxley. He claims to be less than eager, despite the zest with which he parodies Wells and ridicules Henry Ford. The more convinced Huxley becomes of the accuracy of some of his forecasts, the more uncomfortable he sounds.

For the epigraph to *Brave New World*, Huxley quotes Nicolas Berdiaeff's *The End of Our Time* (1927), which claims that "Utopias are realizable. Life marches towards them."[29] By utopias, Berdiaeff surely meant negative totalitarian ones like the World State that Huxley was concocting. The Russian religious philosopher hoped that twentieth-century intellectuals would "find a means of avoiding utopias and of returning to a non-utopian society less perfect and more free." When Hitler, Mussolini, and Stalin appeared as the century unfolded, Berdiaeff sounded increasingly prophetic. Yet it is not clear to what extent Huxley's novel is endorsing Berdiaeff's fears as opposed to redirecting them. *Brave New World* portrays "the truly revolutionary revolution" that goes "beyond the mere politics and economics" that interest most despots. Ironically, the so-called *life* sciences (biology, physiology, psychology), Huxley warns, will try "to modify the natural forms and expressions of life itself," to alter "the souls and flesh of human beings" (*BNW*, x, xi). In short, life is indeed marching towards utopia, but neither towards the scientific paradise Wells desires nor the kind of bad place Berdiaeff fears. It is moving towards a state of affairs that Huxley insists will be much worse.

Moreover, this calamity was approaching faster than originally calculated. In 1946, "only fifteen years" after quoting the Russian, Huxley changed his projection from "six hundred years into the future" to "within a single century" (*BNW*, xv). In the second paragraph of *Brave New World Revisited* (1958), penned "twenty-seven years" after his first dystopia, Huxley updated his prediction again. This time he anticipated a brave new world in his lifetime or in that of his grandchildren (see *BNWR*, 1). Huxley began his lecture on "A Second Visit to a Future World" with another update: the modern world was running with "growing speed" towards a "terrifying future" formerly foreseen "in a distant age" ("Second," 23). In place of Wells the cock-eyed optimist, Huxley presents himself as an increasingly frightened Cassandra.

Before pointing out how the "prophecies made in 1931 are coming true much sooner than [he] thought they would" (*BNWR*, 1), Huxley spends two pages at the start of *Brave New World Revisited* dismissing Orwell's *Nineteen Eighty-Four* as a false alarm. In retrospect, Huxley realized, *Brave New World* can be read as a rebuke to Orwell as well as a rebuttal of Wells, even though *Nineteen Eighty-Four* and *A Modern Utopia* have little in common, the latter's promises being too good to be true, the former terrible in the wrong way. By 1958, it seems clear to Huxley that predictions in *Brave New World* regarding such things as "Mortality," "Over-Organization," and "Hypno-paedia" are holding up better than those in Orwell's novel. Admittedly, *Brave New World* is older by sixteen years and a second world war has intervened, yet only *Nineteen Eighty-Four* seems dated.

Huxley virtually incorporates his 1949 letter to Orwell:

> George Orwell's *1984* was a magnified projection into the future of a present that contained Stalinism and an immediate past that had witnessed the flowering of Nazism. *Brave New World* was written before the rise of Hitler to supreme power in Germany and when the Russian tyrant had not yet got into his stride. In 1931 systematic terrorism was not the obsessive contemporary fact which it had become in 1948, and the future dictatorship of my imaginary world was a good deal less brutal than the future dictatorship so brilliantly portrayed by Orwell. In the context of 1948, *1984* seemed dreadfully convincing. But tyrants, after all, are mortal and circumstances change. Recent developments in Russia and recent advances in science and technology have robbed Orwell's book of some of its gruesome verisimilitude. A nuclear war will, of course, make nonsense of everybody's predictions. But, assuming for the moment that the Great Powers can somehow refrain from destroying us, we can say that it now looks as though the odds were more in favor of something like *Brave New World* than of something like *1984*. (*BNWR*, 2)

The difference is that where the letter quoted earlier is a bit disingenuous, the passage from *Brave New World Revisited* sounds a note of resignation. In a contest Huxley has no desire to win, the "odds," ironically, are in his "favor." In short, there are only two possible scenarios. Either the world will blow itself up, in which case something like the society in *Ape and*

Essence will be all that is left, or the march towards a brave new world will accelerate. In any case, Orwell's projection finishes a poor third.

Ironically, despite peering into the future, Orwell overlooked the inevitability of change. His novel, Huxley contends, is too tightly tied to the context in which he was writing it. Although still "gruesome," its "verisimilitude" has steadily diminished because recent dictatorships have begun to realize what future tyrannies will know for a fact, namely, that "government through terror works on the whole less well than government through the non-violent manipulation of the environment and the thoughts and feelings of individual men, women, and children" (*BNWR*, 2). Hence "the old-fashioned, *1984*-style dictatorship" of Hitler and Stalin has lost out to "the Brave New Worldian nightmare" towards which events "seem to be pushing us all" (*BNWR*, 3, 4). Huxley not only resented being pushed; he also regretted having to point out how much more correct *Brave New World* was than *Nineteen Eighty-Four*. Not just a poignant prophet,[30] he was always a reluctant one: "I am," he confessed, in his "Second Visit" lecture, "in the rather unpleasant position of the prophet of doom, who, against his will, sees some of his prophecies coming true" ("Second," 24). Had Huxley lived longer, he would never have seen actual societies remodeling themselves after Pala. Regretfully, Huxley acknowledged that life marches towards negative utopias, but it does not, perhaps cannot, emulate positive ones, which therefore remain hypothetical or soon become so.

To underscore the theoretical nature of their enterprise, utopists often deliberately undermine their own credibility. Such undermining is a tell-tale indication that one is reading hypothesis rather than prediction. Fabricating a utopia, the utopist in effect signals the reader, is an intellectual game both are playing; its outcome is designed to self-destruct upon closer examination—hence it was never intended for implementation, no matter how persuasive its schemes sound or how thoroughly they contradict the alternative societies in other utopias. Whenever a utopia discredits itself while discrediting rivals, an idea of the perfect place gives itself away as a tall tale, daydream, nightmare, or fantasy. More plausible than other implausibilities, it nevertheless insinuates that it is still ultimately imaginary, that is, highly unlikely to be found or to come to fruition in the real world.

Beginning with More's *Utopia*, utopias frequently masquerade as travelogues, unverifiable records of fantastic journeys. The colossal liars who spin these tales either never ventured to the far-away places they meticulously describe or grossly exaggerate such exploits, sometimes both. Who believes that Gulliver actually voyaged to Liliput, Brobdingnag, Laputa, and the Country of the Houyhnhms, four alternative societies he allegedly visits? Raphael Hythloday tells More about Utopia, but his entertaining account of a fabulous island, where he spent "five years and more" (*U*, 52), is about as trustworthy as Gulliver's descriptions of his travels. Apparently, one of the smartest men in sixteenth-century Europe has been duped into writing a pack of falsehoods. Or else More is even slipperier than Hythloday, who may be a useful figment of the author's imagination, much as Gulliver is of Jonathan Swift's. That is, each allows his author to have his say while avoiding responsibility. Even Plato is difficult to pin down: the *Republic* is Socrates's brain child; Plato claims merely to be his amanuensis. Can one accept as genuine More's regret over Hythloday's failure to divulge the part of the world in which "Utopia is situate" or "in what sea the island standeth" (*U*, 8)? More promises to supply this information later, provided "Master Raphael" has not "died at sea" or returned permanently to Utopia (*U*, 138), either of which is a strong possibility.

The self-scuttling of an improbable journey never entirely disappears from modern British literary utopias, no matter how predictive they become, which means that their fundamental nature remains hypothetic. They are forever akin to the imaginary journey and the tall tale. One has only the word of an unnamed dinner guest that H. G. Wells's Time Traveller ever visited the Eloi and the Morlocks. The Traveller, if he ever existed, has gone back to the future,[31] probably for good, just as Hythloday may have returned to Utopia. Bedford, another unreliable Wellsian narrator, cannot produce the sphere made of Cavorite in which he and Cavor voyaged to the moon to visit an imaginary society inside it. A mischievous boy has flown off in the sphere. Cavor, Bedford's fellow-explorer, has remained among the moon's Selenites. To discourage future visitors, they "swarm upon him" (*FMM*, 160) just as he is about to transmit the formula for Cavorite.

Subtle variations on the underminings in prior utopias keep all three of Huxley's loosely in the travel tradition. His use of the undermining ploy becomes increasingly subversive, rendering his utopias, both negative and positive, inherently imaginary. When Bernard Marx and Lenina Crowne invite the Savage from a primitive reservation in New Mexico to the London of A. F. 632, it is as if John, journeying by rocket, were a time traveller into a future distant as the moon. Bernard actually tells John that he feels "'as though [they] were living on different planets in different centuries'" (*BNW*, 101). Huxley parodies *Men Like Gods*, in which Mr. Barnstaple and companions are miraculously whisked to a Wellsian positive utopia centuries forward in time. Barnstaple's faith in humanity's progress is buoyed by the Wellsian future he inspects; great things are in store for human beings if they follow Wells's advice. A disillusioned John, trapped in Huxley's derisive version of a Wellsian World-state, commits suicide.

The Time Traveller fights a pitched battle to fend off a horde of Morlocks, the disgruntled blue-collar workers of tomorrow. The Savage's battle with "one hundred and sixty-two Deltas" at the Park Lane Hospital is a travesty of the Time Traveller's heroics (*BNW*, 171). The Traveller's struggle to protect an effete humanity from a degenerative sub-species seems ludicrous when rewritten as John's attempt to recall the dim-witted Deltas to "something fine and noble": he tries to curtail their drug dependency by disrupting a "'[s]oma distribution'" (*BNW*, 172). In Huxley's World State, an irreverent redoing of the Wellsian corporate future, society's dirty work is done by mindless drudges bred to be dumber and more intractable than Morlocks. That John's fantastic journey by rocket from Malpais to A. F. 632 culminates with his death makes him more unprodu-cible than Hythloday, Gulliver, or the Time Traveller.

In *Ape and Essence*, Alfred Poole travels by boat from New Zealand to California; the latter was obliterated by atomic bombs during the Third World War. In effect, Poole and his colleagues, who are searching for survivors, sail back in time to the Stone Age. Theirs is definitely an imaginary journey. It takes place only in a discarded film script by William Tallis, which spills out of a garbage truck taking it and other rejected scripts "'to the incinerator'" (*AE*, 9). Having rescued "the text of 'Ape and Essence,'" the narrator states: "I print [it] [...] as I found it, without change and without comment" (*AE*, 23). Is a film script the narrator claims to have saved from incineration more plausible, more worth attending to, than Higgs's unreliable translation of the *Book of the Machines*, which Butler's protagonist comes away with from Erewhon? Or than Richard Sympson's declaration that he is publishing the papers of a "retired gentleman," Mr. Gulliver, a person allegedly "distinguished for his Veracity" (*GT*, viii)?

The script for *Ape and Essence* depicts a dystopian nightmare that Huxley believed the Hollywood dream factory of the nineteen forties would never dream of filming. All his life he was drawn to popular formats in which to raise serious intellectual issues and convey disconcerting messages. For years he struggled to recast *Brave New World* as a Broadway play, perhaps a musical.[32] Using a popular format, he realized, would gain him greater access to all sorts of non-readers, even if the usage was simultaneously serious and parodic. The format would still be recognizable even when turned against itself in, for example, a movie retaining all the features of a popular film while alarming and dismaying everyone it entertains.

Himself unsuccessful as a screen writer,[33] Huxley was disappointed with the typical Hollywood product. Disguised as a film script for an intentionally bad movie by 1940s box-office standards, his ninth novel calls for the kind of grave moving picture he felt ought to be made if a third world war was to be averted. It would issue a stern warning of impending doom, something few movie-goers expected to hear.[34] A script almost certain to result in commercial disaster—hence on its way to the incinerator—is, paradoxically, a potentially salvationary work of art. It puts to shame an industry that prefers more palatable projects. Not only does *Ape and Essence* challenge Wellsian visions of a peaceful future world made steadily more perfect by the material sciences; it also transpires within a popular framework of the 1930s and 40s (i.e., a movie) that is being satirized for moral cowardice.

Plausibility is dealt another blow after Poole and Loola escape from the ape-like society in and around Los Angeles. They stumble upon "a slab of weathered concrete, standing crookedly at the head of an ancient grave"; it belongs to "'William Tallis, 1882–1948'" (*AE*, 152), who has been dead for more than a century and a half. In the final paragraph of a dead man's film script, two characters in it come across his tombstone; they do so in a rescued typescript that the unnamed narrator, presumably Huxley, publishes in the year of its alleged author's death. Poole and Loola can have no idea who Tallis was. Nor can they possibly see themselves as characters he created. Only the narrator perceives these remarkable coincidences. If the world war Tallis predicts has happened and the simian society Poole discovers comes into being, there is no way Tallis's script would have survived. Tallis's world, which is also the narrator's real world, and the imaginary world of 2108 intersect and overlap in self-reflexive ways that, although startlingly effective to read, are not always easy to sort out, much less credit.

No utopia before *Island* deliberately undermines its own credibility as relentlessly; it is the most subtly self-undercutting utopia ever, a deceptive actuality that, much to the reader's consternation, turns into an insupportable hypothesis. To preserve its integrity, Pala has become "the forbidden island," closed to Westerners (*I*, 6). Caught in a "black squall out of nowhere"[35] while sailing, alone, Will Farnaby is an unwelcome traveller, a journalist whose sinking boat is washed ashore on Pala's "only sandy beach" (*I*, 6). For the next fourteen chapters, as Will recovers from his nearly fatal accident, he learns the virtues of Palanese society, which gradually emerges as Huxley's idea of the perfect place. Ironically, his arrival also encourages Pala's pro-oil minority to betray the heretofore isolated island to European commercial interests, namely, Joe Aldehyde's South East Petroleum, which seeks oil concessions. Farnaby holds a "roving commission" from Aldehyde to obtain oil leases (*I*, 269). The more attractive Palanese society seems both to Farnaby and Huxley's readers, the more untenable it is becoming, until neighboring Rendang, a military dictatorship on good terms with Aldehyde, overruns it in the final pages.

Huxley, it turns out, only appears to be creating a new Garden of Eden; all the while he simultaneously undercuts its viability by chronicling what turns out to be the last days of Pala, in effect writing Pala's obituary, another "paradise lost," as he himself described it (*W/F*, 199). Ironically, Farnaby is genuinely rehabilitated, restored to physical health by the enlightened Palanese, who also rejuvenate him spiritually. Yet Huxley calls him "the serpent in the garden" (*W/F*, 199), whose assurances of support from South East Asia Petroleum to the pro-oilers facilitate utopia's demise. Compared to More's Hythloday, Wells's Time Traveller, or Swift's Gulliver, Farnaby seems a more realistic personage, hence more plausible; for a time Pala is as real a place, it seems, as London or Paris. But the island Will visits is regrettably a society vanishing before the reader's eyes. Ultimately, it becomes as imaginary, i.e., as non-existent, as More's Utopia because Huxley believes the world is too corrupt to tolerate such a perfect place.[36]

The questioning of a utopia's credibility hardly begins with Huxley. However, on three occasions he addressed it differently and more cleverly than most. In *Island*, the credibility issue peaks: watching Pala's viability crumble, no matter if the island is skillfully presented, is an acutely unpleasant experience, an undermining less amusing but more ironic than More's or Swift's, hence unlike that in any predecessor. It recalls underminings in More and Butler but is more painful than either. In More, the explorer has vanished; in *Island*, Farnaby gets to stay but utopia vanishes.[37]

With the advent of predictions, dating becomes important.[38] Hypothetical or strictly imaginary utopias seem to exist out of time; often they are not precisely located either. Their authors cultivate a certain indefiniteness. But dating is vital to the predictor's credibility, especially in regard to negative utopia: supplying a date for its actualization imparts a sense of urgency to a dire forecast. The shorter the time line, the graver the warning. Wells's Time Traveller visits "'the world of Eight Hundred and Two Thousand Seven Hundred and One'" [802,701] (*TM*, 60)—a safe estimate. No one reading *The Time Machine* in 1895 would expect to see if Wells's timetable for humanity's decline was accurate. On the other hand, Orwell's inversion of the year in which he was writing in order to provide *Nineteen Eighty-Four* with a title gave his nightmare greater immediate impact than Wells's; unfortunately, it left his prophetic novel only thirty-six years to fulfill itself. That some of Orwell's major concerns, such as his fear of intrusive surveillance techniques and of the debasement of language for political purposes, continue to disturb suggests he saw beyond the deadline in his title.

For positive utopias, dates signify confidence; the utopist dares to specify when his vision will come true. In *Looking Backward*, Edward Bellamy's Julian West sleeps "exactly one hundred and thirteen years, three months, and eleven days" from 1887 to "the year 2000" (*LB*, 39). He awakens in a highly centralized, rationally organized, managerial society run by industrial officers who resemble the *samurai* in Wells's *A Modern Utopia*. Like Orwell's, Bellamy's time has run out. What he foresaw for America in 1887 and what Orwell predicted for Europe after World War Two are so radically different that both could never happen. Writing in 1905, Wells sets *A Modern Utopia* in "the year 2100" (Haynes, 88). Bellamy's utopia should have been here nearly two decades ago, whereas Wells's, with which it has much in common, still has more than eighty years to realize itself. Yevgeny Zamiatin sets *We* in the 2500s, so he predicts that it will take Wells's scientific utopia four centuries to turn into the dystopic One State. The perils of dating—deadlines create a sense of time having run out or soon to expire—outweigh the major advantage, namely, greater immediacy, a sense of imminence, whether of fear in negative utopias or optimism in their positive counterparts.

Otherwise unlike, D. H. Lawrence's *Lady Chatterley's Lover* and Orwell's *Animal Farm* are dystopian novels that share a disregard for futuristic dating. Both are situated in the present, the nineteen forties for Orwell, the mid-twenties in Lawrence. Basically a beast fable, *Animal Farm* is also an allegory, the revolt of the animals on Mr. Jones's Manor Farm a satiric replay of the Russian Revolution, which Orwell saw as a failure. For Lawrence, thanks to Clifford Chatterley and his ilk, industrial dystopia has already arrived in the north of England. Deformed and misshapen, coal miners in Tevershall and steel workers from Sheffield have been reduced to sub-human status; worse off than Wells's Morlocks, they are a setback for evolution. "God alone knows where the future lies," Lawrence wrote, as if reprimanding predictors. For him the current situation was terrible enough: "smoke and glare" from coal-mines and steel-works (*LCL*, 145) sickening workers and polluting the atmosphere. Setting a negative utopia in the present can be more apocalyptic than long-range forecasts such as *Ape and Essence* or *The Time Machine* in that the worst has already happened (or is happening); the author fears it may prove irreversible. Opening the reader's eyes to a disaster already in progress in the here and now, its seriousness being somehow overlooked or underestimated, makes dystopias like *Lady Chatterley's Lover* and *Animal Farm* more date conscious, that is, more aware of the pressing reality of the present moment, than their allegedly far-sighted rivals.

Discarding B. C. and A. D., Huxley sets the World State in A. F. 632, six centuries plus thirty-two years after "'[t]he introduction of Our Ford's first T-model […,] the opening date of the new era'" (*BNW*, 43). Henry Ford introduced the model-T in 1908; by A. F. 632, it is actually 2540, more than five centuries in the future. Fourteen years after *Brave New World* was published, however, when Huxley wrote the "Foreword," he began moving the date for the World State forwards: "I projected it six hundred years into the future," he remarks. "Today it seems quite possible that the horror may be upon us within a single century" (*BNW*, xv). By 1958, he feared it might befall his grandchildren (see "Second Visit," 23). An overly organized society (i.e., an oppressive tyranny), a caste system with obligatory servitude thanks to methodical conditioning, chemically induced happiness, and the sleep-teaching of orthodoxies were all "just around the corner" (*BNWR*, 2).

Repeatedly carrying forward the date for the advent of the brave new world allowed Huxley to enhance his credibility; he keeps apologizing not for being wrong but for being more prescient than he had taken credit for or wanted to be. When the "Foreword" appeared in the 1946 American edition, Huxley had things both ways, far and near. Within the text, the year is a distant A. F. 632, a long-range prediction meant to sound like Wells. Thanks to Huxley's "Foreword," however, dystopia was also less than a century away, nearly as imminent as Orwell's Oceania and allegedly getting closer all the time. Will the World-state materialize in 2100 and look like Wells's modern utopia, or, by 2540, will the World State resemble the brave new world, the latter a parodic deflation of the former? Or will the question be answered in Huxley's favor as soon as 2032?

Agreeing with Wells's son, Anthony West, J. R. Hammond argues that *Men Like Gods*, the novel that goaded Huxley into writing *Brave New World*, is actually "pessimistic"; its optimism is deliberately overdone so as to caricature not only William Morris's *News from Nowhere* and Bulwer Lytton's *The Power of the Coming Race* but also the implausible developments in Wells's own *A Modern Utopia* (see Hammond, 136–37).[39] Was Wells capable of such self-deprecation? If so, it does not matter so much whose timetable holds up, his or Huxley's. *Brave New World* would be rendered superfluous, a parody of a parody.

Ape and Essence begins on "the twentieth of February, 2108" when the New Zealand Re-Discovery Expedition reaches North America (*AE*, 28). The nuclear apocalypse that wiped out most of civilization must have happened at least a decade after 1945, when World War II ended, but prior to the start of the twenty-second century. California is no longer radioactive and the New Zealanders can safely reconnoiter. Setting the novel more than one hundred and fifty years in the future without dating the day the bombs dropped left Huxley with a flexible timespan: the disaster described in the novel could be imminent in 1948 or decades off, a cause for worry either way. In *Island*, Huxley destroys utopic Pala in real time, i.e., the present. Neighboring Rendang invades in the closing pages. "The work of a hundred years destroyed in a single night" (*I*, 294), Huxley laments. Koot Hoomi, the Rani's bogus spiritual director, allegedly first appeared to her "'"on the twenty-third of November 1953,"'" and she has been crusading in his name for eight years (*I*, 50). The date in the final chapter, therefore, is 1961. Pala has lasted just over a hundred years since 1850 when Dr. Andrew MacPhail and the island's Raja teamed up. Perhaps it is no coincidence that Huxley dates the start of his imaginary utopia in the period just prior to *Erewhon*, that is, two decades before the age of prediction began. The historical Pala of 1850 is one of the last pre-Butlerian hypothetical utopias; its inception precedes Wells's attempt to modernize, i.e., actualize, utopia. Published in 1962, *Island* marks the end of the prediction cycle that Butler began and Wells accelerated.

Assigning dates for utopia to materialize can be tantamount to revaluation of a rival. When timetables conflict, only one can be correct; this is even truer if they overlap. Butler dates the "revolution," the civil war between machinists and anti-machinists, roughly "five hundred years" before Higgs's arrival (*E*, 170). But in *News from Nowhere* (1890), when a dream vision transports Guest to the year 2102, William Morris's protagonist finds himself back in a fourteenth-century milieu very different from Butler's New Zealand during the same period. The victorious anti-machinists "wrecked all the more complicated machines, and burned all treatises on mechanics, and all engineers' workshops" (*E*, 171). *News from Nowhere* looks back to the England of the century before More when capitalism had yet to replace feudalism. In this pre-industrialized, pre-commercialized past, mercantilism—the producing, buying, and selling of goods strictly with a view to material gain—was still in its infancy; labor was done for pleasure, not just for profit. "How strange it would be to us," Morris explains in "The Hopes of Civilization," to "be landed in fourteenth-century England" before "commercial contract and cash payment began to take the place of the old feudal hierarchy" (*NN*, 311–12). Butler's author of *The Book of The Machines* and Morris's dreaming Guest both harken back to the same time when they believe society went astray. But doing without machinery as the Erewhonians have done for centuries, Morris objects, is not the same as achieving perfection. The latter entails replacing the current economic system with one that is older but allegedly superior. From the historian Hammond in 2102, Guest learns that the socialist revolution took place in 1952. By 2102, Nowhere's inhabitants have enjoyed 150 years of utopia; Morris's first readers still had sixty-two years to wait.

Unlike Higgs, Guest travels entirely in his mind, his sojourn in the socialist future a dream-vision from which he is foredoomed to awake. His dream is a self-undercutting device. Nevertheless, *News from Nowhere* establishes itself at Butler's expense in that it claims to look backwards more positively in order to depict a saner machineless society, and proposes Karl Marx, not Darwin, as the foundation figure for modern utopian thought. It nominates the *Communist Manifesto*, not *The Origin of Species*, as the more trustworthy text. In a classless society that values work and workers, machines stand no chance of taking over.

Morris's Guest, Bellamy's thirty-year-old Boston gentleman, and Wells's Sleeper, who awakens in the twenty-first century in *When the Sleeper Wakes* (1899), all sleep their way into futures that Huxley's negative utopias either preclude or are about to cancel. It is 2000 in *Looking Backward*, 2102 in *News from Nowhere*, 2100 in *A Modern Utopia*. Then, says the dystopian in Huxley, society will either destroy itself, as happens sometime before 2108 in *Ape and Essence*, or be on its way to becoming the World State by A. F. 632, i.e., 2540. Negative highlights in Mond's English history lesson, all of them contrary to Bellamy, Morris, and Wells, include the Nine Years' War from 2040 to 2049 (A. F. 141; see *BNW*, 38), suppression of all books published prior to 2058 (A. F. 150); and the search for *soma* begun in 2080 (A. F. 178), the "'perfect drug'" with which to stupefy an entire society (*BNW*, 45). Along with these unfortunate events, the machine-gunning of 800 Simple Lifers and the "famous British Museum Massacre" of some 2000 protesters combine to rule out a Lawrentian simple-life alternative and culture in general.

On the other hand, in replacing A. F. 632 with 1984, Orwell claims to be warning against a clear and present danger instead of trying to alarm readers about a threat several centuries in the future. There can be no World State, Orwell tells Huxley, once Oceania materializes. Orwell's impending timetable automatically discredits Wells, Morris, and Bellamy along with Huxley. If he is correct, none of them can be right. Set in the 1950s, however, Huxley's positive utopia reclaims the here and now. Pala is not only preferable to Morris's socialist revolution, which did not happen in 1952, but it can be had without waiting until 2100 as Wells must. Pala only lasts as long as it takes Bellamy's protagonist to awaken—Rendang's invasion destroys "the work of a hundred years [...] in a single night" (*I*, 294). But, even if the island is reduced to a hypothesis, the chants of its mynah birds, "'Here and now, boys; here and now, boys'" (*I*, 6) continue, constantly reminding the Palanese of a human being's never-ending utopian potentialities.

H. G. Wells invited scornful responses to his utopias and scientific romances not just by publishing extremely optimistic forecasts such as *Men Like Gods*, although that was apparently the last straw for Huxley, but also by denigrating Samuel Butler's *Erewhon* and William Morris's *News from Nowhere*. Confident that history would never verify either of these alternative societies, Wells sparked the process of revaluing rival utopias that would continue well into the twentieth century. In *The Time Machine*, for example, when the Traveller reaches the year 802701, he finds a future that neither Darwin's theory of evolution, which preoccupied Butler, nor Marx's brand of communism, which exercised Morris, can explain, much less redeem.

Instead of hearty Erewhonians or artistic socialists, Wells's protagonist encounters the "'indolent,'" "'easily fatigued'" Eloi, "'four feet high,'" "'indescribably frail,'" and the "'ape-like'" Morlocks, who prey upon them (*TM*, 34–35, 41, 63). These simian creatures may be descendants of the machinists whom the anti-machinists vanquished in Erewhon's civil war. The fragile Eloi, walking works of art but quite useless otherwise, are a parody of Morris's industrious pre-Raphaelite craftsmen.[40]

Wells warns Butlerians against abandoning or restricting technology. Without talented technocrats to develop machinery intelligently, society will regress into two distinct species: not machine-lovers and machine-haters as in Erewhon, but into a helplessly effeminate leisure class and a base, dehumanized work force. Eloi sunbathe and eat fruit in the "'dilapidated'" Upper-world, its machines and buildings in a state of "'ruinous splendour'" (*TM*, 40, 42). Blind as moles in the daylight, Morlocks tend life-sustaining "'ventilation'" equipment in subterranean "'wells'" more forbidding than "'the mechanical kingdom'" that the author of *The Book of the Machines* dreaded (*E*, 81).[41]

In the Palace of Green Porcelain, the Time Traveller finds "'big machines [...] greatly corroded and many broken down'" (*TM*, 92). It is as if he has wandered into the Erewhonian "town museum," which contains "broken machinery of all descriptions [...,] many of our advanced inventions," Higgs reports, but "several hundred years old, [...] marred and broken" (*E*, 60). Eloi and Morlocks, Wells insists, have made a fatal mistake by emulating Erewhon. The "'big machines'" having been "'broken,'" Eloi become dependent upon Morlocks, who are no better than servants of the minimal amount of machinery still essential for survival. Wells, not Higgs or the author of *The Book of the Machines*, claims to have best described a future that has neglected its machinery.

After seeing the Eloi, the Time Traveller posits "'the sunset of mankind'"—"'humanity upon the wane'" (*TM*, 45). Evolution, he speculates, has described a parabola; following a steady, linear ascent, "'the work of ameliorating the conditions of life'" reached "'a climax'"; then came subsidence. Darwin was wrong to imagine evolution as an unlimited process.[42] It follows that Butler's fears are wide of the mark. If "'we cannot calculate'" any major "'advance in man's intellectual or physical powers,'" as Butler claims, it is because the supply of evolutionary energy will eventually be exhausted; hence, reasons Wells, it is absurd for Butler to predict "'far greater development [...] in store for the machines'" (*E*, 172, 177).

The Time Traveller's experiences also reverse Marx: instead of a classless society, the gap between "'Haves'" and "'Have-Nots'" has steadily widened (*TM*, 68–69). *News from Nowhere* to the contrary, pleasure and work remain polar opposites. The Time Traveller likens the "'prettiness'" of the do-nothing Eloi to "'Dresden China.'" They are not pre-Raphaelite craftsmen, but resemble things finely made, as if by them. Never precisely classified, Morlocks remind the Traveller of monkeys, lemurs, spiders, ants, "'human rats,'" etc. (*TM*, 102). A blue-collar nightmare, these "'Under-grounders'" (*TM*, 70) come topside after dark to devour the seemingly elite but technologically illiterate Eloi, who are worse off than cattle.

In 802701, the Time Traveller realizes, Have-Nots literally live off the Haves, consuming their flesh, just as the Haves of Wells's day thrive upon Have-Nots economically. The breeding and slaughtering of Eloi by Morlocks accounts for there being no "'aged'" or "'infirm'" among the former, and for the "'extinction'" of horses, cattle, sheep, dogs, and fish (*TM*, 59, 40). Natural selection has triumphed insofar as the edible Eloi are more fit for consumption than the animal species they render superfluous. While the Eloi "'above ground'" were "'pursuing pleasure and comfort and beauty,'" the Morlocks below were "'getting continually adapted to the conditions of their labour'" (*TM*, 69), this degeneration a grimly ironic specialization that parodies survival of the fittest. The Time Traveller calls the Eloi–Morlock arrangement the "'working to a logical conclusion [of] the industrial system of today'" (*TM*, 70), which it therefore implicitly condemns. The outcome in 802701 of conditions in 1895 bears little resemblance to Marx's predictions or Morris's dream vision, both of which Wells encourages readers to disbelieve and discard, along with Higgs's (and possibly Butler's) dislike of machines.

Huxley argues that *Erewhon*, *News from Nowhere*, and *The Time Machine* are deceptively forward-looking; instead, they rehash strictly nineteenth-century anxieties, to which they remain closely tied. They are still working out the logical consequences of a book published in 1859 and of the nineteenth century's Industrial Revolution, whereas the brave new world is the product of what comes next, developments over the next seven centuries: a future society based on discoveries to be made in the future. In short, says Huxley, neither the "sciences of matter" (the natural sciences represented by Darwin) nor political scientists such as Marx will shape tomorrow. The real culprit will be the life sciences, "the sciences of life" (biology, physiology, psychology) (*BNW*, x), which can alter human nature. Contrary to Butler, Wells, and Morris, where utopia actually backpedals several centuries, the seventh century after Ford belongs to experts in bio-engineering and psychological conditioning. The brave new world, Henry Foster enthuses, has ventured "'out of the realm of mere slavish imitation of nature,'" that is, obedience to natural laws and scientific theories such as evolution, "'into the much more interesting world of human invention'" (i.e., eugenics, behaviorism) (*BNW*, 9), which overrides nature. It was a waste of breath for Wells to quarrel with Butler and Morris over Darwin and Marx, all five of whom are of little consequence in the World State by A. F. 632.

Marx survives only as Bernard's surname; Darwin Bonaparte is "the Feely Corporation's most expert big-game photographer" (*BNW*, 207). Neither brave new worlder seems to know anything about his illustrious namesake; nor will either match his namesake's accomplishments.[43] Darwin Bonaparte's masterpiece is a film titled *The Sperm Whale's Love-Life*, science reduced to pornography (see *BNW*, 208). Although the historical Lenin capitalized on Marx's theories, Bernard's infatuation with Lenina Crowne lacks socio-economic significance and is mainly a source of sexual frustration.

The reservation at Malpais may be read as Huxley's opinion of Morris's arts-and-crafts utopia. Obviously, no place named the bad place can be utopic. Old Mitsima teaches John "'to work the clay'" and "'to make the bow'" (*BNW*, 110–11), but real primitives and, by extension, all forms of primitivism, stink. Huxley's ultra-clean, disease-free World State makes nonsense of Morris's hygienic medievalism, for which a New Mexico Savage Reservation is allegedly a more truthful analogue. Confronted with Indians who "smelt stronger and stronger," not to mention "the dirt, […] the piles of rubbish, the dust, the dogs, the flies," Lenina holds "her handkerchief to her nose" (*BNW*, 89–90), the correct response to a realistic version of Morris's idea of a retrograde utopia.

"The Natural History of the Selenites," chapter 23 of H. G. Wells's *The First Men in the Moon* (1901), approximates a text-within-the-text like *The Book of the Machines* in *Erewhon* or Goldstein's treatise on oligarchy in *1984*. Actually, this history is only an abstract of messages Cavor broadcasts from the moon, a planet he and Bedford discover to be "a kind of super ant-hill" inhabited not by rational animals (Gulliver's talking horses) but by rational insects—ants allegedly "higher than man" in "intelligence, morality, and social wisdom" (*FMM*, 147).[44] Bedford has returned to earth but Cavor remains behind to study further the Selenites' social system. His ambivalent responses create the sort of intellectual confusion that Butler generates by having Erewhonians stand one Victorian practice after another on its head.

According to Bernard Bergonzi, H. G. Wells considered *The First Men in the Moon* his "best scientific romance" (Bergonzi, 156). Arguably, *Brave New World* is as much a satiric reply to *First Men* as it is an irreverent response to both *A Modern Utopia* and *Men Like Gods*. Huxley's revaluative parody got out of control because it grew from an attack on *Men Like Gods* into an all-out assault on the early Wells. Just as Huxley sensed a totalitarian dystopia lurking within Wells's World-state, he found *First Men* curiously ambivalent, ostensibly negative yet compromised by the mixed feelings that Wells's protagonists have about several of its problematic features. When Selenite civilization contributes extensively to the brave new world, Huxley subtracts ambiguities to reveal unattractive oncoming possibilities that he implies Wells secretly admired.

Cavor's transmissions about marvelous ants are not just "t*ant*alizing;" they seem about to usher in, says Cavor, "such a change in human conditions as mankind has scarcely imagined heretofore" (*FMM*, 147). The brave new world is Selenite civilization writ large because Wells's moon novel contains a prophecy in graver danger of coming true than its utterer realized—or may consciously have desired. In Bedford's opinion, Cavor's "fragmentary" accounts are coherent enough to "give a vague, broad impression of an altogether strange and wonderful world with which our own must now prepare to reckon sooner or later" (*FMM*, 147). The adjectives in Huxley's title—"brave," "new"—sound like an ironic, albeit oblique, allusion to Cavor's description of a "strange and wonderful world."

Ant hills in Huxley's World State sit above ground, tall as skyscrapers. London's Central London Hatchery and Conditioning Centre, for instance, is a "squat grey building of only thirty-four stories," presumably one of the smallest high rises (*BNW*, 1). Nevertheless, Huxley describes "lower-caste activity" in Fordian London as "ant-like pullulation" (*BNW*, 60). And he called *Brave New World* an "attempt to re-create human beings in the likeness of termites" (*BNWR*, 19). Thanks to the Selenite model in *The First Men in the Moon*, the brave new world's Central London Hatchery may be likened to a giant termitary; there it manufactures Alphas and Betas to be managers and technicians and hatches Gammas, Deltas, and Epsilons to staff its workforce.

Both Selenite society and brave new world want every citizen to be "'a perfect unit in a world machine'" (*FMM*, 143). Wells, not Huxley, seems to endorse this objective. The brave new world's methods, however, are more efficient, more advanced, a satiric elaboration designed to discredit its inspiration. Selenites undergo "'training,'" "'education,'" and "'surgery'" until no one has "'ideas'" or "'organs'" for anything but a specific predetermined function (*FMM*, 143). The brave new world's superior breeding allows Huxley to ridicule Cavor's account: it "'consists of a series of arrests of development'" (*BNW*, 3) that eliminate the need for corrective surgeries but are no less inhumane. To obtain "'future sewer workers,'" for example, bottles containing Epsilons receive "'less oxygen'" (*BNW*, 10). "'The lower the caste, […] the shorter the oxygen,'" Henry Foster explains; "'Nothing like oxygen-shortage for keeping an embryo below par,'" he adds (*BNW*, 10).

For a Selenite mathematician's brain to grow, his limbs must be made to "'shrivel, his heart and digestive organs [to] diminish'" (*FMM*, 143). It follows that the Grand Lunar, the Selenite equivalent of a World Controller, is bodiless, nothing but a large brain that must be sprayed with water regularly to keep from overheating. Selenite minders of mooncalves are "'induced to think and live like a mooncalf.'" Here, too, the brave new world exceeds its model, bringing out its worst implications. Bottles of future rocket-plane engineers are given extra surrogate when "'upside down'"; they will be "'only truly happy when they're standing on their heads'" repairing "'the outside of a rocket in mid-air'" (*BNW*, 13). Bottles of miners, "predestined" for the tropics, alternate between hot and cold tunnels; "[b]y the time they [are] decanted," they have developed "a horror of cold" (*BNW*, 12).

Cavor tells of coming upon "'young Selenites, confined in jars from which only the fore limbs protruded, who were being compressed to become machine-minders.'" The "'extended hand'" is to be "'highly developed […] while the rest of the body is starved'" (*FMM*, 145). Everyone in the brave new world begins in a bottle but physical deformation is unnecessary. On three tiers of racks covering three separate floors, bottle babies travel "two thousand one hundred and thirty-six metres" to the Decanting Room. They emerge undeformed but physically conditioned to perform their tasks; then their minds are "made to endorse the judgment of their bodies" (*BNW*, 12). Every common Selenite may be "'exquisitely adapted to the social needs it meets'" (*FMM*, 145) but never as meticulously or as smoothly as the typical brave new worlder.

In a "'vast,'" low cavern, Cavor reports discovering "'prostrate figures sleeping under an opiate until the moon had need of them'" (*FMM*, 146). In the brave new world, every workday ends with distribution of the *soma* ration, the entire work force being addicted to a nightly dose. With just enough workers to produce the exact amount of required goods, the brave new world is a machine never in need of spare parts. It drugs workers in order to cope with the problem of leisure, that is, to avoid having to amuse citizens when they are not working, playing mindless games, or fornicating. There is never a work shortage or a surplus of workers in a brave new world that is the Selenite society brought to greater perfection.

Impressed, Cavor decides that it is better to "'drug the worker one does not want […] than to expel him from his factory to wander starving in the streets'" (*FMM*, 146). Similarly, he thinks it may be "'more humane'" to reduce youngsters to machine-minders with enlarged hands than to follow "'our earthly method of leaving children to grow into human beings, and then making machines of them'" (*FMM*, 145–46). Cavor suggests that a comatose worker may be preferable to a discharged laborer and that malforming children could be less cruel than deforming adults. Asked which is better, the Selenite system or current practice, the reader is surprised into endorsing the former, which means the moon community is an ironic improvement, not a worsening, and therefore a future utopia that Cavor, if not Wells, recommends.

Unlike Cavor, who has mixed feelings, brave new worlders such as Henry Foster and the Director of Hatcheries and Conditioning sound unequivocally proud of the Fertilizing Room, the Embryo Store, the Decanting Room, the Neo-Pavlovian Conditioning Rooms, the Social Predestination Room, hypnopaedia, Bokanovsky's Process, Podsnap's Technique, etc. Nor does an army of Predestinators and Fertilizers weary of supervising "gallery above gallery" of assembly-line conveyors that carry bottle babies towards "[i]ndependent existence—so called" (*BNW*, 8). The lecture tour in the first two chapters of *Brave New World*, followed by Mond's history lesson in chapter III, are heavily indebted to "The Natural History of the Selenites," except that Huxley's elaborations remove Cavor's positive second thoughts. The removals make the Selenite system appear primitive by comparison with the World State but no less ominous; they imply that Wells nevertheless accepts it even if not wholeheartedly. Stifling his misgivings, Cavor calls Selenite civilization a "'wonderful social order'" (*FMM*, 145); this declaration gave Huxley the opportunity to treat Wells's fantasy and its ironies as a rival utopist's misguided prediction that could lead to a brave new world.

Wells anticipates high-speed monorails, the electric blanket, vacuum cleaners, social security numbers, a "minimum wage," and the chunnel (see *AMU*, 45, 104, 105, 139, 164, 241). His modern utopia teems with accurate predictions. Like those just listed, however, they promote convenience and bodily comfort. Having proclaimed that in his utopia "there are no qualitative questions [...], but only quantitative adjustments," Wells disregards intangibles to stress, instead, "the material ends of mankind"; he exudes confidence in his utopia's ability to improve the "conditions of physical happiness" (*AMU*, 37, 84, 65). Huxley's parody of Wells's World-state is a materialist's pseudo-paradise in which hedonism is compulsory. Consumerism has become the official religion. Mustapha Mond defines "'the conscription of consumption'" whereby "'[e]very man, woman and child [is] compelled to consume so much a year in the interests of industry'" (*BNW*, 40). In *Brave New World*, Helmholtz Watson writes a poem, disdains mindless diversions, and begins to cultivate a soul—all three of which, Huxley believes, would be treasonous in the Wellsian future inasmuch as all pertain to the spirit and none involves consumption.

In utopia, Wells pontificates, "love-making is no concern of the State's" (*AMU*, 206). Wrong, Huxley replies. As in Zamiatin's One State and subsequently in Orwell's Oceania, the individual's private activities are the first to be regulated throughout the brave new world. The goal is to eliminate personal attachments, love especially, lest pairings seem preferable to the common good. The brave new world decrees that "'every one belongs to every one else'" (*BNW*, 31) but this ostensible liberation actually entails the loss of freedom of choice. Sexual persecution is likely to begin early, says Huxley. A howling little boy, "'reluctant to join in the ordinary erotic play'" of young brave new worlders, is carted off to the Assistant Superintendent of Psychology "'to see if anything's at all abnormal'" (*BNW*, 24).

Paradoxically, promiscuity, if mandatory, can be as constraining as chastity once was, Huxley contends. Unrestricted sex becomes one of many diversions that keep brave new worlders from thoughtful solitude. Insomuch as birth control is universal, no connection any longer exists between sex and procreation. No matter how much *soma* Lenina takes on her date with Henry Foster, she would never forget "to take all the contraceptive precautions prescribed by the regulations": "Malthusian drill three times a week" has made "the taking of these precautions [...] automatic" (*BNW*, 64), that is, machine-like. In a world state such as Wells desires, Huxley points out, sex, even if it seems uncontrolled, is likely to be as subject to authoritarian rules and regulations as everything else.

It follows that Wells has not solved "the riddle of [...] marriage and motherhood" as he claims (*AMU*, 180). His solution, Huxley objects, is neither the only one possible nor the most expedient. The brave new world simply abolishes both problems—marriage and motherhood, and it cancels home too, an institution which Mustapha Mond denigrates as a "stiflingly over-inhabited [...,] understerilized prison" (*BNW*, 28). Instead of viewing motherhood as a profession and paying mothers a salary, as Wells proposes, the brave new world demotes "'mother'" to a "smutty word" (*BNW*, 28). Children are produced and educated scientifically without benefit of marriage or mothers. As highly organized as the World-state is, says Huxley, Wells ought to have thought of this. Marriage, motherhood and individual households go counter to the "world-wide synthesis of all cultures and polities and races" that Wells insists is the World-state's primary goal (*AMU*, 344).

His modern utopia, Wells vociferates, is "an adult world" whose *samurai* seek "a transcendental and mystical God" (*AMU*, 315, 302). Not very likely, counters Huxley. Mustapha Mond exiles Helmholtz Watson, the brave new world's only incipient mystic. Otherwise, the lowest common cultural denominator prevails. In a society without museums, concerts, books and art galleries, upper castes must recreate identically with the lower orders. All attend the latest "Feely," a pornographic bastardization of *Othello* (*BNW*, 140). Alphas and Betas must play two rounds of golf every day, just as Deltas and Epsilons do.[45] "'Civilized infantility'" is the rule. The "'duty'" of Alphas is "'to be infantile'" after working hours "'even against their inclination'" (*BNW*, 129, 81), Mond explains. The more child-like a society, says Huxley, the easier it is to please and control.

The World-state, Wells emphasizes, is not "an untidy nursery" (*AMU*, 232). But in Huxley's opinion, it may well be a tidy one. Surely Wells's statement inspired one of Huxley's finest satirical metaphors for life in the brave new world. Besides being a gargantuan factory and a multi-storied termitary, Fordian London resembles a gigantic nursery. "Outside, in the garden [of the Central London Hatchery and Conditioning Centre], it was playtime [. . .;] six or seven hundred little boys and girls were running with shrill yells over the lawns, or playing ball games, or squatting silently in twos and threes among the flowering shrubs" (*BNW*, 23). On the Centre's fifth floor, "Infant Nurseries" teem with "crawling babies" being conditioned to dislike flowers and books (*BNW*, 14–15).

A "period of education and growth [. . .] prolonged to as late a period as possible and puberty correspondingly retarded"—these are Wells's recommendations for enriching life in the World-state. No rationalized society, Huxley responds, could afford to be so impractical. One of the brave new world's goals is to "discover a technique for shortening the period of maturation" for its workers: at Mombasa, scientists have "produced individuals who were sexually mature at four and full grown at six and a half" (*BNW*, 10–11). Regrettably, "[s]ix-year-old men and women" are "socially useless," stupider than Epsilons, Mr. Foster admits. So the search continues for "the ideal compromise" between "adults of twenty," the age at which one is considered "fully grown," and "adults of six" (*BNW*, 11).

Wells's use of the word "retarded" presumably gave Huxley the idea for "'bokanovskification,'" a "'series of arrests of development'" (i.e., retardings) used to "'check the normal growth'" of Gammas, Deltas, and Epsilons. Once "bokanovskified," the D.H.C. explains, each egg "will proliferate," producing anywhere "[f]rom eight to ninety-six buds," every one of which "will grow [. . .] into a full-sized adult" whose intelligence is kept "'below par,'" the "'lower the caste,'" the less intelligence (*BNW*, 3, 10). Instead of having their puberty delayed, brave new worlders take lessons in "Elementary Sex" almost immediately. Even in their sleep, thanks to hypnopaedia, "little boys and girls" are taught to value uninhibited sexual activity. It distracts Alpha and Epsilon alike from seeking additional growth and education.

One finds "great variety of costume" in Wells's World-state (*AMU*, 227). Huxley removes this unnecessary obstacle to the oneness that Wells desires. Brave new worlders dress in one of only five colors, all Deltas in khaki uniforms, for example, to promote solidarity with one's caste.[46] Huxley rewrites Wells's "classification of temperaments" (*AMU*, 265) as what it really is: a "'Caste System'" (*BNW*, 38) of five classifications in place of

Wells's four. Poietic, Kinetic, Dull, and Base yield to Alphas, Betas, Gammas, Deltas, and Epsilons. Only the Base are objectionable to Wells because they are immoral. Huxley's castes all seem to be amoral.

Except for Alphas and Betas, however, there is no sex outside one's caste. Wells rules out "special breeding" in favor of "classes to which people drift of their own accord" (*AMU*, 266). Huxley revises such accidental sorting into the rigorous breeding program Wells's classifications seem to require. On love-making, marriage, motherhood, puberty, education, the class system, and a variety of related subjects, Huxley rewrites and corrects Wells, frequently reusing the latter's allegedly utopic materials to describe negative developments, outcomes considered more likely than Wells's or more in unacknowledged accord with his intentions. Repeatedly, Huxley charges Wells with never sensing the potentially disastrous outcomes of his own designs. According to Krishan Kumar, Yevgeny Zamiatin contends that Wells's "basic purpose was anti-utopian"; that is, no matter what their stated goals, his works have negative connotations and must be rewritten to bring out their underlying intent (Kumar, 227). But Huxley insists that *Brave New World*, not Zamiatin's *We*, better shows readers the calamities to which Wellsian policies and predictions will lead.

Reviewing Bellamy's *Looking Backward* in 1889, William Morris was appalled by its author's enthusiasm for "ever fresh developments of machinery" and "the organization of life and necessary labour [...] by a huge national centralization" (*NN*, 357–58). Clive Williams finds Morris's definition of "machinery" broad enough to include not just "the literal mechanization of all production," but also "the rationalization of society by bureaucratic control" (*NN*, xxxiv). In a clamor of competing voices, Morris can be heard condemning the same advances that worried Butler's Higgs, only to be shouted down by Wells, the twentieth century's strongest advocate of rationalization.[47] In *A Modern Utopia*, Wells entrusts the World-state to a ruling class of technocrats precisely of the sort that Morris despises. The *samurai* achieve greater community stability and a higher standard of living through minimum waste of effort and material; labor is organized scientifically, products standardized, all processes of production and marketing streamlined. Wells foresees and encourages the reconfiguration of society by an intellectual aristocracy. This directorate resolves all conflicts between governments, different economic systems, and competing individual businesses. In *Brave New World*, Wells's *samurai*, their altruism now suspect, become the Ten World Controllers; by *Nineteen Eighty-Four*, as the Inner Party, they have sunk even further below ideal administrators.

Instead of fading away as Marx predicted, the state, in Wells's future, swells to become world-wide, conducting itself as smoothly and profitably as possible for the general welfare of the human race. Utopia, Wells informs Morris, will not be a socialist commune; contra Butler, it can never be machineless. Instead, it must run "like a well-oiled engine" (*AMU*, 171). In speaking about machines, Butler's Higgs laments that "'there seem no limits to the results of accumulated improvements'" (*E*, 186). When Wells sees no limitation to the invasion of life by machinery (see *AMU*, 98), he converts Butler's warning into a shibboleth. In the brave new world, Huxley attempts to silence Wells by exaggerating Morris's fears and Higgs's anxieties. The literal mechanization of all production, something that Wells anticipates but that Butler and Morris dread, expands in Huxley's world to include reproduction; bottle babies amount to a rationalization of the birth process.[48] Huxley invites readers to ponder whether the mechanical production of brave new worlders is the realization of Butler's worst nightmare or the triumphant, long-anticipated removal of the last barrier in the way of Wells's prophecy—or both. Either way, it constitutes rationalization *ad absurdum*, which is meant to make rationalization seem undesirable *per se* as a path to utopia.

For Higgs, the paranoid translator of *The Book of the Machines* in Butler's *Erewhon*, evolution and the Industrial Revolution are forever linked. Rapidly evolving machines are allegedly the next phase of evolution, the force that energizes their progress. Huxley deplores "this dreadful religion of the machine [which] will end by destroying the human race" (*MN*, 180–81). But his response to Butler's pseudo-scientific fears of an increasingly superior machinery is religio-philosophical. In the contest with machines for continued control of the process of evolution, the human race, Huxley speculates, may yet win, thereby rendering Butler's anxieties irrelevant.

"'Is it not possible then,'" Butler's machine-hater theorizes, "'that there may be even yet new channels dug out for consciousness, though we can detect no signs of them at present?'" (*E*, 172) "'[W]hy,'" he asks, "'may not there arise some new phase of mind which shall be as different from all present known phases, as the mind of animals is from that of vegetables?'" Looking for prototypes, "traces of the approach of such a new phase of life," the author of *The Book of the Machines* finds them in "the higher machines" (*E*, 173).

Huxley's redoing puts such foolish ideas to rest: Helmholtz Watson's incipient mysticism is the only truly worthwhile new channel for consciousness. Otherwise bleakly pessimistic about humanity's chances, *Brave New*

World nevertheless posits Watson as the next step for evolution. Through his poetry and the creative urge that inspires it, he has begun to experience "some intensification and refining of consciousness, some enlargement of knowledge" which the unnamed author of a paper titled "'A New Theory of Biology'" posits as "the purpose of life" (*BNW*, 145). Granted, Mond censors the paper, but he cannot keep the reader from seeing it. When he sends Watson to the Falklands, Helmholtz becomes a prototypic islander, a forerunner of Huxley's enlightened Palanese.

Early in *Brave New World*, Watson queries his friend, Bernard Marx:

> Speaking very slowly, "Did you ever feel," he asked, "as though you had something inside you that was only waiting for you to give it a chance to come out? Some sort of extra power that you aren't using—you know, like all the water that goes down the falls instead of through the turbines?" He looked at Bernard questioningly. (*BNW*, 57)

Eventually, Helmholtz rearranges his body chemistry, writes a poem about the pleasures of solitude (i.e., contemplation), and shows promise of evolving, as did Huxley, from poet to mystic. It is, he informs Bernard, "'[a]s though I were beginning to be able to use that power I feel I've got inside me—that extra, latent power'" (*BNW*, 149). That "'something inside,'" Watson may gradually discover, is the particle of the Divine Ground allegedly in every individual and anxious to "'come out'" and connect with the Godhead. In a society that promotes a phony happiness— "'everybody's happy now'"—only Watson, having written his breakthrough poem, seems "profoundly happy" (*BNW*, 62, 149).

Contra Butler, Huxley offers a new biological theory that builds on Darwin's; he uses a machinery metaphor ("'turbines'") to describe its workings. In effect, as Watson writes his heretical poem about "'a presence'" (*BNW*, 148) he encounters when silent and alone, he taps into the human race's reservoir of unused evolutionary energy to expand the scope of his awareness. Despite the Time Traveller's encounter with listless Eloi and regressive Morlocks, plenty of this "'extra power'" (*BNW*, 57) remains available, says Huxley. Thanks to it, the next phase of evolution will likely be a step forwards mentally, psychologically, and spiritually. Watson learns to redirect through the turbines some of the "'water that goes down the falls'"; hence the "'new channels […] for consciousness'" that Butler's Higgs suspected might materialize in higher machinery are discernible in the brave new world's chief candidate for enlightenment.

In *We*, Zamiatin identifies "'entropy and energy'" as the only "'two forces in the world'" (Z, 165). The danger is that the latter will yield to the former; that is, that the heresies necessary to keep society in a constant state of turmoil and revolution will harden into stifling orthodoxy as evolution itself becomes stagnation. This has happened in the One State. Rebuffing Zamiatin, Huxley uses Helmholtz Watson to assert that energy is never lost. As Watson's namesake, Hermann von Helmholtz, demonstrated, energy stymied at one point in the system always reappears elsewhere.[49] Thus when Watson discontinues mindless exertions such as games and sex, the unused energy fuels a creative drive that is ultimately spiritual. The poet listening for his muse is not unlike the mystic awaiting enlightenment. "'[W]e cannot calculate on any corresponding advance in man's intellectual or physical powers which shall be a set-off against the far greater development which seems in store for the machines'" (*E*, 177), *The Book of the Machines* warns. On the contrary, Huxley protests, one can and must. John the Savage is a Lawrentian throwback, an atavistic dead end instead of a prerunner or prototype; Watson, although often laughable as in his failure to appreciate *Romeo and Juliet*,[50] is the "'corresponding advance'" Butler looked for, the new channel to the real future.

In *A Modern Utopia*, Wells reduces evolution to open-endedness: the ideal of perfection grows ever clearer to a technologically improving society that is always kinetic.[51] Better, Huxley replies, to have some idea of evolution's ultimate goal; then one can devise the best means to reach desired ends. The Palanese know man's Final End, the achievement of participatory union with the Divine Ground. Ultimately, Huxley instructs Wells, salvation is individual not social or communal. Therein lies a crucial difference between philosophers and utopists. As a member of both contingents, Huxley tries to reconcile their views: a society is utopian only if, as on Pala, conditions prove conducive to individual salvation, only if they facilitate the spiritual development of all members. Conversely, no society whose members are not seekers of enlightenment can ever improve substantially. How can there be unlimited social and political improvements, Huxley in effect taunts Wells, if they can never bring the fullest measure of mental and spiritual advancement (mental and spiritual becoming at some point virtually synonymous)?

When Huxley invents Pala, he expects readers to remember how members of the ruling Party in Orwell's Oceania pervert Watson's success: they turn his recipe for expanding consciousness into an exercise for gaining greater control. This, Orwell warns Huxley, is what will more likely happen to Freud's idea of sublimation[52] in the malevolent dictatorship of the future. "Chastity" is compulsory in *Nineteen Eighty-Four* and "promiscuity" an "unforgivable sin," so that sexual energy can be rechanneled into "the Two Minutes"—frenzied daily outbursts of hatred for Goldstein or for Eurasia or Eastasia, depending on which Oceania is currently at war with.

The Palanese, by contrast, have mastered "the redirection of power" that Watson discovered. This enables Huxley to reverse Orwell and further discredit Butler. As Mr. Menon explains to Will Farnaby, "'You take the power generated by fear or envy or too much noradrenalin'" and "'instead of repressing it [...], you consciously direct it along a channel where it can do something useful'" (*I*, 212). Butler's channels have been reduced to one, but every Palanese is "'consciously'" in control of the power Watson felt was being wasted. Every Palanese can do with his internal energies what only Watson seems capable of in the brave new world: he spends on meditation and writing poetry the effort he used to squander on attending committees, making love, and playing Escalator-Squash. Huxley claims to know more about channels for consciousness (i.e., energy and evolution) than Butler and Zamiatin combined. In the exchange involving Wells, Butler, and Orwell, Huxley, thanks to the Palanese, typically has the last word.

In a letter for 12 December 1962, Huxley classifies *Island* as "a kind of pragmatic dream—a fantasy with detailed and practical instructions for making the imagined and desirable harmonization of European and Indian insights become a fact" (*L*, 944). Pala is first and foremost a case of wishful thinking, yet Huxley feels that it could also serve as a handbook. A bundle of paradoxes, this hybrid is a "dream" that is "pragmatic," a "fantasy" that is "practical"; it can resolve the competition between hypotheses and predictions by remaining "imagined" (i.e., imaginary), while becoming "a fact" to the extent that it provides details and instructions for a hypothetical "harmonization" of East and West. In particular, *Island* completes a cycle by brokering a peace between modern British utopias and twentieth-century science and technology, which, despite Wells, had been at odds since *Erewhon.*

Erewhonians fear being conquered by their machines and so destroy most of them. In *The Time Machine*, the absence of a responsible technology turns Butler's machinists and anti-machinists into cannibalistic Morlocks and effeminate Eloi respectively. In *A Modern Utopia*, the continued advance of machinery is seen as a positive and allowed to proceed unhindered. By A. F. 632, however, machines control production and reproduction, having taken over the life process itself. Only on Pala, says Huxley, does one find a truly appropriate, people-friendly technology: instead of Butler's technophobia or Wells's industrial technocracy, a healthy, sustainable ecosystem ensures social, political, and environmental progress. Unlike the Pyrrhonic aesthete who wrote *Brave New World*, the author of *Island* is never anti-science. Thankfully, oil-rich Pala simply refuses to grant leases to exploitative Western companies such as Joe Aldehyde's Southeast Asia Petroleum.

The Palanese only "'industrialize in spots'"; still, they manage to "'attack on all the fronts at once'": experimental farming, preventive medicine, population control through the governmental distribution of contraceptives, "'streamlined'" techniques for buying, selling, profit sharing and financing, lessons in ecology for the children in Mrs. Narayan's grade school, never "'[i]ndustrialization for industrialization's sake'" (*I*, 66, 147, 43). Even Pavlov has been rehabilitated. Gone are the Neo-Pavlovian conditioning rooms wherein infants are taught to abhor books and flowers. Palanese use Pavlovian conditioning "'purely for a good purpose,'" to foster "'friendliness and trust and compassion,'" not to sell "'cigarettes and vodka, and patriotism,'" not "'for the benefit of dictators, generals, and tycoons'" (*I*, 195).

Similarly, the Palanese develop a benign caste system based on the individual's physiology and temperament. From the age of "'four and a half and five,'" all Palanese children are tested, then educated, in the manner best suited to their "'shape'" (i.e., physique) and mentality (*I*, 154–56). For example, those with a love of power, of "'being the boss,'" learn to "'canalize'" their energy on to "'strenuous and violent tasks'" (*I*, 157) instead of becoming bullies and tyrants. Although Huxley does not apotheosize Dr. William Sheldon, the Palanese have certainly read his two classics, *The Varieties of Temperament* and *Varieties of Physique*; they base their categorizations of Palanese youths upon "the psychological classification of Sheldonian types."[53] Huxley considered this a more reliably scientific system of determining mind and body type than Wells's division of modern utopians into "four main classes" (*AMU*, 265). In A. F. 178, Mond lectures, "'[t]wo thousand pharmacologists and biochemists'" began six years of research to produce *soma*, the "'perfect drug'" to banish glumness (*BNW*, 45). No telling how many scientists were required, but Pala's *moksha*-medicine does much more; it affords glimpses of the Beatific Vision.

In sum, details and instructions for building a utopia like Pala abound in *Island*. Unfortunately, so do negative guidelines such as the Spring and Summer Catalog from Sears, Roebuck and Co., which Murugan reads while "pretending" to study "'Elementary Ecology'" (*I*, 135). The catalog features guns, boats, and motor scooters, whetting one's appetite for "'possessions'" instead of blessedness (*I*, 136–37). When he becomes raja, Murugan plans to make "'nerve gas'" and other "'[c]hemical and biological weapons'" (*I*,

43) that will destroy Pala's uniquely cordial relationship with science and technology, putting them and utopia at odds once again.

After 1900, moderns increasingly took their novels inside. Interiority—articulation of the individual's internal life—became the primary goal. Novelists ventured into Stephen Dedalus's mind or into the subconsciouses of Mrs. Ramsay and Molly Bloom—or into enigmatic recesses such as the heart of darkness and the Marabar Caves. Disputes about the status of external reality—i.e., whether the human situation was improving or worsening—had been implicit in much Victorian fiction[54]; now such disagreements were considered less important than psychological investigation. Consequently, such disagreements were mostly relegated to supposedly less experimental writers, utopists obsessed with future states, not inner ones.[55]

Just as Victorian realists argued among themselves as to whose view of social conditions was most accurate, the modern utopist claims that his depiction of the future is more credible than the conceptions of his rivals, which in effect he revalues and hopes to replace. For example, Orwell believed the sexual ethic in *Nineteen Eighty-Four* more credible and a more likely development than the unrestricted promiscuity of brave new worlders. Would a populace best be kept from being troublesome by having unlimited sex or none at all? Huxley replied by denigrating the "Puritan severity" of Oceania's sexual prohibitions. In future, he summarized, "the lust for power" is not likely to be "satisfied by inflicting pain" but "by inflicting a hardly less humiliating pleasure" (*BNWR*, 21). As to which is both worse and more plausible, Oceania or the World State, Huxley unhesitatingly endorses the latter.

Much as *Erewhon*, "nowhere" almost spelled backwards, is a mirror image of Victorian England, *Brave New World* has been called "a mirror image" of the "principal conventions of its Wellsian opposite" (Baker, *BNWHSD*, 36), and Pala in *Island* is a mirror image of the brave new world, Huxley's negative utopia in reverse, "mirror image" being practically synonymous with revaluation. Butler's Erewhonians reject the nineteenth century's growing reliance on machinery, but Wells's modern utopia, Mark R. Hillegas observes, "is filled with [...] beautiful machines" for which the utopist has "an obvious liking" (*AMU*, xxi). Erewhonians think Victorians are slaves to their machines; Wells believes Erewhonians fail to appreciate technology. Huxley revalues Wells and, in retrospect, dismisses *Nineteen Eighty-Four* as a misguided counterstatement to *Brave New World*.

"In the primary areas of his scientific interest (biology, physiology, and psychology)," notes one observer, Huxley's *Brave New World* "has dated practically not at all" (Firchow, *End*, 39). On the contrary, his "main argument that man is genetically modifiable and psychologically conditionable has [...] gained in scientific authority." This is despite the fact that *Nineteen Eighty-Four* is Orwell's "reply" to *Brave New World*; it "provides different answers to the same questions [...] [in] a kind of dialogue [...] with Huxley's novel" (*End*, 121). What *Brave New World* did to *Men Like Gods* and *A Modern Utopia*, *Nineteen Eighty-Four* attempts to do to *Brave New World*. The crucial difference is that Huxley's dystopia continues to talk back to Orwell's much more sharply than Wells's utopias talk back to *Brave New World*. As skeptical as Huxley was of making predictions, he grew more and more convinced, ultimately adamantly so, that Orwell, like Wells, was wrong although in the opposite direction. Wells gave readers impossible daydreams; Orwell purveyed the wrong nightmare.

Outraged objections to "almost all modern literature" (Woolf and Joyce especially), namely, that it negates "outward reality" and thus constitutes an "attenuation of actuality," a "rejection of history" (Lukacs, 256, 264), do not apply to modern British literary utopias. In them, "reality" or "actuality" —that is, what to make of social conditions to come—remains paramount, both the principal concern and a bone of contention as divergent assessments of the situation multiply. In twentieth-century utopias, the social conscience, to which Victorian novels gave rise, continues to come to fruition. If the "emergence of a modern urban and industrial society" was strictly "a Victorian affair" (Thompson, 29), utopias from *Erewhon* to *Island* are the chief evaluators of the consequences.

Nevertheless, Huxley tries to have things both ways. His last novel brings the cycle from *Erewhon* to *Island* full circle as battles between hypotheses and predictions come to a close in it; but he also avoids attenuations of reality while investing two of his utopias with elements of interiority. In *Brave New World*, although society's workings are described in great detail, Helmholtz Watson's poem "'about being alone'" ignores external reality, in particular the World State's "'warnings against solitude'" (*BNW*, 148, 149). Two twelve-line stanzas proclaim that "'[a]ll silences rejoice.'" In effect, Watson drops out; he delves into himself and writes a paean to the pleasures of introspection, which he attests surpass those of the flesh. He seems to be on his way to "some intensification and refining of consciousness, some enlargement of knowledge" beyond the brave new world's perverse "faith in happiness as the Sovereign Good" (*BNW*, 145). Huxley implies that a breakthrough such as Watson's is more important than a person's surroundings whether utopic or the reverse. The biology paper that Mustapha Mond censors not only calls for a refining and intensifying; it goes on to suggest that these phenomena are the "goal" or "purpose" of life; this allegedly lies "somewhere outside the present human sphere" (*BNW*, 145), that is, beyond the external world in which utopian endeavors take place, the world Lukacs charged writers like Woolf and Joyce with abandoning.

George Orwell eschews stream of consciousness; he tends to avoid indirect discourse, in which the author records a character's musings, thought by thought, as if he (or she) were thinking out loud. Yet in *Nineteen Eighty-Four* both Winston Smith and Julia regard an individual's interiority, his or her inner space, as the last defense against absolute tyranny. Realizing he is to be shot soon, Winston resolves to keep his interior self "inviolate" (O, 231). He accepts O'Brien's statement that "'[r]eality is inside the skull'" and that "[a]ll happenings are in the mind" (O, 218, 229). So just before the fatal bullet penetrates his brain, Winston vows to entertain a final "heretical thought." Unknown to Big Brother, it would go "unrepented," out of the Party's reach "forever," thereby spoiling its boast that it reforms all dissidents before exterminating them. Julia assures Winston that one's internal self is impregnable: "'It's the one thing they can't do. [...] They can't get inside you'" (O, 137). Whether or not Winston defeats the Party, even if O'Brien never knows it, remains problematic.

Readers get no more than a glimpse of Watson contemplating, but in 1932 Huxley is already flirting with the idea that pursuing enlightenment may be more important than trying to establish the perfect place. This suggestion deals a severe blow to traditional utopianism, especially to Wells's attempts to modernize it by extolling new technologies. Pala, Huxley's final utopia, does additional damage. Ultimately, the paramountcy of internal spiritual growth makes developments in the material world seem immaterial. A place such as Pala is still desirable because it is more conducive to one's spiritual advancement than are the facile comforts of the brave new world. Unlike every previous positive utopia, Pala creates the ideal conditions for individuals to actualize what Huxley calls "latent human potentialities,"[56] that is, it provides the opportunity for the Palanese "to grow to the limits of [their] capacities" (*HS*, 236, 237). Put another way, only the Palanese have activated the ideal relationship between ends and means that Huxley formulated in 1937 between the time he wrote *Brave New World* and added a "Foreword": "How will this thought or action contribute to, or interfere with, the achievement, by me and the greatest possible number of other individuals, of man's Final End?" (*BNW*, ix)[57] This "Final End" is not Wells's implausible idea of a society becoming more and more perfect indefinitely, but "unitive knowledge" once for all of "the transcendent Godhead or Brahman" (*BNW*, ix). If such "knowledge" is the ultimate goal, then Huxley's perfect place, were it to come about, would still be only the means, not an end.

A most unusual utopia, *Island* climaxes with the protagonist's drug-induced journey inside himself instead of to the Falklands or to a community of "'Hots'" (*AE*, 103) in northern California.[58] For modern British literary utopias, *Island*'s final chapter is the epitome of interiority. Thanks to a miraculous drug, the *moksha*-medicine, the mirror image of *soma*, Will Farnaby, an uninvited visitor, caps his mental, physical, and spiritual recovery.[59] A cynic upon arrival, a much improved Farnaby swallows a pill and becomes "blissfully one with oneness" (*I*, 271). He achieves the breakthrough that Watson was striving for in his poem. Huxley calls this union "luminous bliss," "knowledgeless understanding," "undifferentiated awareness" (*I*, 272), three admittedly groping terms for an indescribable state of being superior to that in any prior utopia, indeed, to life on Pala itself. Although Pala is ruined in the final pages when Colonel Dipa's troops invade, Huxley continues to proffer the possibility of internal utopia, the one paradise that apparently can never be lost. "Disregarded in the darkness" after Dipa's cars have passed, writes Huxley, "the fact of enlightenment remained" (*I*, 295). Enlightenment, Huxley maintains, is a "fact"; Pala, the perfect society he constructs around it, remains a hypothesis. Big Brother may (or may not) be able to get inside Winston Smith, but the Palanese, thanks to the *moksha*-medicine, get inside Farnaby. They illuminate him from within, endowing interiority with a spiritual dimension not to be found in Oceania or through the modern novel's use of stream of consciousness.

The first serious utopian in Huxley's fiction is not Mr. Scogan, regardless of the resemblance between the World State in *Brave New World* and "'the Rational State'" he outlines for Denis Stone in chapter 22 of *Crome Yellow*. Admittedly, Scogan's utopia will feature a caste system that separates inhabitants "'into distinct species,'" three in fact to the World State's five. "'[L]abelled and docketed,'" each individual is to "'be given the education suitable to members of its species'" and all will be conditioned "'to believe that they are happy'" (*CY*, 242, 245). But Scogan is just another talker in a discussion novel of ideas. Hercules the dwarf, whose life story Henry Wimbush reads from his *History of Crome*, is a doer. "'[A] pigmy of three feet and four inches,'" he establishes, during his tenure as master of Crome, a household society perfectly suited to his deficiencies: a personalized utopia or "'private world of his own, in which all should be proportionable to himself'" (*CY*, 123, 128). No member of his numerous staff stands "'above four feet high'"; he kept the "'smallest'" breeds of dogs and horses (*CY*, 128). To the extent that all utopias are private worlds set up to cater to the ideas of one alleged sage or a chosen few, Huxley is the only modern British utopist to recognize a connection between eccentricity and utopianism. That is, he realizes that every utopian, especially those in negative utopias, is a bit like Sir Hercules, an egotistic eccentric redesigning the world to favor his own idiosyncratic tastes and capabilities.[60]

Throughout *Brave New World*, Henry Ford is satirized for suggesting that society be reorganized according to the guidelines used to run his factories. "I am now most interested," Ford confessed, "in fully demonstrating that the ideas we have put into practice are capable of the largest application—that they have nothing peculiarly to do with motor cars or tractors but form something in the nature of a universal code" (Ford, 3). The Central London Hatchery and Conditioning Centre, an insult to human nature, is the result: the largest Ford factory ever conceived, but to mass produce brave new worlders, not motor cars and tractors. The American efficiency expert, Frederick Winslow Taylor, believed his principles of scientific management should be applied to "all social activities," in homes, farms, churches, universities and government institutions (Taylor, iv). In *We*, Zamiatin's One State extends Taylor's methods "to all of life, to every step, to the twenty-four hours of every day" (Z, 33). Efficiency techniques are applied to eating, sleeping, and even love-making. Extending Darwinian evolution to machinery in *Erewhon*, Taylorism to all human activity in *We*, and mass production to procreation in the brave new world are three equally reductive misapplications; each is one-pointed and Procrustean, a narrowing disguised as an expansion. Zamiatin's Taylor and Huxley's Ford—each is Sir Hercules writ large. But "Fordism," Huxley informs Butler and Zamiatin, is the worst, a perverse religion that "demands the cruellest mutilations of the human psyche and offers the smallest spiritual returns" (*MN*, 180–81). A utopia inspired by Ford is therefore more dreadful than one indebted to Taylor or one in which machinery is allowed to develop unchecked.

Unfortunately, Pala in *Island* must also bear the stigma of being a private world. Huxley seems to realize that the "forbidden island," closed to outsiders, has cut itself off from the rest of civilization as determinedly (and ultimately as ineffectually) as Sir Hercules remodeled his household. Pala, Mr. Bahu explains, is "'a small island completely surrounded by twenty-nine hundred million mental cases'" who resent it for being "'too rational'" (*I*, 66). As such, it is clearly doomed. Only "'so long as it remains out of touch with the rest of the world, an ideal society can be a viable society,'" Bahu maintains (*I*, 55). Pala seems utopic whereas Sir Hercules is ridiculous, yet both meet the fate Huxley reserves for eccentric escapists. For the dwarf disaster arrives in the person of Ferdinando, a normal-size son. Pala's downfall begins with the advent of Will Farnaby and the prospect of granting Joe Aldehyde's Southeast Asia Petroleum invasive oil concessions.

Modern British literary utopias, it bears repeating, argue among themselves constantly. Each wants to validate its conception of what the future will or should be like by outstripping rival scenarios. From *Erewhon* to *Island*, every major utopist pits his vision of the future against one or more of the futures described by his contemporaries and predecessors. Modern British utopists write with one eye on the future, the other on the futures previously imagined by their rivals. Nearly every modern British utopian's vision of things allegedly oncoming entails a reconsideration of a prior assessment. A future is always being constructed in its own right and at the expense of another future already in print, whose plausibility or desirability it seeks to negate. Paradoxically, the major utopian novels from the first half of the twentieth century are as backwards-looking as they are future-oriented.

Modern British utopists, even someone like Huxley with mixed feelings about making forecasts, proceed as if it is worthwhile to predict the future, yet each foresees, that is, fears or desires, a different future, one that challenges other depictions. Inasmuch as each believes that only he can accurately accomplish what Butler began, he validates and invalidates Butler simultaneously. The future can be predicted, says each utopist, but all predictions other than his own are wrong. According to *The Book of the Machines*, there is only one future to be concerned about. After *Erewhon*, there are many. From among the countless revaluations that make the cycle from *Erewhon* to *Island* a cross between a debating society and a battlefield, five topics that utopists argue over stand out: 1. choice of rulers, 2. fate of couples, 3. texts-within-texts, 4. freedom versus happiness, 5. cures. In each case, on every issue, Huxley strives to have the last word.

Whether stipulating who they believe should run the future or predicting who they fear will do so, no two modern British utopists agree. H. G. Wells's modern utopia is governed by technocrats whom he admires greatly: altruistic lawyers, doctors, scientists—all with extraordinary administrative abilities.[61] Zamiatin, Huxley, and Orwell take turns ridiculing his notions of ideal management. They also contradict each other until Huxley delivers what is meant to be the final say on this subject. Wells devotes chapter nine of *A Modern Utopia*, titled "The *Samurai*," to a "voluntary nobility" (*AMU*, 259) modeled on the Guardians in Plato's Republic and named for feudal Japan's hereditary warrior class.

Democratic elections, Wells explains, cannot provide the "more powerful and efficient methods of control" that "Utopian organization" requires (*AMU*, 258). Only a talented cadre of dedicated public servants can combine "progress with political stability" says Wells (*AMU*, 271). Hence the *samurai*. However, Zamiatin's One State succumbs to totalitarian tendencies he saw lurking in Wells's need for extra powerful and efficient controls. Plato's Guardians reappear in *We* as the "experienced eyes" (i.e., police, spies) of the Benefactor, a dictator whose euphemistic title cannot conceal a resemblance to Lenin (Z, 14).[62] Organization has become regimentation, the ultimate goal of scientific utopias in Zamiatin's opinion. D-503, the state's leading rocket scientist, is a parody of a Wellsian *samurai*. He sings the praises of "the mathematically perfect life of the One State" (Z, 2). Zamiatin's vision of the future and its ruler is simultaneously a negative revision of Wells's.

Huxley warns Wells that his emphasis on control, efficiency, and stability could lead to dystopia. "Stability" is the last word in the first paragraph of *Brave New World* and the climactic third ideal in "the World State's motto" (*BNW*, 1). "'Stability,'" Mond stresses repeatedly, is "'[t]he primal and the ultimate need'" (*BNW*, 34), both alpha and omega. There is no "'inefficiency,'" political or otherwise, in a "'properly organized society like ours,'" Mond asserts. Only a dystopist, Huxley believes, would put stability before increases in knowledge, to which, in fact, it is opposed. Huxley concludes the 1946 "Foreword" to the reissue of his dystopia with an admonition for Wells. The brave new world, he contends, is "one supra-national totalitarianism" that has been "called into existence by the social chaos resulting from rapid technological progress" and "the need for efficiency and stability" (*BNW*, xv).

Mond's history lesson, his impromptu lecture to a group of newly arrived students, explains how the brave new world was established to stop "'The Nine Years' War'" and end "'the great Economic Collapse. There was a choice between World Control and destruction. Between stability and…'" (*BNW*, 39). "'We have the World State now,'" he adds, alluding directly to Wells's modern utopia, the "World-state" (*BNW*, 44; *AMU*, 12). Similarly, Mond's title, "Resident Controller for Western Europe" (*BNW*, 26), is a slap at Wells's call for more efficient controls. These have resulted in "World Controllers," not Wells's self-sacrificing modern *samurai*.

Returning to Wells in *Brave New World Revisited* without mentioning him by name, Huxley allots Chapter III to "Over-Organization," a disaster which Zamiatin also dreads. Huxley calls it the "shortest and broadest road to the nightmare of Brave New World" (*BNWR*, 14). In 1958, as in 1932, Huxley seems convinced, contra Wells, that rapid technological progress threatens stability; inevitably, along with over-population, it leads to a "choice between anarchy and totalitarian control" (*BNWR*, 14), just as Mond maintains in his lecture. Extremely over-organized, the brave new world safeguards stability by regulating the birth-rate and stifling additional scientific advances. Huxley employs all of Wells's key words—progress, efficiency, organization, stability—but they do not fit together nicely as in *A Modern Utopia*. Instead, control and progress are virtually contrapuntal ideas for Huxley, precluding the Wellsian utopia and, possibly, utopia *per se* despite Wells's plans to keep his future society open-ended. Progress minus control, especially control of population, spells chaos, but stability through over-organization puts an end to progress, Huxley informs Wells.

Huxley's parody of a Wellsian ruler is more damaging than Zamiatin's insofar as Mustapha Mond comes across as a round, three-dimensional character.[63] Wells does not depict individual technocrats; his *samurai* are to be thought of collectively, always a group. Admittedly, D-503 is psychologically complex, but Zamiatin's Benefactor remains flat, an undeveloped authoritarian less interesting than the dehumanizing regimen he imposes. He sounds sincere when he claims to have taught everyone "'the meaning of happiness,'" which is also the brave new world's paramount concern. By controlling all thought and movement, he has freed everyone from "'desires'" (Z, 214). Similarly, Mond portrays himself as the servant of "'happiness. Other people's,'" he adds (*BNW*, 187). In the brave new world, he boasts, there is no lengthy "'interval between the consciousness of a desire and its fulfilment'" (*BNW*, 36). But the Controller is an accomplished hypocrite who realizes he serves a bogus ideal, coming as it does at the "'cost'" of change, art, truth, beauty, and science, all of which, he concedes, are "'incompatible with happiness'" and therefore cannot be tolerated (*BNW*, 184). Unlike the Benefactor, Mond sees through the system he administers but endorses it anyway because, surpassing Wells's fondest dreams, it "'has given'" the brave new world "'the stablest equilibrium in history'" (*BNW*, 186).

Unlike Wells's faceless *samurai* and Zamiatin's "bald," presumably ancient Benefactor (Z, 215), Mustapha Mond is a lively presence, vigorous and congenial; when he interviews the Savage, his face beams with "good-humoured intelligence" (*BNW*, 179). This, says Huxley, is what a World

Controller is likely to look like: a deceptively benevolent despot. Surprisingly, Mond has received a good press. "The one character exempted from satire in *Brave New World* is the world controller for western Europe, Mustapha Mond" (Milner, 118). "Of course," agrees a second commentator, "Mond generates sympathy in the reader"; "the secretly free-thinking man is the character in the novel most like ourselves" (McGiveron, 136). But Mond is clearly a satire. He behaves more diabolically than the Arch-Vicar, an actual devil-worshipper who runs things in *Ape and Essence*.

Once a promising physicist, Mond now regards science as an "'enemy'" to be restricted and, if necessary, silenced (*BNW*, 184). Accordingly, he censors an unnamed biologist's paper for rejecting "happiness as the Sovereign Good" (*BNW*, 145). Salvific texts such as *The Holy Bible*, *The Imitation of Christ*, and *The Varieties of Religious Experience* he keeps locked in his safe, out of the hands of brave new worlders (see *BNW*, 189). He exiles Bernard Marx and Helmholtz Watson; and he denies the Savage's request to accompany them, which precipitates John's suicide. To exonerate Mond is to negate one of Huxley's sternest retorts to both Wells and Zamiatin, to the former for being naively adulatory regarding *samurai*, to the latter for creating an utterly charmless villain, as dryly mechanical as the One State's system of life by the numbers. By extension, Mond challenges Orwell's Big Brother, a Stalin-like paragon of masculinity who is probably imaginary, that is, a total fabrication by the ruling Party. He also impugns O'Brien, Big Brother's sadistic agent; O'Brien's seven-year torture of Winston Smith is a prolonged ego-trip that makes the Benefactor's prompt liquidation of dissidents seem benign.

Wells's *samurai* rely on their mastery of "physiological science" to postpone "the years of decay." The process Wells describes is unintentionally comical:

> They keep their teeth, they keep their digestions, they ward off gout and rheumatism, neuralgia and influenza and all those cognate decays that bend and wrinkle men and women in the middle years of existence. They have extended the level years far into the seventies, and age, when it comes, comes swiftly and easily. (*AMU*, 315)

Stability for Wells requires good health; *samurai* are obliged to maintain a wholesome physical condition as long as possible. Wells awards them "a ripe prolonged maturity in an adult world" (*AMU*, 315).

Huxley's satire exposes what he regards as the shallowness of Wells's thinking. His idea of maturity is mostly longevity, objects Huxley. The adulthood of Wells's ruling class seems to amount to preserving good digestion and a full set of teeth. For Wells's *samurai*, says Huxley, well-being, i.e., simply being well, has become the primary goal; adulthood is redefined as reaching one's seventies in good shape, without serious ailments. All brave new worlders, even Epsilons, are "'never ill'" and remain "'blissfully ignorant of […] old age,'" a horror they are seldom allowed to witness (*BNW*, 180).[64] Is such wellness and ignorance the best a utopia can offer?, Huxley asks. In the "year of stability, A. F. 632," it is impossible to tell whether the Director of Hatcheries and Conditioning is thirty or fifty-five. The brave new world conceals or denies the aging process.

Faces of dying patients in the Park Lane Hospital appear "fresh and unwithered"; only their brains and hearts have aged (*BNW*, 164). They seem to be preparing not for death but for a "second infancy" (*BNW*, 164). Brave new worlders, Wells's modern utopians to the contrary, are not encouraged to reach adulthood or prolong it. Instead, they are compelled "to behave out of office hours 'like a babe in a bottle'" (*BNW*, 122). Everyone must maintain "'a proper standard of infantile decorum'" (*BNW*, 81). Self-imposed arrested development rules out mental growth. "'Characters remain constant throughout a lifetime,'" exclaims Mond. If, as he boasts, "'at sixty our powers and tastes are what they were at seventeen'" (*BNW*, 4), adulthood has been reduced to eternal adolescence. All brave new worlders are "'death-conditioned'" not to worry about their mortality for as long as they can. As Bernard Marx puts it, they enjoy "'[y]outh almost unimpaired till sixty, and then, crack! The end'" (*BNW*, 91). The brave new worlder dies as quickly as Wells could desire but does so thoughtlessly. Following some of Wells's pronouncements regarding the life and death of the ruling class, and applying them to the general population, Huxley comes up with a very different, indeed, anti-Wellsian, picture of a future scientifically controlled and administered but not at all attractive.

The competition to describe the directing intelligence of society in future culminates in *Island* with Dr. Robert MacPhail. Huxley imagines the best possible *samurai*; just as in the brilliant but devious Mustapha Mond he created the worst. Principal spokesperson for Pala, Dr. Robert is the island's Prospero: physician, scientist, ecologist, and above all, enlightened sage. For Huxley, he epitomizes the ideal into which Wells never could breathe enough life.[65] Although Dr. Robert has no title and holds no office, he belongs to an elite as hereditary as Wells's: along with the Raja of the Reform, Dr. Robert's great-grandfather, Dr. Andrew, "'invented modern Pala'" (*I*, 34). Evidently, there has been a MacPhail—great-grandfather, grandfather, father—alongside every one of Pala's rajas as a sort of unofficial prime minister. The first pair, a "'Scottish doctor and the Palanese king, the Calvinist-turned-atheist and the pious Mahayana Buddhist'" (*I*,

129), devised the perfect synthesis; they combined the best of modern science from the West with Pala's Eastern Buddhism in order "'to make the best of both worlds—the Oriental and the European, the ancient and the modern'" (*I*, 130). Besides eclipsing Wells's *samurai*, Dr. Robert is the perfect antidote for the Benefactor, the Arch-Vicar of *Ape and Essence*, and Big Brother.

As a physician, Dr. Robert can cure Will Farnaby of injuries suffered in a fall. As a scientist, he can also help to run an Agricultural Experimental Station. As an enlightened sage, he encourages the Palanese to seek "'unitive knowledge'" of the Godhead, to become "'fully human'" (*I*, 141, 143); he can teach them how to obtain "'beatific glimpses'" of the Clear Light and attain "'the wisdom of the Other Shore'" (*I*, 173, 226), gifts totally beyond the grasp of *A Modern Utopia*'s *samurai* and vastly superior to the comfortable but purely materialistic adulthood Wells offers. Most important, Dr. Robert both espouses "'the yoga of everyday living'" and has mastered "'the ultimate science, [...] the science that sooner or later we shall all have to be examined in—thanatology'" (*I*, 152, 144). Pala is the only modern British utopia to prepare its citizens for leaving it in the best way possible. Unlike the brave new world, which tries to trivialize death, Dr. Robert and his daughter-in-law, Susila, specialize in "'the whole art of dying'" (*I*, 246).

Unfortunately, Dr. Robert and Pala both perish, which raises doubts about Huxley's confidence in a perfect place and an ideal *samurai* to administer it. Rescinded, both become hypothetical, unlike Wells's *samurai*, who are supposedly on the way. Dr. Robert's eldest son, Dugald, has died in a climbing accident; Lakshmi, his wife, dies from cancer in the penultimate chapter. In the last chapter, Dr. Robert is summarily shot by Colonel Dipa's invading force from neighboring Rendang, an ignominious death. Murugan, the next raja, is in league with Dipa, so future partnerships between a MacPhail and Pala's king seem unlikely. The novel's final sentences declare that even though "disregarded in the darkness, the fact of enlightenment remained" (*I*, 295), but of five competing alternatives to Wells's improbable *samurai*—the Benefactor, Mond, the devil-worshipping Arch-Vicar in *Ape and Essence*, Dr. Robert, Big Brother—only Huxley's paragon, who wins the competition for best ruler, does not survive.

Modern British utopists hold conflicting opinions about how the leaders of their future societies will combat heresy. Like the quality of its leadership, a society's ability to cope with rebels and dissidents, misfits and malcontents, helps to determine its worthiness to be considered a utopia. The lone malcontent in *A Modern Utopia* is a ridiculous "talkative" person (i.e., a bore) dressed in leather doublet, knee breeches, faded cloak, and sandals (*AMU*, 114). A proponent of "Simple Ways" who subsists on grapes, he rails against machine technology. Wells dismisses this interrupter as a "consummate ass" (*AMU*, 116). For Wells, the real problem is not unorthodox thinkers like this refugee from Morris's arts and crafts society but those he calls life's undesirables: "congenital invalids, […] idiots and madmen, […] drunkards and men of vicious mind, […] cruel and furtive souls, […] stupid people" (*AMU*, 136). The *samurai* send them to "islands of exile" (*AMU*, 147) that prefigure brave new world's, but Wells never explains how such places can function. Zamiatin regards heretics as the world's lifeblood; their heresies supply the energy that forestalls entropy. Nevertheless, he anticipates a One State in which they will be lobotomized or else liquidated in the "Benefactor's Machine" (Z, 232).

Huxley outdoes the Russian three misfits to one. Confident of its invincibility, the brave new world improves upon Wells's island solution: Bernard Marx and Helmholtz Watson are bound for "'an island'" where they will meet "'the most interesting set of men and women to be found anywhere in the world,'" individuals like themselves with "'independent ideas of their own'" (*BNW*, 186). The Falklands are an offshore think tank whose members, Mond realizes, will not have the slightest impact on the rest of the world. Still, this punishment seems like a reward. Orwell scoffs at Zamiatin's fondness for heretics. Compared with Mond's questioning of Watson and Marx, O'Brien's sadistic interrogation of Winston Smith rivals the Inquisition. Given its length and brutality, it can be called the longest way with dissenters. Oceania controls dissent by first stimulating it in order to flush out potential heretics and find greater satisfaction in crushing them.

Only Huxley's Will Farnaby is actually a deviant in a healthy society, a sour pessimist among the enlightened, and therefore genuinely in need of help. In healing Will's spirit, improving his attitude towards life and his opinion of himself, the Palanese achieve a genuine conversion. Thanks primarily to Dr. Robert MacPhail but with the aid of several interlocutors, Will learns the Palanese philosophy of life and grows from jaded cynic to apprentice mystic; he literally sees the light. In *Island*, Huxley invents the only society among modern British utopias whose benign methods of enlightening a misfit and malcontent seem perfect.

In several modern British utopias, a crucial question arises: how will a man and a woman, life's basic social unit, fare? Can they find bodily and intellectual satisfaction? If not, their society is shown to be a fake paradise, a negative Eden, in which, instead of making a new start for humanity, the couple, figuratively its Adam and Eve, are disappointed or disappoint each other, sometimes fatally. Between *Erewhon* and *Island*, the central couple's plight worsens from novel to novel, each redoing of its predicament grimmer than the last. Finally, Huxley reverses previous failures, including the one in his own *Brave New World*, with two positive but still problematic pairings, first in *Ape and Essence* and then in *Island*.

Higgs flees Erewhon by balloon with Arowhena in a mock Ascension. Arowhena becomes Weena in *The Time Machine* where the balloon turns into a mechanical contraption the Erewhonians would probably smash. Wells allows the Time Traveller to return to the nineteenth century but leaves Weena to be devoured by Morlocks. Not "'until it was too late did I clearly understand what she was to me,'" moans the Traveller (*TM*, 62). Zamiatin, the Russian utopist who serves as a connector between Wells, on the one hand, and Huxley and Orwell on the other, felt that Wells, like the Traveller, underestimates the importance of an Eve figure. In *We*, I-330 lures D-503, society's master builder of the *Integral*, into thinking and behaving heretically. When he betrays his temptress and forsakes the chance to recover his individuality, she must "ascend" the Benefactor's Machine, in which she will literally be liquidated, reduced to "a small puddle of chemically pure water" (Z, 232, 48); her rise and her exit parody Higgs's ascension and the Time Traveller's apparatus for escape, neither of which Zamiatin credits.

Ashamed of his lust for "'pneumatic'" Lenina, a promiscuous Eve-figure who attempts to seduce him, John the Savage whips her to death during an impromptu "'Orgy-porgy'" (see *BNW*, 212).[66] Then he hangs himself. In *Brave New World*, the central couple perish ignominiously, one a murder victim and the other a murderer and suicide. Connie and Mellors experience a rebirth of hope and pleasure in *Lady Chatterley's Lover*. However, at novel's end, they are living separately, no longer a couple, having been expelled from the Edenic wood wherein their improvised love rituals brought them back to life sexually. It is uncertain if they can reunite.[67] Politically and sexually, Winston Smith and Julia end up worse off in *Nineteen Eighty-Four* than D-503 and I-330 in *We* or than Connie and Mellors in Lawrence's novel, the two couples whose fortunes Orwell revises downwards. Self-confessed rebels against Oceania's ruling Party, Winston and Julia betray their convictions and each other: "'I betrayed you,' she said boldly. 'I betrayed you,' he said. She gave him another look of dislike" (O, 240). Orwell rejects the idea that a resurgence of physical intimacy can disrupt a negative utopia as it does, if only temporarily, in Lawrence and Zamiatin. A pathetic version of the Lawrentian hero, Winston Smith does not sing the body's praises, instead, he deplores "the treachery of the human body" (O, 86). One's fight is "always against one's own body," he declares; it is easily overwhelmed by pain and the fear of it.

In *Ape and Essence*, Poole and Loola make a ludicrous pair, a caricature of our first parents. Having absconded from the ape-like society around Los Angeles, they head north, looking for a saner, sexually more normal community supposedly "'friendly to runaways from southern California'" (*AE*, 152). Ridiculous or not, Poole and Loola are the first central couple to stick together since Higgs and Arowhena made their getaway. But there is no guarantee the society they seek exists or that "the two lovers" will be able to find it (*AE*, 153). From a world devastated by "weapons of mass destruction" (*AE*, 37), they grope their way towards a rediscovery of "monogamy and romantic love," a situation not quite "analogous to holiness" but that may lead to it (*AE*, 122, 148).

In *Island*, set in the 1950s, Pala is an alternative society rather than a future one. A giant step forwards from Poole and Loola, Will Farnaby and Susila MacPhail are as close to an ideal couple as modern British utopias get. Under the tutelage of a positive Eve figure, Will acquires the moral and spiritual fortitude to cope with the despicable behavior in his past; he overcomes the self-loathing his misdeeds have caused and begins to adopt the Palanese version of the perennial philosophy. By helping him, Susila continues to recover from the sudden loss of her first husband in a mountain climbing accident. Their curative impact on each other is reminiscent of Connie and Mellors, maybe better. During the LSD trip Will takes with Susila as his guide, he opens his eyes[68] to see her "'incredibly beautiful" face (*I*, 288), a foretaste perhaps of the Beatific Vision. Thanks to Susila, Will travels to the kingdom of God that exists within each of us, a journey superior to the Time Traveller's or the Savage's from Malpais to Fordian London or than the New Zealand Rediscovery Expedition's to southern California.

The perfect couple emerge in *Island* and may have a future together. If Farnaby and Susila do make a go of it, they will be the modern British literary utopia's most successful pair, their coupling as much a spiritual as a physical union. Unfortunately, Pala is invaded by Rendang even as Will is completing his *moksha*-medicine experience. Murugan, the new Raja, proclaims "'the United Kingdom of Rendang and Pala'" (*I*, 293), a marriage of hell and heaven. Ironically, the perfect place for the perfect couple ceases to exist. Trumping the competition, Huxley earns the distinction of creating in John and Lenina the most disastrous couple in modern British utopias and in Will and Susila the couple with the best prospects for a harmonious relationship despite Pala's collapse. One could argue that the fates of

Huxley's couples make the World State the worst of the modern British utopias (i.e., the epitome of dystopia) while Pala, clearly the best, is also the frailest.

Modern British utopias often incorporate a text-within-the-text. The protagonist visiting an alleged utopia stumbles upon an explanatory document and the narrative pauses while he peruses it. This essay-like time-saving ploy permits the writer to describe the major features of his imaginary society without constantly having to create more characters and supply additional dialogue. From *Erewhon* to *Island*, several utopists strive to employ the text-within-the-text more effectively than their rivals. The list of notable insertions begins with *The Book of the Machines*, and includes *My Life and Work*, *The Theory of Oligarchical Collectivism*, *A Clockwork Orange*, and *Notes on What's What.*

In *Erewhon*, *The Book of the Machines* warns that rapidly evolving machines will gain control of the human race if societies do not destroy them to prevent a takeover. From this text-within-the-text Higgs and the reader learn why the Erewhonians have so few machines and that societies not yet machineless are in grave danger. But according to Huxley, Butler gets the future all wrong. Contra Butler, Huxley foresees that the apotheosis of the machine is inevitable, but not in the constructive ways that H. G. Wells predicted. In the brave new world, vastly improved and enlarged assembly lines not only control the production of consumer goods but run the reproduction process as well. The Central London Hatchery and Conditioning Centre, a skyscraper of "thirty-four stories," massproduces "scores" of bottle babies. In the biggest Ford factory ever, a "spidery steelwork of gallery above gallery faded away in all directions" (*BNW*, 1, 4, 8).

When the Savage is ushered into the Controller's study in chapter XVI of *Brave New World*, he picks up a copy of *My Life and Work by Our Ford* "published at Detroit by the Society for the Propagation of Fordian Knowledge" (*BNW*, 178), Huxley's parody of the Society for the Propagation of the Christian Faith. A "massive volume bound in limp black leather-surrogate, and stamped with large golden T's," it has replaced the Bible. After reading a few paragraphs, however, John decides that "the book didn't interest him" (*BNW*, 178). His indifference is ironic. Ford's autobiography, widely discussed in its day, is dismissed as uninteresting, but it remains more important than John realizes. If he read further, as Huxley did, he would understand how thoroughly the World State he despises is constructed according to Henry Ford's guidelines for an efficient factory.[69] Huxley never quotes from his text-within-the-text. Still, a mere mention—along with dozens of references to the Controller as "'his fordship'" (*BNW*, 25)—is sufficient to alert readers to the pervasive influence of Ford's organizational practices.

Similarly in *We*, Zamiatin satirizes Taylorism, the scientific management theories of Frederick Winslow Taylor, an American efficiency expert. Wrongheadedly, the One State has applied his time-and-motion studies to "every step" of life (Z, 33) just as the brave new world obeys Ford's precepts in all things whether industrial or biological. The result in *We* is a totally regimented—indeed, robotized—populace, whose every activity from sleeping to eating is rigidly programmed. D-503 calls "Taylor" a "genius" (Z, 33) but his name appears once only and *The Principles of Scientific Management* (1911), his masterwork, is never cited. Huxley considered *My Life and Work* (1913) more pernicious, its potential impact on the future more alarming.

Unlike the texts by Ford and Taylor, *The Theory and Practice of Oligarchical Collectivism* is entirely imaginary, as is its reputed author, Emmanuel Goldstein.[70] In 1949, it was by far the lengthiest text-within-a-text in a modern British utopia. Running over twenty-five pages in most editions, Orwell's inserted text contradicts Mustapha Mond's history lesson in chapter III of *Brave New World.* Disregard A. F. 632, says Orwell, and worry about the horrors in store for the next forty years, in the fifties and sixties especially. "[B]y the fourth decade of the twentieth century," Goldstein writes, "all the main currents of political thought were totalitarian. The earthly paradise had been discredited" (O, 168).[71] The early twentieth century, Orwell continues, was wrong to envision "a future society unbelievably rich, leisured, orderly and efficient—a glittering antiseptic world of glass and steel and snow-white concrete" (O, 156). Orwell rules out H. G. Wells's bright future and dismisses Huxley's parody of it in which "glass and nickel and bleakly shining porcelain" make the Fertilizing Room as "cold" as a morgue (*BNW*, 1). For Orwell, Huxley's parody becomes irrelevant once its target, the Wellsian utopia, is deemed an impossibility.

Oligarchical Collectivism dismisses everybody from Wells to Huxley. Wells idolized machines, for example, whereas Huxley satirized the worship of machinery by misapplying mass production to biology. "The machine" has practically disappeared from Oceania—not because it was evolving faster than humans, as Butler feared, but because, observes Goldstein, it seemed likely to eliminate "human drudgery"; it promised to put an end to "hunger, overwork, dirt, illiteracy, and disease" (O, 156). But if it produced enough wealth to go around, writes Goldstein, the machine would minimize "inequality" and thus threaten "the destruction" of a "hierarchical society" such as Oceania's; power and luxury would no longer remain "in the hands of a small privileged caste" (O, 156). Orwell considers this Inner Party, as he calls it, a perverse rendition simultaneously of Wells's *samurai* and Huxley's World Controllers[72]: it is, says Orwell, the most likely form totalitarianism will take.

As in the brave new world, science in Oceania "has almost ceased to exist" (O, 159). "[T]echnological progress" having been halted, the "tendency towards mechanization" has also been arrested (O, 159, 157). In both places, the goal is stability, which experiments and discoveries can easily upset. But Oceania's stability, Goldstein stresses, is not like the World State's. Science is forbidden in Orwell's dystopia lest it improve the common lot. Orwell's stable future is a world of "chronic shortage[s]"; a "general state of scarcity" prevails (O, 158). The "'conscription of consumption'" *(BNW*, 40)—every brave new worlder is obliged to consume a certain amount of goods annually in order to keep the economy running steadily—has been superseded by an industrial system geared never to produce more than "half the necessities of life" (O, 158). This guaranteed shortfall makes Inner Party members, who enjoy more privileges than both Outer Party members and the even less fortunate "submerged masses" (O, 158), visibly superior.

Instead of Wells's never-ending universal improvement and Huxley's system of complacent castes, Orwell's future society favors "collectivism" (O, 170), a euphemistic term for a regimented, hierarchical community in which a few control all the wealth and property, while the majority is kept abject and miserable. In short, collective means selective. Although supposedly an enemy of Oceania, Goldstein writes about oligarchical collectivism like an insider. Orwell's text-within-a-text is a masterful elucidation—almost a justification—of a form of governance its author, be he Orwell or Goldstein, thoroughly opposes.

Orwell's text-within-a-text shows that he believed himself to be a more realistic historian of the future than prior utopists, better, that is, at presenting things yet to come as if they had already happened. When Bellamy looks backward from the future in *Looking Backward* in order to describe the past hundred years, he sees what he would like to have occur by then. Admittedly, Mond ticks off the major events leading up to the brave new world, a fanciful history of the future. But when Orwell writes about the future in the past tense, the future is indeed in the past: Goldstein seems to be doing political science, the future as history, an extensive record of things that have actually happened. *The Theory and Practice of Oligarchical Collectivism* treats the fifties and sixties the way a historian such as C. L. Mowat writes about

Great Britain since 1914—except that it is only 1949 when Orwell is writing, whereas it is 1971 for Mowat.

Winston Smith's job in the Ministry of Truth is to facilitate the "alteration of the past" (O, 175). In Oceania, "history is continuously rewritten" by civil servants like Winston so that when the Party changes its mind, it can still insist that it has always held its current position (O, 176). "The mutability of the past," as Orwell calls it (O, 176), guarantees that the state was never at odds with its present policies. Apparently, *The Theory and Practice of Oligarchical Collectivism* is exempt from revision. Orwell has it both ways. Oceania can rewrite the past as needed but Goldstein's account of the fifties and sixties stays unchanged. Ford's *My Life and Work* is a "massive volume" attractively bound and sporting "golden T's" (*BNW*, 178). Goldstein's tome is a rare but dilapidated book, a "heavy black volume" bound "amateurishly" with no title on its cover; moreover, it is falling "apart" (O, 151). The Savage tosses Ford's autobiography aside. Orwell does not say what becomes of Winston's copy of Goldstein's book. Its shabby condition suggests that O'Brien has used it often to entice would-be heretics like Winston to step forwards in search of a mythical "Brotherhood" opposed to Big Brother (O, 141). Unlike *My Life and Work* and Taylor's time-and-motion studies, which have done their damage, Orwell's text-within-the-text continues to be a working text, more useful than either predecessor.

Technically, Winston Smith's diary is Orwell's text-within-the-text and Goldstein's book yet another text within it. Surely Winston begins a diary because D-503 kept one. *We* is arguably all text-within-the-text, a novel entirely composed of its protagonist's reflections on life in the One State. The same problem confronts readers of both diaries: how did each find its way into print? Once Winston is scheduled to be liquidated, why would Oceania want his diary preserved? Who publishes D-503's journal and for what purpose? In the dystopia of the future, says Huxley, dissidents will not be able to keep an incriminating diary because they will have no inner lives to confide to its pages. Wisely, Huxley avoids involving his narrator with a text-within-the-text. But his "amused Pyrrhonic aesthete" (*BNW*, viii) is unconventionally omniscient; more in control of his story than either Winston or D-503, he is nevertheless a total skeptic who writes chiefly to share his amusement at the bad turn he thinks things are going to take.

In *A Clockwork Orange*, Anthony Burgess only quotes a single sentence from his text-within-the-text but that brief excerpt provides the key to the novel. Published in 1962, Burgess's dystopia is set in an unidentified city in the England of the near future. Despite a government that aspires to be authoritarian, little Alex and his band of teenage delinquents roam the countryside unchecked, committing random acts of violence. One night they invade the cottage of F. Alexander, a dissident intellectual, beating him up and raping his wife. Little Alex tears up the writer's book manuscript titled "A CLOCKWORK ORANGE," but not before reading "a malenky bit out loud": "'—The attempt to impose upon man, a creature of growth and capable of sweetness, to ooze juicily at the last round the bearded lips of God, to attempt to impose, I say, laws and conditions appropriate to a mechanical creation, against this I raise my sword-pen—'" (*CO*, 27). "'Who ever heard of a clockwork orange?'" Alex innocently asks.

If this pompous, somewhat garbled sentence is indicative of F. Alexander's prose, reading his entire manuscript might be a chore. He seems to be protesting the state's plan to perpetuate itself by turning its citizens into mechanical creatures thoroughly conditioned to be docile and obedient. They will be chemically treated so as to surrender their "'sweetness'" (goodness) automatically, i.e., like clockwork, without having to be constantly squeezed. In Burgess's comic yet terrifying vision of the future, the means to power and stability is neither pleasure (Huxley) nor pain (Orwell) but the fostering of an artificial, drug-induced goodness predicated on the elimination of free will. When the state temporarily turns Alex into a clockwork orange, which is its idea of the "'true Christian'" (*CO*, 128), he has no choice but to turn the other cheek, returning good for evil. He has been transformed into "'a little machine capable only of good'" (*CO*, 153).

Burgess subverts the utopian enterprise by pondering the merits of perfection—whether, as the Prison Charlie (Chaplain) tells Alex, "'[i]t may not be nice to be good'" (*CO*, 97). Indeed, it "'may be horrible'" if there is no other choice and Alex is only good because behaving otherwise literally makes him ill. Our fallibility, the capacity for wrongdoing, for being able to choose "'the bad,'" is all that keeps us human, Burgess decides (*CO*, 96). Being bad sometimes or at least being able to choose to behave badly is therefore good. The "'[d]eep and hard'" question Burgess asks is whether being free to choose unwisely is "'in some way better'" than having "'the good imposed'" upon us (*CO*, 96) in a tyrannical utopia, the only kind he can conceive of, all states being bullies at heart. Imperfection, it follows, may be more utopian than certain kinds of perfection, which are dystopian. In Burgess's future, the concepts of good and bad, sickness and health, perfection and its opposite seem to change places more disturbingly than one's idea of what is a crime and what an illness does in Erewhon.

"'Am I just to be like a clockwork orange?'" Alex cries (*CO*, 126). Fortunately for him but not for society, he recovers his hoodlum instincts. The satiric utopist in Burgess scores a problematic victory for human nature as Alex, his despicable hero, regains his appetite for pathological behavior. Despite being a rapist and murderer, Alex emerges as the novel's true innocent; the state, for all its interest in perfection, appears not just criminal but its designs on human nature are diabolical by comparison. F. Alexander never writes A CLOCKWORK ORANGE. By telling his story, Alex does it for him.

Island is the only modern British utopia that contains a positive, uplifting text-within-the-text, a sort of corrective and last word on the subject. *Notes on What's What, and on What It Might be Reasonable to Do about What's What* redeems the device. It not only counters Henry Ford's *My Life and Work* in *Brave New World*, but outstrips the depressing texts-within-the-text by Zamiatin and Orwell discussed above. The cycle from *Erewhon* to *Island* completes itself when the *Notes* replace Butler's *Book of the Machines*; Huxley can offer a timeless spiritual guidebook by a genuine holy man, Pala's Old Raja, instead of Higgs's translation of a crazy person's rant against Darwin. It wants to save humanity from enslavement to machinery, but only the *Notes* are truly salvific.

Will Farnaby is washed ashore on Pala after a boating accident and quotes "'the beginning of *Erewhon*'" to explain his survival: "'As luck would have it, Providence was on my side'" (*I*, 17). At the urging of Dr. Robert MacPhail, his recuperation includes reading the *Notes* in an effort to overcome a cynical outlook on life more detrimental to his well-being than physical injuries. Just as Higgs learns about the Erewhonians from *The Book of the Machines*, Farnaby absorbs the precepts of Palanese philosophy from the *Notes*. The few essay-like extracts in chapters V, VII, and XI are a recurrent motif or melody. Unfortunately, they are but a fraction of the material from the *Notes* in Huxley's final typescript. His editors persuaded him to eliminate gobs of it and then shortened drastically the passages he retained.[73] In one instance, Huxley reduced "fifteen pages" of typescript to one and a half pages of text in the first edition (Nugel, "Huxley's Revisions," 79). In the typescript, the Old Raja expounds on ways to improve education, ensure accurate use of language, indeed, its preservation, and maximize human potentialities. His ideas echo essays Huxley published in the 1950s and lectures given at Santa Barbara in 1959. Were all cuts restored, the *Notes* would rival in size and exceed in scope Goldsteins's book on *Oligarchical Collectivism*.

As things stand, the Old Raja's pamphlet blends the teaching of Krishnamurti with the wisdom of the Buddha and the central tenets of Vedanta. The Old Raja's grandfather and Dr. Robert's great-grandfather "'invented modern Pala'" in the 1850s (*I*, 34). In 1938, the Old Raja died after a reign of sixty-seven years. His *Notes* are "'just a few pages'" long but explain "'what Pala is all about'" (*I*, 34). Among other things, the passages quoted in *Island* urge the reader to stop behaving like a Manichee, to cultivate ever-greater awareness, to hold onto "Faith" (confidence in one's capacity to become fully human) and avoid "Belief" (words taken too seriously, i.e., dogmatically) (*I*, 85). The Old Raja believed that "quite ordinary people" are "capable of […] fully liberating experiences" (*I*, 176), or as Susila MacPhail, Dr. Robert's daughter-in-law, puts it, that enlightenment is "'[e]verybody's job'" (*I*, 244). Huxley's positive utopia is a community of persons seeking enlightenment individually and collectively; the *Notes* show them the way.

The *Notes* are a unique text-within-the-text because they reverse the traditional perfection process, as is clear from the second (II) of three excerpts that Will reads in chapter V. The Old Raja puts "Good Being" before "good doing":

> […] Good Being results in the most appropriate kind of good doing. But good doing does not of itself result in Good Being. There has never been a society in which most good doing was the product of Good Being and therefore constantly appropriate. This does not mean that there will never be such a society or that we in Pala are fools for trying to call it into existence. (*I*, 35–36)

That "good doing" is "the product of Good Being" means that one must become good before one can "constantly" do good and thereby hope to "call" utopia "into existence."

The *Notes* instruct the Palanese on how to become good enough to create a utopia. As they increasingly cultivate "Good Being," their "good doing," the formation of "appropriate" practices, principles, and institutions for an ideal society, follows inevitably. Pala, the Old Raja emphasizes, is the only society in which, realistically, "good doing" is always the result of "Good Being."[74] Only Pala realizes that human nature must improve dramatically *before* one can devise the perfect system; one cannot expect any system to make human beings perfect. Put another way, no system can of itself produce ideal citizens, but a vastly improved citizenry might just possibly concoct a superior system. As a book of wisdom, the *Notes* are the ultimate in self-help. They seek to make people better, i.e., to make better people, who can then create a more perfect society. They are thus fundamentally unlike what may be called systems-first utopias such as the brave new world, where organizational techniques from *My Life and Work* are employed to reconstitute society along the lines of a Ford factory, or the One State in *We*, in which adherence to Taylor's tables compels every individual to perform every action with maximum efficiency and always on schedule.

Beginning humbly in *Erewhon* when Higgs is nearly jailed for catching cold, modern British utopias feature an ironic cure scene. One society after another reveals that it is not utopia by proposing to rehabilitate a protagonist who seems healthier and saner than it is. Novelists outdo each other trying to invent the most insidious cure scene imaginable; a consensus develops in which nobody in future—no rebel, heretic, dissident or malcontent—will be able to hold out against the almighty state and its appetite for perverse correction.

Yevgeny Zamiatin devised the first full-fledged cure scene. In *We*, D-503 undergoes "the Great Operation" (Z, 180), a lobotomy which the One State prescribes for heretics. In *Lady Chatterley's Lover*, Connie and Mellors must struggle to bring each other back to a healthy physical life in an industrial dystopia determined to ruin human sexuality. In the climactic debate at the end of *Brave New World*, Mustapha Mond tries to convince the Savage to adopt the World State's facile lifestyle.[75] In *Ape and Essence*, Alfred Poole resists the enticements of the devil-worshipping Arch-Vicar. O'Brien's efforts to make Winston Smith "'perfect'" by Oceania's standards go on for years (O, 201). In *A Clockwork Orange*, Dr. Brodsky conditions Alex so that the young "'wrongdoer'" actually gets "sick" at the very thought of behaving violently (*CO*, 126, 139). Finally, *Island* restores the cure scene's integrity: the Palanese genuinely rehabilitate Will Farnaby. Indeed, Pala begins with a cure scene in 1850 when Dr. Andrew MacPhail removed the raja's cancerous tumor. Irony persists, however, in that Pala cures Will yet cannot preserve itself. As the next chapter will show, nothing better illustrates the modern British utopist's penchant for revaluing predecessors than the constant redoing of the cure scene, each utopist striving to be more diabolical until Huxley intervenes with a cure for the cure scene itself. From a minor episode in Butler, the cure scene develops until it takes over most of the narrative in Huxley's last novel. The cure scene in Orwell is lengthy, but *Island* amounts to one long cure scene: the rehabilitation of Will Farnaby as proof of Pala's perfection.

When modern British utopists are not busily talking back to each other, or even while they are, they talk back to themselves, reconsidering, indeed, revising, their prior observations. In *Nineteen Eighty-Four*, Orwell darkens *Animal Farm*. The Inner Party is a more disturbing example than Manor Farm's pigs of how one faction within a revolution to gain equality for all becomes more equal than others. As George Woodcock observes, *Animal Farm* "left out one element which occurs in all [Orwell's] other works of fiction, the individual rebel caught in the machinery of the caste system" (Woodcock, 198). Redoing D-503 as Winston Smith, Orwell remedied a deficiency in *Animal Farm* while implying that Zamiatin's protagonist got off too lightly. Insofar as Winston and Julia are D-503 and I-330 reconsidered as less successful rebels in Orwell's more dystopian dystopia, *Nineteen Eighty-Four* illustrates the modern British utopia's uncanny ability to correct itself even as it asserts its superiority to a rival text.

No one talked back to himself more effectively than Huxley. Brave new worlders and Palanese address similar concerns, but the latter, a systematic revision of the former, handle them wisely. If *Brave New World* is a synthesis of the worst that had recently been thought and said—bad or misapplied ideas from Ford, Freud, Pavlov, and Wells[76]—Pala is an amalgam in response of the best suggestions for revamping society that Huxley had come across in his researches since 1932. But the Palanese also reverse bad choices made by Belial's worshippers in *Ape and Essence.* Adherents to Buddhism and Vedanta, they epitomize the saintly society of which the Arch-Vicar and his followers are a devilish perversion. Pala is the third way missing from both *Brave New World*, which pits Fordian London against primitive Malpais, and from the Huxley canon, which cried out for a positive utopia to offset two negative ones.

According to the account the Arch-Vicar gives Alfred Poole, World War III broke out because Belial persuaded East and West

> "to take only the worst the other had to offer. So the East takes Western nationalism, Western armaments, Western movies and Western Marxism; the West takes Eastern despotism, Eastern superstitions and Eastern indifference to individual life. In a word, […] mankind [made] the worst of both worlds." (*AE*, 136)

Hence the dystopia whose post-war aftermath Poole encounters in *Ape and Essence*:

> "Just think if they'd made the best!" squeaks the Arch-Vicar. "Eastern mysticism making sure that Western science should be properly used; the Eastern art of living refining Western energy; Western individualism tempering Eastern totalitarianism." He shakes his head in pious horror. "Why, it would have been the kingdom of heaven." (*AE*, 137–38)

Ironically, Pala is the Arch-Vicar's worst nightmare. Huxley synthesizes Eastern spirituality and Western know-how; they cross-fertilize each other the way Pala's co-founders did, the "'Scottish doctor [Andrew MacPhail] and the Palanese king, the Calvinist-turned-atheist and the pious Mahayana

Buddhist'"': "'Each became the other's pupil and the other's teacher'" (*I*, 129)—that is how East and West should behave. Huxley redoes the debate between Mond and the Savage as the co-operation of doctor and king. Instead of an intractable counterpoint, he is "'able to reconcile and combine,'" that is, "'to make [Pala] the best of both worlds—the Oriental and the European, the ancient and the modern'" (*I*, 130).

Instead of the brave new world's mind-numbing jingles, Pala offers the mynah birds' continual calls to "'[a]ttention,'" the novel's first and last word (*I*, 295). The Palanese constantly remind themselves to keep mind and spirit uppermost. "'Mother'" is not a dirty word in Pala but remains "'strictly the name of a function,'" Susila explains (*I*, 88); once the child is grown, parent and ex-child can "'continue to see a lot of one another'" or "'drift apart.'" During the child's childhood, he or she belongs to "'an MAC—a Mutual Adoption Club,'" which provides from fifteen to twenty-five homes to choose from. Only in the sense that the child can migrate from one household to another that he or she finds more congenial does everyone belong to everyone else. Gone for good are what Mustapha Mond, speaking as "Our Freud," stigmatizes as "the appalling dangers of family life" (*BNW*, 30), but family life itself survives.

In such an "'inclusive, unpredestined and voluntary family,'" there is no need for "'Freudism'" (*I*, 90). Instead of feeling suffocated and becoming neurotic or nursing Oedipus complexes, Palanese children have "'twenty pairs of fathers and mothers'" to select from; they can change households permanently or for shorter periods, a process that results in a beneficial "'[h]ybridization of micro-cultures'" (*I*, 90). Will calls it "'[m]aking twenty families grow where only one grew before'" (*I*, 89), as opposed to the brave new world, which, having eliminated the family, bolsters its population artificially: cloning procedures are capable of "'[m]aking ninety-six human beings where only one grew before" (*BNW*, 3). In place of "'forty or fifty assorted children of all ages'" in a typical MAC, which Huxley approves of, a "bokanovskified egg" proliferates into "'[n]inety-six identical twins'" (*BNW*, 4), an outcome Huxley abhors.

The brave new world to the contrary, Pala is the opposite of a World State: "'a federation of self-governing units'" with "'no place for any kind of dictator'" (*I*, 149). Instead of compulsory consumerism in support of an obligatory hedonism, the Palanese "'cultivate scepticism'"; their brand of Buddhism "'deplores [...] unverifiable dogmas'" (*I*, 149). It also makes them "'inadequate materialists,'" whereas brave new worlders, obliged to consume a specified amount of goods, are subject to "'the conscription of consumption'" (*BNW*, 40). The big difference is that "Fordism," unlike Buddhism, however skeptical, offers zero "spiritual returns" (*MN*, 180–81).

Butler's Higgs shares the confidence that the author of *The Book of the Machines* expresses in one's ability to predict the future by studying the past. Knowledge of history, coupled with an awareness of how things evolve, provides a sure guide to coming events, Higgs's translation claims. *The Book of the Machines* is in large part a history lesson: the story of how machines developed until the anti-machinists prevailed against them, thereby saving Erewhonians from enslavement to machinery. The brave new world thinks about history differently. In Huxley's dystopia, Mustapha Mond subscribes to "'that beautiful and inspired saying of Our Ford's: History is bunk'" (*BNW*, 26)—Odysseus, Job, Jupiter, Gotama, Jesus, Lear, Pascal and others are "brushed away" like so much dust. When Mond delivers a lengthy history lesson in chapter III, it stresses the brave new world's destruction of history. After the Nine Years' War, Mond expounds, "'a campaign against the past'" resulted in "'the closing of museums, the blowing up of historical monuments […] [and] the suppression of all books published before A. F. 150'" (*BNW*, 42). Contrary to Butler, Huxley thinks that the World State of the future will attain such stability as to have no future (i.e., changes) to predict; also, it will eradicate all history except its own.

In *Nineteen Eighty-Four*, Goldstein's book on *The Theory and Practice of Oligarchical Collectivism* is essentially a history of events between 1948 and 1984, but Orwell writes it in '48 and therefore gives an account of the future as if it were already the past. Orwell rejects the positions taken by Butler and Huxley. The past is neither useful as a basis for prediction nor is it bunk to be disregarded. It is mutable. Oceania changes history at will. Thanks to "the mutability" of the past (O, 25), it has the power to reshape the past into agreement with present policies. When the Party changes its mind and implements a lie, all records are altered until they "told the same tale" and "the lie passed simultaneously into history and became truth" (O, 32). The Party is never wrong because what it professes at any given moment, it can show it has always professed. Those it supports, it has always supported; its enemies have always been its enemies. Persons and events no longer aligned with the party line are erased from the historical record. The Party's slogan is a twofold boast: "'Who controls the past […] controls the future: who controls the present controls the past'" (O, 32). Unlike Erewhonians and brave new worlders, Oceania's rulers need not scrutinize the past for clues to the future nor bother to dismiss the past altogether because, says Orwell, they can always manipulate it to suit themselves. Three-quarters of a century after *Erewhon*, Orwell, consciously or not, wrestles with Butler's legacy: he substitutes the "mutability of the past" (O, 25) for Butler's "'fixity of the future'" (*E*, 190), the former concept rendering the latter dispensable. Butler, Orwell in effect declares, was wrong to say "'the past is unalterable'" (*E*, 189).

To counterbalance Mond's history lesson in *Brave New World,* Huxley offers the glowing account of Pala that Dr. Robert MacPhail gives Will Farnaby in chapter VIII of *Island.* This history lesson is also a handbook on how to found a utopia, i.e., the right way to go about setting up the perfect society. In the mid-nineteenth century, Dr. Robert's great-grandfather, Dr. Andrew MacPhail, and Pala's Raja—the "'Scottish doctor and the Palanese king, the Calvinist-turned-atheist and the pious Mahayana Buddhist'" (*I*, 129)—band together to utopianize Pala. They try "'to make the best of both worlds—the Oriental and European, the ancient and the modern'" (*I*, 130). The resulting synthesis of Eastern religion and Western technology surpasses Erewhon and the World State; compared to Orwell's nightmare society, it is Eden, a paradise regained. Unfortunately, history, as Dr. Robert defines it, is "'the record of what human beings have been impelled to do by their ignorance,'" by stupidity canonized "'as a political or religious dogma'" (*I*, 118). Western industrialists and a militant neighbor combine to bring about Pala's downfall. As if Darwin never happened, the Palanese cannot preserve their "'absurd little island,'" as Susila calls it, in a "'worldwide wilderness of monkeys'" (*I*, 117–18). Farnaby bemoans "[t]he work of a hundred years destroyed in a single night" (*I*, 294). Sadly, Huxley admits that history, even when it is not bunk or mutable, can still be negated.

Zamiatin firmly believed in revolution as a panacea, the only sure way to keep society from ossifying. "'Revolution,'" he wrote, must be "'infinite. There is no final revolution.'"[77] In *We*, the One State is a dystopia because it thinks otherwise; as the novel ends, the Benefactor's forces seem poised to crush the remnants of an uprising "in the Western parts of the city" (Z, 232). A lobotomized D-503, no longer maladjusted or malcontent, sounds confident that the rebels, whom he calls "enemies of happiness," will be executed and that "Reason," his synonym for orthodoxy or the status quo, "will prevail" (Z, 232). "'[O]ur revolution was the final one,'" D-503 insists; "'there can be no others'" (Z, 174), a statement that seals the One State's fate as a bad place. In short, Zamiatin approved of revolutions even though he came to loathe the outcome of the one in Russia and petitioned Stalin for permission to leave the country.

Orwell makes no secret of his admiration for *We*,[78] but on the subject of revolution, he begins talking back to Zamiatin in *Animal Farm*. During the Spanish Civil War, Orwell observed that the communists seemed more intent on purging their own ranks than on defeating General Franco. Similarly, Lenin's radical left-wing took over the Russian Revolution in 1917; then, after Lenin's death, Stalin demoted and eventually deported Leon Trotsky, Lenin's ally, much as Napoleon ousts Snowball. Orwell tells Zamiatin that there definitely is a final revolution. It is the revolution within the initial revolution, the internal power struggle that determines which party or faction within it will assume control of it. Whether constant or periodic, Orwell lectures Zamiatin, upheavals staged by heretics and rebels are always fundamentally flawed, hence no antidote for the entropy of orthodoxy. He writes *Nineteen Eighty-Four* not just to alert England's socialists to the dystopian direction being taken by the Russian Revolution, but to discredit Zamiatin and the revolutionary process per se. The same winnowing by which the pigs at Manor Farm exalt themselves to the detriment of the other animals occurs in *Nineteen Eighty-Four*: in the mid-1960s, writes Goldstein, one witnessed "the great purges in which the original leaders of the revolution were wiped out once and for all" (O, 64).

When Huxley weighs in on the subject of revolutions in his "Foreword" to *Brave New World*, he dismisses both Zamiatin and Orwell for looking backwards, basing their fears for the future on recent events instead of worrying about those still impending. Huxley claims to have described in *Brave New World* what society will be like after the "most searching revolution," the "really revolutionary revolution" that will "modify [...] life itself"; in the brave new world, he repeats, one witnesses "the ultimate, personal, really revolutionary revolution" in psychology and physiology that changes "the souls and flesh of human beings" (*BNW*, x, xi), that alters not just the quality of life but the very nature of it. No more "inefficient" measures such as "persecution" and "liquidation" (*BNW*, xiii). Future totalitarians, Huxley foresees, will sponsor "a greatly improved technique of suggestion," drugs "less harmful and more pleasure-giving than gin or heroin," "a foolproof system of eugenics" that guarantees a "scientific caste system" and encouragement of "sexual promiscuity"—all to make docile citizens who "love their servitude" (*BNW*, xiii-xiv).

"Meanwhile," says Huxley, thanks to Hitler and Stalin, "we are in the first phase of what is perhaps the penultimate revolution" (*BNW*, xi), the one prior to the coming of the brave new world. Unfortunately, Zamiatin and Orwell got stuck in these preliminaries: Orwell claims to know more than Zamiatin about the way revolution works, whereas Huxley's claim is to have grasped the final revolution, whose nature Orwell misunderstood and whose existence Zamiatin denies. So why read Zamiatin and Orwell, Huxley asks, when they can only depict "a superficial, external revolution"? To understand the "deep, personal revolution" in store for "human minds and bodies," he strongly recommends *Brave New World* (*BNW*, xiv) for information if not prevention.

In "Latent Human Potentialities," the final lecture in a series at the University of California in 1959, Huxley concedes that "[w]e can learn quite a lot in the field of love from some of the primitive peoples" (*HS*, 249). This is a surprising statement from the creator of Malpais, the Savage reservation in *Brave New World.* However, when Huxley talks back to himself on the subject of primitives, the Palanese are enlightened primitives, not "columns of dark blood" like the Indians in D. H. Lawrence's *The Plumed Serpent* (*Plumed*, 48). Never mindlessly promiscuous, as are brave new worlders, Huxley's islanders are ardent lovers, experts on what Susila MacPhail calls "'the Art of Loving'" (*I*, 105); but their finest innovations involve what Huxley in his California lecture terms "love and knowledge" or love as a means to greater spiritual awareness (*HS*, 249).

As his primary example of "primitive intelligence," Huxley cites Margaret Mead's description of "the amazing practices" of the Arapesh, "a tiny tribe in New Guinea, an essentially non-violent and co-operative society" (*HS*, 250). Bent on "encouraging and implementing" friendliness and love, the Arapesh mother,

> when nursing her baby, will continuously murmur the words "good, good," and while the baby is sucking the milk and the mother is murmuring, she will rub the child against the family dog, or against the family pig, or against a human being in the family circle or even outside the family circle, so that the child is brought up with a kind of conditioned reflex for feeling confidence and love and the goodness of other people. (*HS*, 250)

On Pala, as Will watches, Vijaya rubs his baby's back while the mother whispers, "'Good father, good, good…'" (*I*, 194). Then they rub a parrot's feathers against the child's skin while repeating "'Polly's a good bird.'" The Palanese "'picked up the idea'" from a tribe in New Guinea, who "'believed in love'" (*I*, 195), Vijaya explains. They "'[s]troke the baby" while its feeding and rub his body against "'the animal or person'" they "'want him to love'"; "'let there be a warm physical contact between child and love object,'" Vijaya declares, so that "'[f]ood plus caress plus contact plus 'good' equals love.'"

Huxley not only borrows from his lecture on "Human Potentialities," he also rewrites positively the scene in the brave new world's Neo-Pavlovian Conditioning Rooms where alarm bells and electric shocks teach the babies to dislike books and flowers. As the Director's helpers "'rub in the lesson,'" the babies' bodies "twitched and stiffened": "Books and loud noises, flowers and electric shocks—already in the infant mind these couples were compromisingly linked," the D.H.C. explains. Brave new worlders "'grow up'" with "'an 'instinctive' hatred of books and flowers'" (*BNW*, 16). If people are alive merely to consume things, as the brave new world maintains, then the love of books and flowers must be abolished; it "keeps no factories busy," the D.H.C. points out (*BNW*, 17), not to mention that one might read something heretical.

Will calls Vijaya's technique "'Pure Pavlov'"—that is, Pavlovian conditioning purified, redeemed and done right. "'Pavlov purely for a good purpose […,] for friendliness and trust and compassion'" (*I*, 195) instead of for hate, the D.H.C.'s preference. Shanta proceeds to rub the child against Toby, the family dog, and then permits Will, someone outside the family circle, "to stroke the child's tiny body" while she whispers "'good man'" (*I*, 195), thus repeating almost literally the actions of the Arapesh woman.

Whether ideas are helpful or harmful, Huxley stipulates, "depends entirely on what we regard as the end and purpose of human life" (*HS*, 55). It follows that only someone who knows this "end and purpose" can devise the perfect place. Towards the end of his life, Huxley revised his concept of the utopist: he must know man's Final End. Unlike the brave new worlders, who misapply Freud and Pavlov, only such a utopist can ask if a given idea contributes to the desired end. Friendship, trust, compassion—these Palanese synonyms for love replace D. H. Lawrence's emphasis on intuition, spontaneous emotion, and sensuality; they are hallmarks of the seeker after enlightenment, the person desirous of realizing to the fullest his (or her) human potentiality. Conditioned reflexes are a fact of life, Huxley lectured, "so we may as well see that our conditioned reflexes are good rather than bad" (*HS*, 250), a precaution taken by the Palanese, thereby reversing brave new worlders. Vijaya might as well be speaking of the latter when he rules out using Pavlov "'for brain washing, […] Pavlov for the benefit of dictators'" or World Controllers (*I*, 195). That utopia is the place that best actualizes a human being's "potentialities," his (or her) physical, intellectual, and spiritual capabilities, is Huxley's final contribution to utopian thinking, a demanding ideal not to be found in Butler or Wells and certainly not even to be looked for in Zamiatin and Orwell.

Orwell scoffs at the idea of a "world in which everyone worked short hours, had enough to eat," and flew his (or her) own "airplane" (i.e., helicopter) (O, 156). This is precisely what Alphas and Betas do: "'Seven and a half hours of mild, unexhausting labour,'" after which he (or she) ingests *soma*, plays games, and enjoys "'unrestricted copulation'" (*BNW*, 183). To Orwell, it must have seemed as "if leisure and security were enjoyed by all alike" in the brave new world, whereas in a truly "hierarchical society" such as he foresees, a "small privileged class" or caste like the Inner Party will monopolize power (O, 156). When it comes to caste systems in the imminent totalitarian state, Orwell claims to be the expert, not Huxley.

"The unforgiveable crime" in Oceania is "promiscuity between Party members," an offense Julia claims to have committed "'scores of times'" (O, 57, 104). Probably, she exaggerates. But totalitarian states, Orwell promises, will not endorse unrestricted fornication. Where the brave new world cheapens Lawrence's ideal of a warm physical relationship between one man and one woman, Oceania simply forbids it. Huxley's World State eliminates the consequences of having sex: no venereal disease, no ties, no responsibilities for raising children. Oceania finds it safer "to remove all pleasure from the sexual act" (O, 57), an approach borrowed from Western Christianity.

Brave new worlders copulate constantly with whomever they choose; there is not much danger of anyone forming a close, personal, monogamous relationship that might supersede loyalty to the state. Oceania prefers to destroy "the sex instinct" itself; it "created a world of its own which was outside the Party's control" (O, 110). Promiscuity, Orwell tells Huxley, is a tremendous waste of energy. In Oceania, the "hysteria" that "sexual privation produced" has been "transformed into war fever and leader worship" (O, 110), a case of sublimation that would impress Our Freud. Enforced chastity and mandatory promiscuity prove equally painful. One can inflict pleasure. Orwell shows the reader Winston lusting for Julia, but Huxley's picture of Bernard Marx forced to couple with Morgana Fairchild is equally disquieting: "Those black eyebrows of hers—that eyebrow, rather—for they met above the nose" (*BNW*, 66).

Like the brave new world, *Nineteen Eighty-Four* is an industrial dystopia. But just as it substitutes pain for pleasure and mandatory abstinence for rampant promiscuity, Oceania emphasizes deprivation instead of plentitude. In the truly effective totalitarian state, Orwell tells Huxley, there can be no abundance of goods. Plenty, like pleasure, interferes with the diminishment of freedom. Oceania's workers are kept in "poverty and ignorance" lest they become "too comfortable, and hence, in the long run, too intelligent" (O, 157). The Party and the World State face the same problem: "how to keep the wheels of industry turning" (O, 157). Brave new worlders are compelled to use up all they produce, whereas Oceania's workers, like those in Eurasia and Eastasia, are barely allowed to consume at all.

Orwell foresees no "return" to "the agricultural past, as some thinkers about the beginning of the twentieth century dreamed of doing" (O, 157). Heedless of the Erewhonians' warnings and deaf to Mellors's protests as well, the new order will not become "industrially backward"; on the contrary, it furthers "the tendency toward mechanization" that Butler feared and Morris abhorred. "The dangers inherent in the machine are still there" (O, 156), Orwell admits, but evolving into something superior to the human race is not one of them. Nor does Oceania fulfill Wells's "vision of a future society unbelievably rich, leisured, orderly and efficient" (O, 155–56). It sanctions "technological progress" only "when its products can in some way be used for the diminution of human liberty" (O, 157).

For its machines to "keep on turning—for ever" (*BNW*, 33), the brave new world institutes "'the conscription of consumption'": everyone must "'consume so much a year'" (*BNW*, 40). It will be easier, says Orwell, to restrict the distribution of goods than to monitor output or match it to demand. Oceania manages "to use up the products of the machine without raising the general standard of living" (O, 155). It expends labor power "without producing anything that can be consumed" (O, 157). All but "the bare needs of the population" are "consumed through continuous warfare" (O, 157). Workers remain busy turning out the same items (armaments) over and over. For this system of recurring shortages to function, Orwell foresees three states, not one, of which two must always be at war with the third.

Controlling an alleged utopia's means of production and regulating the emotional lives of its citizens (i.e., sex and the psyche) are seemingly unconnected activities. The first is a Marxist concern, the second of more interest to Freudians. Nevertheless, similarities exist. In both instances, the brave new world and Oceania pursue a consistent policy. Oceania always opts for restriction where the brave new world endorses a liberation that seems equally coercive: mandatory copulation versus enforced celibacy, compulsory consumption as opposed to systematic deprivation. In an all-intrusive state that tells the populace what to think, which will be worse?, Huxley and Orwell ask readers and each other.

Every major modern British utopia wants to be considered the most accurate account of things as they will, or should, become. Is it to be Our

Ford's world or Big Brother's, Pala or Oceania, Wells's World-state, Huxley's World State, or Zamiatin's One State? Chronological and anti-chronological disagreements erupt, ranging backwards from Huxley and Orwell to Zamiatin, Wells, and Butler, as well as forwards from them to Huxley, Orwell and Burgess, whose revisions their earlier works still contradict. Once Orwell talks back to Huxley, it becomes possible for *Brave New World* to critique *Nineteen Eighty-Four*, if one revisits the former upon reading the latter, as indeed Huxley did. An informal quarrel materializes.[79] If ideas in a utopia remain compelling even when assailed by successors, the book can speak out of the past to challenge works in the present.

To become part of the modern British utopian tradition means to participate in an ongoing conversation and thus remain rereadable; a perennial utopia must chastise utopias already in print and arouse the ire of future utopists who will keep them alive by arguing with them in turn. Unfortunately, this is not always the case. Charlotte Perkins Gilman's *Herland*, for example, fails to get caught up in the tradition. A feminist utopia about a perfect, all-female society, *Herland* can be read as a satirical revaluation of a heretofore almost exclusively masculine genre. But although written in 1915, well within the cycle from *Erewhon* to *Island*, it never registers with subsequent utopists; most ignore it.[80] Yevgeny Zamiatin, on the other hand, reaches the west in translation—into English in 1924 and Czech three years later—but his place in the canon of modern British literary utopias is assured, thanks to his fascination with Wells and the impact of *We* on *Brave New World* and *Nineteen Eighty-Four*. A Russian novel joins the tradition as a textual bridge from Wells to Huxley and Orwell while Gilman remains outside. Huxley and Orwell both re-examine *We* extensively while presuming to correct and improve upon its author's views. Zamiatin suspects that the Wellsian scientific utopia, administered with mathematical precision, must quickly deteriorate into a totalitarian nightmare. He introduces the first full-fledged ironic cure scene in which a misguided society imposes its will upon a heretic healthier than it is. Such a scene becomes obligatory in nearly every subsequent utopia, negative or positive. Equally important, Zamiatin poses two perennial questions for modern British utopists—freedom or happiness, which should a utopia promote? Can it deliver both?

Utopian fictions have a bigger problem with the issue of freedom versus happiness than do ordinary novels. For their societies to be perfect, they feel obligated to guarantee both yet usually wind up embracing one at the other's expense. In that case, the problem becomes which to choose, assuming either is good enough without the other. Zamiatin thinks Wells underrates the gravity of the dilemma, which the One State in *We*, mistakenly according to Huxley, claims to have resolved. In the brave new world, freedom and happiness are regarded as counterpoints like passion and reason, body and mind. Oceania subsumes the quest for freedom and happiness to its lust for power. Only the enlightened Palanese in *Island* seem to have found the answer; sadly, it does not hold up under stress from the outside world.

In the second chapter of *A Modern Utopia*, titled "Concerning Freedoms," Wells promises that "the maximum general freedom" will be provided in the World-state and "the conditions of physical happiness will be better understood" (*AMU*, 34, 65). According to Mark R. Hillegas, Wells was deeply concerned with "the problem of freedom versus happiness" (*AMU*, xii), but happiness seems to be synonymous with comfort or bodily well-being. Thus, Zamiatin accuses Wells of turning a complex philosophical problem into a simple physical one with better technology as the solution. In the One State, the *Integral*, Zamiatin's version of a time machine, is being designed to subjugate other planets still "living in the primitive condition of freedom"; D-503's spaceship will "compel them to be happy," i.e., to emulate "the mathematically perfect life of the One State" (Z, 1, 2).

For Zamiatin, the problem originated with Adam and Eve. R-13 summarizes:

> "Those two, in paradise, were given a choice: either happiness without freedom, or freedom without happiness. There was no third alternative. Those idiots chose freedom, and what came of it? Of course, for ages afterward they longed for the chains. The chains—you understand? That's what world sorrow was about. For ages! And only we have found the way of restoring happiness." (Z, 61)

According to R-13, all the world's miseries have been caused by freedom of choice.[81] However, the One State has reversed the decision of Adam and Eve; it has eliminated "'confusion about good and evil'" by choosing for everyone, thereby making everything "'childishly simple'" again (Z, 62). In "'[o]ur unfreedom'" lies "'our happiness,'" R-13 declares.

For the One State, the Garden of Eden was utopia as long as Adam and Eve did exactly as instructed. Ever since they ate forbidden fruit from the Tree of Knowledge, everything has gone to hell. But with the Benefactor in charge and the Guardians as his helpers (i.e., guardian angels), R-13 maintains that the One State has been able "'to conquer the devil,'" who tempted Adam and Eve with "'a taste'" of "'ruinous freedom'" (Z, 61). "'Now everything is fine—we have paradise again'" (Z, 61), R-13 concludes. Zamiatin, of course, is being ironical: for him, despite R-13's disapproval, Adam and Eve are heroes; our first parents were the first heretics, whose rebellion destroyed the world's first utopia, the freedomless Garden of Eden.

The idea of paradise regained scarcely applies to D-503. Briefly he aligns himself with the rebel group Mephisto (short for the devil Mephistopheles) and trysts with I-330, the novel's *femme fatale*. But his defection leaves him miserably confused until he recovers his happiness by forfeiting his freedom of thought: he submits to a state-sponsored lobotomy. In future, Zamiatin unhappily decrees, happiness may only be possible without freedom, as Adam and Eve should have known.

In the brave new world, "'everybody's happy now,'" as Lenina declares (*BNW*, 62). She has heard these words "repeated a hundred and fifty times every night for twelve years." Huxley claims to know more than Zamiatin about making happiness compulsory. In the World State as opposed to the One State, "sleep-teaching, or hypnopaedia" (*BNW*, 18), Huxley informs the Russian, will easily make artificial, unexplained happiness universal. In the climactic debate that fills the penultimate chapter, John the Savage says, "'I want God, I want poetry, [...] I want freedom'" (*BNW*, 197). Mustapha Mond accuses him of "'claiming the right to be unhappy.'" The novel builds to a stalemate, leaving readers with a counterpoint to contemplate. Evidently, one cannot have both happiness and freedom, yet neither is completely satisfying without the other, Huxley decides. Therefore, utopia seems impossible. Not only is there no third choice, Huxley tells Zamiatin in 1932, but, contrary to R-13, neither choice is the right one. In the 1946 "Foreword" to the reissue of *Brave New World*, Huxley regrets offering the Savage "only two alternatives" when "a third alternative" was badly needed (*BNW*, vii, viii). Zamiatin ought to have searched for it harder, Huxley implies, the way he was beginning to do in the "Foreword."

When Orwell joins the conversation, *Nineteen Eighty-Four* overrules *We* and *Brave New World* simultaneously. As O'Brien lectures and tortures Winston Smith to make him "'sane'" by Oceania's standards (O, 209), Winston rationalizes that the Party seeks power "for the good of the majority" (O, 216). He thinks it believes that the "frail" and "cowardly" masses "must be ruled over" by those "stronger than themselves." The "choice for mankind," Winston tells O'Brien, "lay between freedom and happiness" and the Party must have decided that, "for the great bulk of mankind, happiness was better" (O, 216). Winston, however, is not happy. Furthermore, for offering this "'stupid'" explanation, which echoes R-13 and Mustapha Mond, he is punished severely; O'Brien pushes the lever of the pain machine "up to thirty-five" and the shock nearly kills Winston (O, 217). The perfectly totalitarian state, says Orwell, is not interested in providing either freedom or happiness. Its only concern is acquiring and keeping "'"power entirely for its own sake"'"—as an "'"end"'" in itself, not a "'"means"'" (O, 217). According to Orwell, Zamiatin and Huxley did not correctly identify the goal of dictatorships; consequently, like Winston, they ask the wrong questions.[82]

For Huxley, who has the last word, *Island* is a third option several times over. Pala emerges from the third of Huxley's utopias as the ideal alternative to both the brave new world and to *Ape and Essence*'s post-apocalyptic society. Huxley's third try also provides "a third alternative" to "primitive" Malpais and an allegedly "utopian" World State, a way through the "horns" of the Savage's "dilemma" (*BNW*, viii). Finally, it contains Huxley's definitive alternative to Zamiatin and Orwell. The former contends that future societies will be forced to choose a mechanical happiness; the latter denies that tomorrow's dictatorships will have any interest in keeping its citizens free or happy.

Mr. Bahu, Rendang's cynical ambassador to Pala,[83] admits that Pala, which he is conspiring to overthrow, is an "'"enchanting island,"'" one that is "'"perfectly designed to make every man, woman, and child [...] as perfectly *free* and *happy* as it's possible to be"'" (*I*, 55; italics added). Huxley believes Pala's policies and politics are "'"admirably well adapted to achieving these two goals,"'" namely, "'"freedom and happiness"'" (*I*, 55), a former counterpoint which no previous utopia, negative or positive, could resolve. The Palanese whom Farnaby encounters—Dr. MacPhail, Susila, Vijaya, even Lakshmi, who is dying—seem liberated from life's sorrows and therefore happy. (The only exceptions are Murugun and the Rani, malcontents incapable of appreciating the Palanese way of life.) Unfortunately, as Bahu observes, "'"the outside world"'" is "'"closing in on this little island of freedom and happiness,"'" an ideal allegedly "'"no longer viable"'" on a mad planet (*I*, 56). When neighboring Rendang overruns Pala, Huxley's solution to the problem of freedom versus happiness becomes hypothetical once more, as insubstantial as the refuge he contemplated as a third choice for the Savage in the 1946 "Foreword" to *Brave New World*. From *A Modern Utopia* through *Island*, an acceptable combination of freedom and happiness remains an impossible dream.

In sum, Huxley brings the cycle from *Erewhon* to *Island* to a close by resolving a number of key issues; he had the last word in several ongoing discussions. Only the Palanese, for example, can truthfully claim to be both free and happy, even if not permanently. Of all the couples the success of whose relationship tests the Edenic potential of an imaginary society, only Will Farnaby and Susila MacPhail, his spiritual guide, stand a decent chance of going forwards even if Pala does not survive. Pala's Dr. Robert MacPhail eclipses Mustapha Mond, the Benefactor, the Arch-Vicar, and Big Brother as the ideal administrator. Huxley created both the worst (Mond) and best (Dr. Robert) manager of an allegedly utopic society. Were the Old Raja's pamphlet not truncated, the *Notes on What's What* would resemble even more closely venerable texts such as *The Cloud of Unknowing*; as it stands, Huxley's text-within-the-text reduces to absurdity perfidious guidebooks by Henry Ford, Frederick Winslow Taylor, and Emmanuel Goldstein.

The end of a cycle does not mean the end of a genre. But with the uniquely interactive utopias from *Erewhon* to *Island*, a chapter of Western thought has come to a close. So far, postmodernism and its aftermaths have not produced utopian writings of comparable quality in Great Britain or outside it. Nothing equivalent to *Brave New World* or *Nineteen Eighty-Four* has appeared. Immensely readable texts, such as Margaret Atwood's *The Handmaid's Tale* (1985) and its less interesting sequel, *The Testaments* (2019), have garnered attention; however, their hold on the popular imagination seems unlikely to unseat Huxley or Orwell,[84] whose works have become part of everyday language. When commentators, upset by problematic discoveries or undesirable current events, exclaim "O brave new world," the reference is to Huxley, not Shakespeare. Similarly, "Orwellian" is a favorite adjective to describe untoward political developments. Single-issue utopias, such as Ernest Callenbach's *Ecotopia*, which focuses on ecology, disregard Huxley's warning to would-be utopists that "'[s]cience is not enough, religion is not enough, art is not enough, politics and economics are not enough [...]. Nothing short of everything will really do'" (*I*, 134). Contrary to the quote from the *Los Angeles Times* on its cover, *Ecotopia* is not "'the newest name after Wells, Verne, Huxley and Orwell.'" Not even Kurt Vonnegut's once popular *Player Piano*, which its author claimed "'ripped off the plot of *Brave New World*'" (quoted in Coverley, 136), has managed to remain influential.[85] So too with Dave Eggers's *The Circle* (2014), which reads more like an imitation of Orwell than a revaluation.

Texts that hover around the modern utopian tradition without expanding it or achieving full scale participation, that is, without extensively revaluing any of the writers discussed in this essay or revising each other, include Olaf Stapledon's *Last and First Men* (1930); Katherine Burdekin's *Swastika Night* (1937); B. F. Skinner's *Walden Two* (1948); Ray Bradbury's *Fahrenheit 451* (1953); Evelyn Waugh's *Love Among the Ruins* (1953); William Golding's *Lord of the Flies* (1954); Ayn Rand's *Atlas Shrugged* (1957); Pierre Boulle's *Planet of the Apes* (1963); Robert Rimmer's *The Harrad Experiment* (1966); Ira

Levin's *This Perfect Day* (1970); Octavia B. Butler's *Parable of the Sower* (1993); Ernest Cline's *Ready Player One* (2011); Boualem Sansal's *2084: The End of the World* (2015); Bill Broun's *Night of the Animals* (2016); David Means's *Hystopia* (2016); Dan Vyleta's *Smoke* (2017); and Ben H. Winters's *Underground Airlines* (2017). Most of these novels are not trying to depict an alternative future to be desired or feared; instead, the novel's action simply transpires in a radically different context, a dystopian setting. In short, these books present societies that are neither a model nor a critique. Books by William Gibson and Ursula Le Guin neither prescribe nor proscribe. Skinner is a behavioral psychologist whose utopia *Brave New World* may be said to have precluded. In her introduction to *Swastika Night* (xii-xiii), Daphne Patai discusses several similarities between it and *1984*; they do not amount to a major reconsideration. Nor is Sansal's *2084*, except for its title, an extensive updating of Orwell. Citizens in Levin's future world are kept "healthy" and happy by periodic injections (*Perfect Day*, 84); "Incurables" (i.e., "undruggables") are allowed to escape to islands whose inhabitants the High Council considers "sick." These similarities to *Brave New World* are, however, superficial.

In 1905, Wells declared that old-style utopia was dead: no more "Nowheres" such as "men planned before Darwin quickened the thought of the world" (*AMU*, 5). Plato, More, Cabet, Campanella and their ilk were all passé. In *A Modern Utopia*, that is, with Wells's ideas for an actual place, a new dispensation was beginning. Wells's proclamation overlooked Butler's *The Book of the Machines*, which claimed to see the future; it also slighted Bellamy, who is merely mentioned in the list of defunct utopists (see *AMU*, 8). Yet on 30 March 1888, Edward Bellamy wrote the *Boston Transcript* that *Looking Backward* is "intended in all seriousness, as a forecast, in accordance with the principles of evolution, of the next stage" in humanity's industrial and social development (*LB*, 220). One should take note of Bellamy's conviction that social evolution and industrial revolution have become synergistic. For both Bellamy and Wells, the end of so-called old-fashioned utopia was also a fresh start. No such new "stage" is evident in the current situation.

No sooner had Wells penned *Men Like Gods* (1923) than *Brave New World*, in Peter Firchow's opinion, signaled what he called the *end* of utopia. His title means that Huxley's book marked the end of a period of unqualified optimism, of unfounded faith in science to bring about stability and guarantee happiness—in short, the end of belief in human perfectibility. Fearing changes in human nature itself, Huxley, says Firchow, shows us a "vision of the end of the world as we know it" (*End*, 10). When Orwell chimes in, he claims that *Nineteen Eighty-Four* puts an end to "'stupid hedonistic Utopias that the old reformers imagined'" (O, 220). Like Wells, he may be referring to pre-Darwinian texts but one need not exclude the World State from his edict. Huxley did not consider the brave new world "'hedonistic'"; compulsory pleasure can degrade and humiliate just as much as pain.[86] But the adjective "'stupid'" suggests Orwell believed societies like Huxley's were simply mindless, whereas his dystopia was a real, diabolical threat. According to Francis Fukuyama's chapter titled "A Tale of Two Utopias," *Brave New World*, not *1984*, "was right, that the most significant threat posed by contemporary biotechnology is the possibility that it will alter human nature and thereby move us into a 'posthuman' stage of history." In the posthuman future, human potentiality becomes irrelevant (Fukuyama, 7).

The end of the literary utopia has been announced more often than the death of the novel, mostly however by political scientists who are thinking of it as an actual place. "Utopian alternatives to the current political and economic systems seem utterly impossible" writes Robert T. Tally, Jr., in 2013; "radically alternative places and futures" are "inconceivable" (Tally, 10, 11). We have come, says Tally, to "the end of the utopia." The utopian impulse itself is supposedly dead. Post-modernity "is characterized by a profound inability to imagine any alternatives" (Tally, 21, 22). After World War II, Merlin Coverley adds, "the utopian tradition had exhausted itself" (Coverley, 161). Some now argue for utopia as "a method rather than a goal," that is, for a "creative" sociology rather than full-scale visions of alternative societies (Levitas, 149). Judith N. Shklar goes furthest by tracing "the gradual decline of rational political optimism since the Enlightenment" (Shklar, x). Shklar's title, *After Utopia*, reverberates throughout Coverley's "Afterword: The Death of Utopia," and in such titles as Russell Jacoby's *The End of Utopia*, John Gray's chapter on "The Death of Utopia" in *Black Mass*, and Tally's on "The End of Utopia at the Present Time."

On the other hand, the golden age of literary utopia, from the 1870s to the 1960s, *Erewhon* to *Island*, encompasses the very period Shklar identifies as its sharpest decline. Could it be, one wonders, that utopia is "inextricably tied […] to modernity" (Tally, viii) and the imperative to make it new? Clearly, the British utopia has weathered the modern outburst of prediction that begins with Butler and Wells. Perhaps one should be on the lookout for a new outburst. In the meantime, it will be necessary to revisit *Brave New World* periodically, as did Huxley, to see how civilization is faring. Arguably, it would be wisest to reinstate permanently the idea that the best place must be no place, i.e., purely imaginary, as Huxley was inclined to think. Doubtless there will be additional attempts to fuse prediction and hypothesis, using different amounts of each each time until the perfect hybrid evolves. To the extent that *Island* effects a compromise between More and Butler, it may be as good a hybrid as can be expected. Only a diminished civilization, one fears, no longer produces utopias; it has given up on describing perfection, not just on attaining it. Kumar's assertion that utopias remain valuable to make one "think about possible worlds, [inventing them] for our contemplation and delight" ("Apocalypse," 219) is the position Huxley finally adopted when assessing human potentialities. Whatever happens, his influence on the future of utopian literature is apt to be no less imposing than the impact of his thinking on the future itself.

Nevertheless, the tricky question remains: are utopias possible? Might one still be on the way? In 1962, Huxley answered the first question in the negative insofar as *positive* utopia is concerned. Huxley's reduction of Pala from prediction to hypothesis corroborates the anti-utopia consensus of writers such as Tally, Coverley, Shklar, Jacoby, and Gray. But he said "yes" to the second question in 1932 and again in 1948 and '58 if it refers to *negative* utopia. Huxley never ceases to worry that, thanks to breakthroughs in technology and enabling advances in the life sciences, negative utopia (i.e., dystopia) is becoming increasingly plausible, whereas positive utopia continues to be as elusive, indeed, as illusory, as ever, either unrealizable or unsustainable.

Even positives in *Brave New World* Huxley presents negatively.[87] The paper on "A New Theory of Biology," which redefines "the purpose of life" (*BNW*, 145), is summarily censored; no one in the World State besides Mustapha Mond will ever read it. Books about spiritual growth by Cardinal Newman and Maine de Biran are kept locked in the Controller's safe (see *BNW*, 190). Helmholtz Watson's poem on the beauty of introspective solitude, a prerequisite for enlightenment, gets him banished; brave new worlders will never hear this poem recited. It is relatively easy to tamper with human nature in detrimental ways, Huxley opined, but seemingly impossible to engineer a universal change of heart.

For Huxley, the challenge was to combat negative developments while preserving positive utopia as a literary forum for discussing what constitutes the perfect place. He sounds like the author of *The Book of the Machines* when he states that "it is perfectly possible to understand current trends, foresee their probable ends, and try to think of ways of preventing negative outcomes" ("Second," 29).[88] On the other hand, Huxley the anti-predictor warned in a 1942 letter, "the one thing that can certainly be said [about the future] is that we are totally incapable of foreseeing it accurately" (*L*, 483).

In any case, prevention is never an irrational screed as it was for Butler. In *Brave New World Revisited*, for example, Huxley tries to ward off the serious consequences from overpopulating the planet and squandering its resources, the causes of a twofold crisis few commentators were as aware of as he was in the 1950s.[89] It is always negative utopia that must be forestalled. Positive utopias, Huxley consistently argues, should remain hypothetical. One must remember that Huxley describes Pala as "an imaginary island between Ceylon and Sumatra" (W/F, 198), a realistic but unreal place between two actual locales.

Generally overlooked is the implication in *Brave New World*, seconded more clearly throughout *Island*, that positive utopia must be nowhere—not a place at all—not just because it is implausible but because it is better thought of as an internal state, a state of mind variously described as heightened awareness, unspeakable bliss, in short, enlightenment. Pala seems vastly superior as a temporal place because it offers its inhabitants a pathway to their ideal internal state, liberation as the "Sovereign Good" first adumbrated by the unnamed biologist in *Brave New World* (*BNW*, 145). If utopia is ultimately more psychological than topographical, as much internal as external, then the entire utopian enterprise, the search for perfection in time and space, becomes suspect, perhaps quixotic. Huxley's 1932 flirtation with the idea that life's purpose, man's Final End, the "unitive knowledge of [...] the transcendent Godhead," lies "outside" the current human sphere (*BNW*, ix, 145), and his collapsing of Pala thirty years later may be seen as interrelated acts with a common denominator: profound mistrust of the temporal order; this is commendable in the mystic, essential to the perennial philosopher, but detrimental in, possibly fatal to, the would-be utopist.[90] Had Huxley, who died in 1963 at age sixty-nine, lived into his seventies, one doubts he would have penned another utopia.

---

1 The term "positive" utopia seems redundant if one thinks of utopia as a perfect place. Most commentators prefer dystopia to "negative" utopia. Huxley found both terms useful; see his 1963 lecture on "Utopias, Positive and Negative" ("Utopias," 1–5).

2 In the "Foreword" Huxley wrote in 1946 for an American edition and reprinted in the 1950 edition of *Brave New World*, the text cited throughout this chapter, he adopts the persona of "the amused, Pyrrhonic aesthete" (*BNW*, viii). A follower of the Greek philosopher Pyrrho, founder of skepticism, who taught that nothing can be known with certainty, Huxley's Pyrrhonic aesthete is the rough equivalent of Sir Thomas More's elusive Raphael Hythloday and Samuel Butler's unstable Higgs. He is not a leg-puller like More and Butler but a complete skeptic whose aesthetics are always ironic, i.e., intended to amuse and disconcert rather than edify.

[3] Huxley gave his lecture in November; *Brave New World Revisited* appeared a month earlier. The lecture was the third visit.

[4] David Bradshaw argues that Wells and Huxley had several common goals; therefore, says Bradshaw, *Brave New World* is not a "straightforward send-up of the futuristic dispensation" in Wells's optimistic utopias (*The Hidden Huxley*, 37). Actually, as utopists, they shared a number of concerns but took increasingly different positions.

[5] See Meckier, "Our Ford, Our Freud," *MSN*, 131–64.

[6] But see David Lorenzo's attempt to distinguish "utopian stories" from "dystopian" ones and both from "satirical" utopias (Lorenzo, 5). Or consider M. Keith Booker's discussion of Lyman Tower Sargent's three-part "scheme": Euotopia or positive utopia, Dystopia or negative utopia, and Anti-utopia (*Dystopia*, 6). Still useful is Northrop Frye, "Varieties of Literary Utopia," 323–47. Also see Gregory Claeys's exhaustive yet inconclusive essay on what he calls the "definitional controversy": "The Literary Dystopia: Problems of Definition" (Claeys, 284). Claeys seems undecided whether *Brave New World* is utopian, dystopian, or an "astute combination" (361). Hence for him "The Huxleyan Conundrum" (357–87). Much of his *Dystopia: A Natural History* consists of listings, with brief comments, of several hundred largely unreadable dystopias. Claeys's ambition is "to synthesize the literary and historical approaches to the concept" of dystopia (7). This 556-page tome falls short because Claeys is a competent political scientist but less trustworthy as a literary critic.

[7] Chatto and Windus, Huxley's English publisher, issued *Ape and Essence* in 1949; in America, Harper's edition came out in 1948.

[8] See Marovitz, "Aldous Huxley and the Nuclear Age," *Critical Essays*, 195–207, and "*Ape and Essence*: Fright or Fantasy?," *NMTE*, 159–73. In both, Marovitz claims Huxley did not know how to handle the nuclear threat—with a dystopian warning or a grotesque tragicomedy. Perversely, Theodor Adorno finds *Ape and Essence* improbable and *Brave New World* oversimplified (see Adorno, 116). Overlooked has been Huxley's regret that "there is no reference in my fable [*BNW*] to subliminal projection. It is a mistake of omission which, if I were to rewrite the book today, I should most certainly correct" (*BNWR*, 69).

[9] Robert V. Hine positions this "isolated" community "in the San Joaquin Valley" (Hine, 21).

[10] Aldous Huxley, *Island* (New York: Bantam, 1963), 75, 78. [*I*]

[11] See Meckier, "Utopian Counterpoint and the Compensatory Dream," *SS*, 175–206.

[12] Pala is often cited as a third alternative. For example, it has been called "the third way between the capitalist and communist versions of industrialism" (Mathisen, 57–58).

[13] Orwell found *Ape and Essence* "awful," a pornographic novel reeking with sex. See *In Front of Your Nose*, 539.

[14] In *Honey for the Bears*, when Alexei Prutkov declares "It's all the State. There's only one state," be it Russia or America, Anthony Burgess echoes Huxley's remarks on "statism" (*HB*, 82).

[15] By "narco-hypnosis" Huxley means sleep-teaching; "hypnopaedia" comes from the Greek *hypno*, a combining form meaning "sleep," and the Greek word *paideia*, which means "child-rearing," "education," and is a derivative of the word for "child."

[16] Roslynn D. Haynes credits Wells with being "able to think in a completely new way about the future"; his works mark "the introduction into literature of a new awareness of the future" (Haynes, x, 2).

[17] George Kateb's phrase comes from his study *Utopia and Its Enemies* (Kateb, 17).

[18] Peter Raby quotes Butler's letter to E. M. S. Savage: "'*Erewhon* is out, and will be advertised tomorrow'" (Raby, 119).

[19] See for instance George Dyson, *Darwin Among the Machines*. It takes its title from Butler's 1863 essay as it tries to determine whether computers can think for themselves. Martin Rees foresees a future dominated by electronics, i.e., machines with AI, artificial intelligence; see *On the Future Prospects for Humanity*.

[20] "An irony of history," according to Hans-Peter Breuer and Daniel F. Howard, "is that one of *Erewhon*'s most ardent admirers was Aldous Huxley, grandson of Thomas Huxley, the Darwinian biologist whom Butler considered one of his chief enemies in the quarrels about evolution" (Breuer/Howard, 35). In his introduction to the Limited Edition Club's *Erewhon* (1934), Huxley praises Butler's satire on "excessive zeal," hence the hidden pun in New Zealand (new-zeal-land), the alleged model for Erewhon. Butler wrote *Erewhon Revisited* thirty years after *Erewhon*, the same time span between *Brave New World* (1932) and *Island* (1962), in which Will Farnaby twice quotes *Erewhon*. See Aldous Huxley, "Butler's *Erewhon*," 49–54, and Sieger, 243–72. Sieger likens Will Farnaby in *Island* to Butler's unnamed protagonist.

[21] "The concept of an evolving utopia in which the ideal of perfection is itself changing," Haynes argues, is "a Wellsian innovation in the history of utopian thought" (Haynes, 22); Hillegas calls it "Wells's transformation of the utopian tradition" (*AMU*, xi).

[22] Krishan Kumar denies Watson's importance: "Huxley shows us little meaning or significance in his revolt […]. [Watson] remains frozen in his development, unlikely to influence anyone by his verses in praise of solitude" (Kumar, 279–80). Surely the deportation of its most promising citizen is part of Huxley's indictment of the World State.

[23] If utopia for More is hypothetical, the good place that exists no place, then numerous utopian experiments between his *Utopia* and Butler's *Erewhon*, especially those throughout the nineteenth century, may be dismissed as misunderstandings of More. Settlements based on the phalansteries of Fourier, and the pipedreams of Cabet, or Robert Owens's New Lanark, and even the Oneida Community, which Huxley admired, were mostly quixotic, unsuccessful attempts to actualize nowhere, to turn hypothetical places into real ones.

[24] When "newly arrived students" tour the Central London Hatchery and Conditioning Centre, Huxley writes, "machinery faintly purred" (*BNW*, 4). Tiers upon tiers of racks filled with test-tubes make a mockery of frightened Erewhonians smashing their machines. Ironically, the atmosphere in the brave new world's "Fertilizing Room" is "frozen, dead." Workers in white overalls

and "corpse-coloured" (*BNW*, 1) gloves resemble ghosts, as unnatural in their way as spider-like Morlocks who tend machines in Wells's *The Time Machine.*

25 Wells defines utopia as a society that converts "all the available energy in nature to the material ends of mankind" (*AMU*, 84).

26 "A modern utopia," Wells boasted, should feature "the evolving interplay of unique individualities" (*AMU*, 33).

27 R. S. Deese's study of Aldous and Julian, *We Are Amphibians*, is one-phibian short (see Deese). This paragraph and the seven preceding it have been excerpted (and revised) from Jerome Meckier, "Aldous Huxley and Utopia: Five Assertions," *Aldous Huxley: East-West Centenary Essays*, 193–200.

28 It is these negative developments that Martin Green refers to in 1965 when he notes that *Brave New World*'s "prophetic voice has remained surprisingly contemporary, both in its particular forecasts and its general tone of serious alarm" (*BNWR*, v). Strangely, David Leon Higdon states that "Huxley was not engaged in guessing what shapes human society might take in five or six hundred years [...]. He was depicting a world that already largely existed in the 1920s and 1930s" (Higdon, 25). Even more curious is Judith N. Shklar's opinion that *Brave New World* "is not a picture of a totalitarian state" because "it offers no insights into totalitarian systems" (Shklar, 155). But Kumar echoes Green when he argues that Huxley "most keenly anticipates the more pernicious characteristics of twenty-first-century society" ("Apocalypse," 226). In *The Last Utopians: Four Late Nineteenth-Century Visionaries and Their Legacy*, Michael Robertson mistakes the beginning of the cycle my book describes for its end (see Robertson). Ignoring Butler and Wells, its progenitors, it concentrates on Bellamy and Morris instead of *Erewhon* and *A Modern Utopia*, texts that were seminal for twentieth-century thinkers like Zamiatin, Huxley, and Orwell. The real issues at the turn of the century were the impact of proliferating technology and the ongoing socio-political consequences of Darwin's theories. Along with Ray Bradbury, Huxley could say "I'm a preventer of futures, I'm not a predictor of them," although one must sometimes predict what one is trying to prevent (Bradbury, 195).

29 My translation of Berdiaeff's French.

30 Gerald Heard alleges that Huxley, the poignant prophet, moved from satire in *Brave New World* to prophecy in *Island* (see Heard, 49–79).

31 Mark Hillegas calls *The Time Machine* "the first well-executed, imaginatively coherent picture of a future worse than the present." In "imaginative qualities," he says, it "excels" *We* and *Brave New World*, "being both more successful in domesticating the incredible and more poetic in its conception" (Hillegas, 34).

32 See Meckier, "Afterword."

33 See Chapter 4 of Dardis, 183–216.

34 Hollywood has turned out a number of successful apocalyptic films. Stanley Kubrick's *Dr. Strangelove* is the best example. Usually, however, such films are not serious cautionary tales. Instead, they offer the vicarious thrill of participating in a disaster one can walk away from unscathed at film's end—or else someone saves the world.

35 Huxley's use of "nowhere" is probably coincidental although Farnaby likens his providential arrival on Pala to Higgs's in Erewhon (see *I*, 17).

[36] Perhaps unwittingly, Wells underscores the inherently hypothetical nature of a utopia such as *Island* when he muses that "a Utopia is a thing of the imagination that becomes more fragile with every added circumstance, that, like a *soap-bubble*, it is most brilliantly and variously coloured at the very instant of its dissolution" (*AMU*, 352).

[37] One had best disregard Frank Kermode's derogatory opinion of *Island* as "one of the worst novels ever written" (Kermode, 472–73).

[38] All following calculations were made in 2018–2019.

[39] Hammond quotes from *Principles and Persuasions* (1958), in which West claims that Wells "'parodied'" the "'unpracticality and unreality of his idealism'" (Hammond, 137). Nathan Waddell agrees: "that Wells's narrator is denied a permanent residence in that [perfected] state [i.e., a Modern Utopia] hints at the impracticality" of its prophecies (Waddell, 17).

[40] In one instance, Huxley corroborates Morris. Reviewing Bellamy's *Looking Backward* in 1889, Morris cautioned that the "multiplication of machinery" would reduce human labor to a minimum, forcing laborers to find pleasure away from work (*NN*, 357), as happens in *Brave New World*. Not only is there demand for almost constant diversion but some forms of recreation, golf for example, are mandatory. Huxley deplores the "futility of Shakespeare and the triumph of mass over high culture" (James, 33), a widespread dumbing down that includes motion pictures, to which the brave new world adds "feely effects" of scent and physical sensations (*BNW*, 139). It all starts when Morris warns against the "utopianization" of work (see Breton, 43).

[41] Note the author's pun on his own name. Apparently, the future cannot do without "wells"—H. G. Wells, that is.

[42] In "Zoological Regression" (1891), Wells pictured the popular conception of evolution, namely, that "the great scroll of nature has been steadily unfolding to reveal a constantly richer harmony of forms and successively higher grades of being."

[43] See Meckier, "Onomastic Satire," *MSN*, 185–224.

[44] Like Butler, Wells relies heavily on Swift. Just as Gulliver alienates the king of Brobdingnag with a "historical account" of Europe's "last century"—"an heap of conspiracies, rebellions, murders, massacres, revolutions, banishments" (see Book 2, Chapter 6)—Cavor disgusts the Grand Lunar with a history of "'earthly War'"; he begins with the "'invasions and massacres'" of Huns and Tartars, describes the Crusades, and finishes with "'the Battle of Colenso'" (*FMM*, 157). No wonder the Selenites prevent Cavor from instructing other earth-dwellers how to reach the moon.

[45] See "Golf in *Brave New World*," chapter 3 below.

[46] All Alphas wear grey, Betas blue, Gammas green, Deltas khaki, and Epsilons black (see *BNW*, 21). For even greater uniformity, everyone in Zamiatin's One State wears "pale blue unifs" (*Z*, 5), uniforms that are literally uniform.

[47] For a discussion of Wells's principles of rationalization and the argument that Huxley, supposedly "the greatest anti-Wellsian of them all," was not always unsympathetic to them, see Bradshaw, *The Hidden Huxley*, 31–43.

[48] James Sexton provides a useful definition of rationalization in "*Brave New World* and the Rationalization of Industry," *Critical Essays*, 88. Rationalizers want to put everything in society—business, government, private lives—on the most logical and efficient basis they can devise.

[49] For a fuller analysis of Watson's poem, one is reminded to see Meckier, *PM*, 252–4, and *MSN*, 195–96.

[50] Conditioned to accept promiscuity, Watson, who has slept with "six hundred and forty different girls in under four years," "broke out in an explosion of uncontrollable guffawing" at the thought of an "idiotic girl" not allowed to have sex with anyone she wants (*BNW*, 57, 151). "Tybalt lying dead, but evidently uncremated and wasting his phosphorus" also convulses him.

[51] According to Bernard Bergonzi, "the combination of almost limitless scientific possibilities with large-scale social engineering was to produce the characteristic 'Wellsian' utopia, adumbrated first in *A Modern Utopia* in 1905" (Bergonzi, 171).

[52] Sublimation involves the displacement of energy from a frustrated desire, the deflection of energy into intellectual, humanitarian, cultural, and artistic pursuits (see Hall, 82).

[53] For Sheldon's classifications, see *L*, 486–87, and Bedford, I, 352.

[54] George Eliot, for instance, concludes *Middlemarch* by expressing her faith in the "growing good of the world" (*Mm*, 613). In *Bleak House*, when Joe dies, the outraged narrator's exclamation that the poor are "dying thus around us every day" (*BH*, 611) indicates that Dickens puts little stock in a steady amelioration. For a discussion of utopianism within Victorian realism, in particular the argument that many Victorian novels have a utopian or dystopian thrust depending on whether the author believes social conditions are improving or worsening, see Meckier, *Hidden Rivalries*, 5–6.

[55] Supposedly "narrow and inward-looking," modernism in Nathan Waddell's opinion was not "indifferent to exterior realities." Conrad, Lawrence, and Joyce, he argues, expressed "interest in utopia" (Waddell, 1, 5). D. H. Lawrence often fantasized about establishing "Rananim," an ideal community "far from England" (Worthen, 157).

[56] "Latent Human Potentialities," a preoccupation of the later Huxley, was the subject of one of Huxley's lectures at Santa Barbara in 1959.

[57] See Huxley's study of *Ends and Means* (1937), which has a utopic subtitle: "An Enquiry into the Nature of Ideals and into the Methods employed for their Realization." Despite its title, there can be only one "Final End."

[58] Intense promiscuity throughout *Ape and Essence* and the brave new world may be a satirical dismissal of Wells's *First Men in the Moon*, whose Selenites, says Huxley, comprise "an insect society in which love is perfectly unnecessary" (*MN*, 97).

[59] For an extended analysis of Farnaby's drug trip, see Meckier, "Conradian Reminders in Aldous Huxley's *Island*," *MSN*, 274–92. To Susila MacPhail's query—"'Where are you now?'"—a drugged Will answers, "'In heaven, I suppose'" (*I*, 271).

[60] For an analysis of Sir Hercules's story, see Meckier, *SS*, 14–15.

[61] One commentator describes the "experts" who rule the World-state as "a functional elite" whose supervision is "paternalistic" (Hillegas, xv, xvi, xvii).

[62] Wells was favorably impressed by Lenin, whom he interviewed during a visit to Russia. In *Russia in the Shadows* (1921), Wells dubs Lenin "The Dreamer in the Kremlin." See Hutchings, 87.

[63] Peter Firchow suggests that the ten World Controllers in *Brave New World* are "modeled on the pope and cardinals of the Church of Rome" (*End*, 33).

[64] At Malpais, when Lenina encounters an example of "extreme old age," an Indian with a "profoundly wrinkled" face, a "toothless mouth," his body "bent and emaciated," she asks "'What's the matter with him?'" Bernard replies: "'He's old, that's all'" (*BNW*, 90). But, like Lenina, who is horrified, "he too was startled." At the Park Lane Hospital, the Delta twins, being "'death-conditioned,'" are "alarmed" at the sight of "flaccid," senile Linda: "They had never seen a face like hers before" (*BNW*, 166).

[65] Dr. Robert has his detractors. Dominic Baker-Smith refers to "that know-all Dr. Robert" (Baker-Smith, 111).

[66] Never identified by name, John's victim wears Lenina's outfit: "green velveteen shorts, white shirt, and jockey cap" (*BNW*, 211). When she falls while fleeing the Savage's assault, she appeals for help to "'Henry, Henry!'"—presumably Henry Foster, her golf date in chapter IV.

[67] See Meckier, "Satire as 'Discriminative Sympathy,'" 128–29.

[68] Opening one's eyes is not always a fortuitous occurrence. In Morris's *News from Nowhere*, Guest's relationship with Ellen—they are another failed couple—ends abruptly when he wakes in his own bed and wonders if he has had "a vision rather than a dream" (*NN*, 228). In *Looking Backward*, Bellamy's protagonist has a bad dream in which he wakes up back in the nineteenth century. Then he reawakens still securely in the utopian future he woke up in after sleeping a hundred years. Farnaby's experience with Susila is best of the three.

[69] To appreciate the extent of Huxley's satiric use of Ford's ideas in *Brave New World*, see Meckier, "Debunking Our Ford," *MSN*, 121–30. Huxley often inserted texts within his text, such as "The Autobiography of Francis Chelifer" in *Those Barren Leaves* and Philip Quarles's "Notebook" in *Point Counter Point*. *Brave New World*'s texts-within-the text include an excerpt from the biology paper Mond censors and lengthy quotations from books by Maine de Biran and Cardinal Newman. *Brave New World Revisited* would make an excellent text-within-the-text if it were incorporated in a novel a chapter at a time. The outline of Nowhere's history that old Hammond sketches for Guest in chapters xvii and xviii of *News from Nowhere* is the equivalent of a text-within-the text. It anticipates Mond's history lesson in *Brave New World* and the sections that Winston Smith reads from Goldstein's book in *Nineteen Eighty-Four*. *The Origin of Species* and *Capital*, seminal works by Darwin and Marx, are texts present implicitly in *Erewhon* and *News from Nowhere* respectively, just as ideas from Ford's autobiography and Taylor's efficiency studies infiltrate *Brave New World* and *We*. Through a "specious use of analogy" (*E*, x), supposedly the satirist's real target in chapters 23–25 (and not Darwin), Butler has the author of *The Book of the Machines* demonstrate that there is "'enough analogy existing at the present moment'" between the way humans have evolved and the speed with

which machines are developing "'to make us feel seriously uneasy about the future'" (*E*, 185). Using "'seriously'" as part of the joke on Darwin is a nice touch. In *Brave New World*, machines take over not by reproducing themselves the way Butler's paranoid author feared, but by assuming control of the reproduction process: "The principle of mass production at last applied to biology" (*BNW*, 5) involves another specious analogy. Marx's ideas about the worth and dignity of labor and the working class pervade "a Socialist future" in *News from Nowhere* (*NN*, xxi). In Wells's *The Time Machine*, the future repudiates Marx and Darwin both.

70 O'Brien refers to it reverently in italics as "'*the book* [...,] Goldstein's book'" (O, 146). Later he tells Winston "'I wrote it. That is to say, I collaborated in writing it'" (O, 215).

71 Orwell alludes to William Morris's *The Earthly Paradise* (1868–70). Actually, the adventurers in Morris's poem never find the fabled Earthly Paradise "where none grow old."

72 Goldstein's "new aristocracy," the Inner Party, an elaborate parody of Wells's *samurai*, is "made up for the most part of bureaucrats, scientists, technicians, trade-union organizers, publicity experts, sociologists, teachers, journalists, and professional politicians," all of whom, however, are power-hungry, not altruistic (O, 169).

73 Bernfried Nugel reports that Huxley's British and American editors felt "the novel contained too much philosophical exposition." Nugel argues that by "deleting large portions of the *Notes*," Huxley "greatly detracted from the coherence and effectiveness of *Island* as a whole" ("Huxley's Revisions," 69, 90).

74 Peter Firchow calls Pala "a realistic, if not a real, utopia." It is Huxley's "vision of what a realistic utopia might be like" ("Brave at Last," 160, 157).

75 "Facile," meaning too easy, undemanding, but not necessarily inexpensive. When the Savage claims "'Nothing costs enough here'" (*BNW*, 196), Henry Foster puts the price of the new Conditioning Centre at "'[n]ot a cent less'" than "'[t]welve and a half million,'" presumably dollars not pounds since Henry uses the word "cent." When Bernard Marx, visiting Malpais, "suddenly remembered that he had left the Eau de Cologne tap in his bathroom [...] running," he "saw the needle on the scent meter creeping round and round" (*BNW*, 83). So there are steep individual utility bills.

76 As a combination of the worst features of Nazi Germany and Stalinist Russia, Orwell's synthesis in *1984* is powerful but not nearly as extensive.

77 This is Zamiatin's opinion of revolution in his essay "On Literature, Revolution, Entropy and Other Matters" as quoted in Mira Ginsburg's introduction (Z, x).

78 Orwell praised *We* in a review for the *London Tribune* (4 January 1946), acknowledging his indebtedness. Despite Huxley's denials, Orwell stuck to his assertion that "*Brave New World* must be partially derived from it" (*In Front of Your Nose*, 72). According to Peter Firchow, Orwell "argues mistakingly [...] that Aldous Huxley had read *We* and borrowed from it" (*MUF*, iii, note 17). In *The End of Utopia*, Firchow again insists that "Huxley had not read *We* at the time he was writing *Brave New World*" (*End*, 121). However, George Woodcock

states that Huxley "borrowed copiously" (Woodcock, 209). Robert S. Baker analyzes Huxley's and Orwell's responses to Zamiatin and concludes that charges of "systematic plagiarism directed against both writers are false" (*BNWHSD*, 39). Revaluation is often misunderstood as thievery. Reworkings on Huxley's part are irreverent borrowings. "Unanimity Day" in *We* (Z, 136), for example, surely inspired the "Solidarity Service days" that Bernard Marx must attend every second Thursday *(BNW*, 65). Both services are ridiculous pseudo-religious rituals. Reluctantly, poor Bernard must go to twenty-six more than the annual ceremony D-503 looks forward to. For a discussion of what she calls parallels between *We* and *Brave New World*, see Beth Cooke, *Human Nature in Utopia.*

79 See Meckier, "What the Books Were Always Saying," 39–48.

80 In her introduction to *Herland*, Ann J. Lane argues for the utopian novel's "uniquely feminist expression" as a tradition of its own (Gilman, xx). The dozen examples of novels by female authors she cites mostly come from the 1970s; they do not talk to each other. Nor do they take issue with Wells or with Huxley and Orwell.

81 In *A Clockwork Orange*, Anthony Burgess insists that our freedom to choose, even if wrongly, is what prevents society from becoming dystopia. The best world, it follows, is an imperfect world. Burgess's views not only challenge those of Zamiatin, Huxley, and Orwell but question the value of perfection itself.

82 For George Woodcock the major difference between *1984* and previous utopias is that "the pretense of providing happiness as a compensation for the loss of freedom is not maintained" (Woodcock, 215).

83 Bernfried Nugel argues that Bahu was an afterthought. Huxley decided "to introduce a new character even after he had already written a considerable part of the whole book." See "Aldous Huxley's 'Introduction of a Brand New Personage,'" 132.

84 The blurb on Atwood's book cover promises that "[j]ust as the world of Orwell's *1984* gripped our imagination, so will the world of Atwood's handmaid" (*Handmaid*). This has not happened.

85 *Player Piano* is more derivative than revaluative. For example, everything in the United States is done by machines. PICACXIV is busy "deciding how many refrigerators, how many lamps, how many turbine-generators, how many hub caps, how many dinner plates, how many door knobs, how many rubber heels, how many television sets, how many pinochle decks—how many everything America and her customers could have and how much they would cost. [It] would decide for the coming years how many engineers and managers and research men and civil servants, and of what skills would be needed in order to deliver the goods; and what I. Q. and aptitude levels would separate the useful men from the useless ones" (V, 117). Vonnegut borrows the notion of conscriptive consumption and blends with it the mass production of a work force. Actually, "the divine right of machines," as Vonnegut calls it, sounds more like Wells's dream and Butler's worst fear.

86 "In *1984*," Huxley notes, "the lust for power is satisfied by inflicting pain; in *Brave New World*, by inflicting a hardly less humiliating pleasure" (*BNWR*, 21). Thomas E. Ricks calls the pleasure-pain antithesis "a false distinction"; flirting

with *double think*, he explains how "both men are right" (Ricks, 257). Mond's goal, like Big Brother's, is to stay in control.

[87] On the other hand, Huxley does not simply provide three dissidents (Marx, Watson, the Savage) to Zamiatin's one (D-503); he also sprinkles positive thoughts and heretical behavior throughout his text. These are flaws in the brave new world's system. They keep the World State from being perfect according to its own precepts. For examples: Fanny Crowne has maternal urges and must be given "'a three months' Pregnancy Substitute'" for her health (*BNW*, 31). And Lenina exhibits monogamous tendencies by going out exclusively with Henry Foster for four months, a dating pattern Fanny calls "'horribly bad form'" (*BNW*, 32). Even an Epsilon-Minus Semi-Moron, a liftman, reveals a religious propensity: whenever he opens the elevator gates atop the building on a sunlit afternoon, he cries "'Oh, roof!' [...] in a voice of rapture" (*BNW*, 49).

[88] Possibly it is no coincidence that the golden age for modern literary utopias began in 1872 with Butler and that, thanks to a series of great inventions, the decade 1866–76 was the start of the most amazing period of activity and development in the world's history, an "enormous wave of inventiveness" (Smil, 308, 277).

[89] See *BNWR*, Chapter 1 ("Over-Population"), 1–10.

[90] In *After Many a Summer*, Mr. Propter tells Pete Boone that "'time is evil'" whereas "'[a]ctual good is outside time'" (*AMS*, 106, 108). This is Huxley's final take on the temporal order, which the modern satirical novelist used to rely on to administer comeuppances to miscreants and malefactors at the appointed time. Yet Propter is a bit of a utopist: he provides cabins for migrant workers' families and tries to interest them in "'Jeffersonian democracy'" (131).

Chapter Two

Cure Scenes

In the prototypical cure scene from Samuel Butler's *Erewhon* (1872), confusion develops as to what constitutes sickness and what health. Shortly after Higgs stumbles upon Erewhon, he is "nearly imprisoned" for catching cold (*E*, 67). On the other hand, Mr. Nosnibor, "'lately recovered from embezzling a large sum of money'" (*E*, 68), continues to be greatly respected because in Erewhon, sickness is a crime; crime is considered a sickness. Victorians punished criminals severely but coddled the sick. Butler laughed at both countries but especially at Britishers like Higgs, who "cannot bear having much to do with people who think differently" (71). The real danger, Butler surmised, was that in the future the state might manipulate concepts of sickness and health to enforce its policies: conformity would be regarded as healthy; anyone disagreeing would have to be cured.

Yevgeny Zamiatin's *We* (1924) was the first major utopia to replace Butler's playful ambivalence with painful ironies.[1] The government is clearly the sick party, not D-503, whom it presumes to cure. The totalitarian One State coerces a deviant back into the fold by persuading him that he has fallen ill. Its cure makes it impossible for D-503 not to embrace the government's perverse doctrines ever after. In the novel's thoroughly absurd happy ending, a lobotomized D-503 and the One State seem pleased with each other.

The One State's totally regimented citizens have numbers in place of names. All wear the same "pale blue unifs" (uniforms) (Z, 5) and do everything with mathematical precision, even chewing each mouthful of food a prescribed number of times. They obey the Benefactor unreservedly. D-503, the One State's leading scientist, is building "the *Integral*," a rocket ship designed to "subjugate" planets "still [...] living in the primitive condition of freedom" (Z, 1).[2] I-330, a *femme fatale*, awakens the heretofore rational D-503's second self, which proves to be poetic and sensual. Confused, he consults a doctor: "'You're in a bad way!'" he is told; "'You have developed a soul'" (Z, 89). "'Is it very dangerous?'" D-503 inquires. "'Incurable'" is the unfortunate reply.

Actually, the One State, fearing an "epidemic" of "soul sickness" (Z, 91, 195), has devised an invidious cure: surgical "'excision of the imagination'" (Z, 81), whereby the last traces of one's creativity and rebelliousness are removed. Being "ill," D-503 becomes convinced, means acquiring "individual consciousness" (Z, 128) in lieu of universal depersonalization. Such awareness is "merely a sickness," he decides, just "a miserable little nodule in the brain" that one can be "cured of" by its extraction (Z, 180). Tied to a table, D-503 is "subjected to the Great Operation" (Z, 232). "I am well," he subsequently writes in his diary without a trace of regret: "a kind of splinter was pulled out of my head," which now "feels light and empty" (Z, 231), hardly the ideal mental state. D-503 tells the Benefactor "everything" he knows about I-330 and her confederates, the Mephi,[3] who are promptly condemned as "enemies of happiness" (Z, 232). In *We*'s cure scene, which is both scary and funny, sickness and health trade places more disconcertingly than they do for Butler's Higgs. By its method of curing D-503, the One State indelibly stamps itself a negative utopia.[4]

In the first of the three climactic cure scenes in *Brave New World* (1932), John the Savage disrupts distribution of the daily "*soma* ration"[5] to the menial staff of the Park Lane Hospital for the Dying, an unpromising setting for a cure. "'Lend me your ears,'" John begins; "'Don't take that horrible stuff. It's poison.'" He insists he has "'come to bring [them] freedom'" (*BNW*, 173) by ending the drug dependency that keeps them happily servile. Unfortunately, the "khaki mob" of maggoty twins prefers euphoria to independence. "Exasperated" by such "brutal stupidity," the Savage begins throwing pill-boxes of *soma* out the window (*BNW*, 175). When the infuriated Deltas charge, John is soon discarding *soma* with one hand and punching "the indistinguishable faces of his assailants" with the other (*BNW*, 175). The disturbance quickly escalates into a riot as a well-meaning visitor fails to cure a group of dystopia's unheeding citizens of their *soma* addiction.

"A full head" taller than his attackers, John swings away at a swarm of "less than human monsters" mad enough to "kill him" (*BNW*, 171, 174, 175). At once ludicrous and frightening, Huxley's cure scene parodies the funeral oration Mark Antony delivers after Caesar's murder: "Friends, Romans, Countrymen, lend me your ears!" He subtly convinces the Plebeians that Brutus and his allegedly "honourable" accomplices are actually "traitors."[6] Like John, Antony achieves a different result from his ostensible purpose but does so intentionally. Huxley's Shakespeare-quoting Savage, an outsider who fails to impress the society in which he finds himself trapped, winds up fighting the workers he intended to save.[7]

No one gets cured in the two cure scenes with which *Brave New World* ends. In Chapter XVI, Mustapha Mond banishes Helmholtz Watson to the Falklands for fighting alongside John at the Park Lane Hospital. Watson is clearly not about to be reformed. The World State seems more anxious to purge itself than to discourage Watson's new-found penchant for solitude and independent thought. As in Zamiatin, the unhealthy party here is the government. Exile to an island, Watson's punishment, is less draconian than

D-503's lobotomy, but it reveals an unsound society's determination to maintain a meretricious status quo by deporting its healthiest citizens. The World State is more demented than the One State. This "insane" utopia (*BNW*, viii), as Huxley calls it, dispenses with the one person who might do it some good. A nascent poet-mystic, Watson has begun pursuing loftier ideals than the brave new world's limited concept of "happiness" as "well-being," i.e., bodily health.

Island exile may be more prize than punishment, an ironic misfortune.[8] Although Watson selects the "'thoroughly bad climate'" of the Falklands over the Marquesas or Samoa—allegedly it will prove more conducive to composing—Mond calls it "'really a reward'" (*BNW*, 186, 187). Along with Bernard Marx, Watson is

> "being sent to a place where he'll meet the most interesting set of men and women to be found anywhere in the world. All the people who, for one reason or another, have got too self-consciously individual to fit into community-life. All the people who aren't satisfied with orthodoxy, who've got independent ideas of their own. Every one, in a word, who's any one." (*BNW*, 186)

"'I almost envy you,'" Mond concludes. The "'almost'" is worrisome, but Watson seems destined to associate with talented misfits like himself, a blessing in disguise. If he continues to poeticize, he will make himself sicker by brave new world standards. Ironically, island exile can only aggravate the so-called illness it purports to cure.

In the novel's best-known cure scene (Chapter XVII), the World Controller, speaking for the brave new world, tries unsuccessfully to convert an outsider to its spurious views. Parallel lines, Mond and John the Savage argue to a stalemate, neither convincing the other, which leaves readers with a counterpoint instead of resolution. Freedom, which John champions, and happiness, the World State's *summum bonum*, turn out to be as contrapuntal in Huxley's opinion as Fulke Greville found "passion and reason, self-division's cause."[9] Apparently, one cannot have both of the former simultaneously yet neither satisfies without the other.

Mond advocates a prelapsarian happiness. Blissfully ignorant, thoroughly conditioned to glorify their lot as the best possible, brave new worlders enjoy the "'perfect health'" that Adam and Eve knew before the Fall; an unquestioning happiness predicated on the absence of "'inconveniences'" (*BNW*, 196, 197) such as sin, introspection and, above all, suffering. "'People are happy'" in the brave new world, Mond boasts; "'they're never ill'" (*BNW*, 180). Happiness means never getting sick, never having to worry. John objects that life on such terms is "'too easy'" (*BNW*, 196), mindless and meaningless. "'I want freedom,'" he declares, such as our first parents acquired by eating forbidden fruit from the Tree of Knowledge. Mond accuses John of "'claiming the right to be unhappy,'" i.e., the right to grow old as did Adam and Eve, to contract typhoid, syphilis, and cancer, to suffer "'unspeakable pains of every kind'" (*BNW*, 197). "'I claim them all,'" says the Savage at last. At the end of a debate supposed to win John over to the World State, he embraces every known sickness and disease rather than become a healthy brave new worlder.

Huxley outdoes Zamiatin with three cure scenes as variations on a theme: not a single genuine cure is effected. John the Savage fails to liberate the Deltas; given "a fresh supply of pill-boxes," they are soon "kissing and hugging one another" (*BNW*, 176). Watson may signal the next evolutionary advance for humankind, an expansion of consciousness. Yet even if he becomes poet laureate of the Falklands, maturing into a full-fledged poet and mystic by actualizing the "'extra latent power'" (BNW, 149) he senses within,[10] his breakthrough can have little impact on the brave new worlders left behind. The debate between Mond and the Savage improves upon *We*, wherein the Benefactor invites D-503 to "argue" with him (Z, 213), then brushes aside his objections.[11] Huxley's World State is irrevocably certified as a dystopia when the incurably disillusioned Savage hangs himself rather than continue to live there.

D. H. Lawrence believed that, by 1928, an industrial dystopia already existed for dehumanized coal miners in and around Nottingham as well as for the deformed steel-workers from Sheffield.[12] The former appear as permanently "blackened" as the countryside, whereas the latter are "weird, distorted, smallish beings" who frighten Connie (*LCL*, 142, 143). In *Lady Chatterley's Lover* (1928), industrialists such as her husband have sucked the vitality—the instinctive, passionate side of human nature—out of Tevershall's work-force. Thanks to their underground existence, Sir Clifford's miners have been reduced to "less than humanness" (*LCL*, 143); this "new race" of dwarfish "creatures" seems worse off than Wells's subterranean Morlocks, whom they resemble, or Huxley's subhuman Deltas.

Unlike the Time Traveller, Connie need not journey into the distant future to learn "what has man done to man" (*LCL*, 143). A simple car ride through "the long squalid straggle of Tevershall" gives her a sense of the future as "utter negation" (*LCL*, 142). Under conditions that continually imperil "the life of the body," destroying its "living intuitive faculty" (*LCL*, 219, 142), Mellors and Connie, Sir Clifford's wife and his gamekeeper, struggle to resurrect each other: each strives to bring the other back to the fullness of physical life. Despite their adulterous affair, they are the only ones who remain faithful to the feelings and instincts industrial society has betrayed. Inspired by Mellors, Connie goes so far as to predict victory, complete recovery for life-worshippers like herself and Mellors: the body "'"is really rising from the tomb,'" she cries (*LCL*, 220).

By novel's end, Connie and Mellors develop into full-blown life-worshippers, ardent proponents of unrestricted physical awareness here and now, in which "the body is really wakened to life" (*LCL*, 219). They accomplish this by violating taboos, not just the one prohibiting adultery but also England's supreme sexual taboo forbidding sodomy—anal copulation with a member of the opposite sex. Through a startling transgression comparable to Adam and Eve's, Lawrence sought to liberate society-in-general along with Connie from all self-imposed constraints due to guilt or fear. Living with Clifford and his ilk is literally killing Connie. Her health, her state of mind as well as her physical condition, deteriorates rapidly until Mellors begins giving lessons in love. He is still bitter from his failed marriage to Bertha, so Connie in effect forces him to wake up and make a new start. Their mutual restoration culminates in an intense cure scene on their "last night" in Mellors's hut before Connie and Hilda leave for Venice.

The irony in Lady Chatterley's cure scene is that through perversity, that is, by means of what society considers sick behavior, lies a path to physical, bodily health, not to mention a peace of mind akin for Lawrence to spiritual contentment. Two malcontents in an industrial dystopia cure each other by violating society's ultimate taboo. Indirectly, almost in Connie's own words, Lawrence recounts her "night of sensual passion":

> [S]he was a little startled, almost unwillingly, yet pierced again with piercing thrills of sensuality, different, sharper, more terrible than the thrills of tenderness, but, at the moment, more desirable. […] [S]he let him have his way, and the reckless, shameless sensuality shook her to her foundations, stripped her to the very last, and made a different woman of her. […] Burning out the shames, the deepest, oldest shames, in the most secret places […] to burn out the false shames and smelt out the heaviest ore of the body into purity. […] [T]he shame died […]: the deep organic shame, the old, old physical fear which […] can only be chased away by the sensual fire, […] by the phallic hunt […]. She felt, now, she had come to the real bed-rock of her nature, and was essentially shameless. (*LCL*, 231–32)

Almost painfully, Connie savors a sexual emancipation that Lawrence believed all persons must experience, in one form or another, if they are to recapture the shamelessness that Adam and Eve knew prior to original sin. Thanks to Mellors, Connie regains a certain paradoxical "purity," complete freedom from "the old, old physical fear," namely, fear of the physical; in short, she recovers a utopian state of bodily wellness not unlike bliss.

Without this state, says Lawrence, there can be no ideal place. Shaken "to her foundations," having reached down to "the real bed-rock of her nature," Connie sheds the last of her inhibitions; decisively uninhibited, she turns into "a different woman," someone completely cured, entirely healthy, indeed, virtually reborn. Ironically, her transformation, a form of enlightenment, takes place amidst the "nightmare" of a dystopia that threatens to engulf her as modern life becomes increasingly "mechanical" (*LCL*, 143, 146), more and more hostile to all things physical. Mustapha Mond, one recalls, censors a heretical paper that dared to posit the "refining of consciousness" as life's purpose (*BNW*, 145). Lawrence's heroine finds the "refinements of passion," unimpeded delight in the body from moment to moment, quintessential for living well even in dystopia.

Regrettably, Connie's redemptive feat remains a secret from everyone except Mellors. Not rebels so much as social outcasts thanks to Connie's infidelity, their really serious offense goes undetected[13] by a society whose mores seem impervious to change. The only chance Mellors and Connie have of not being the last full-bodied man and woman is to transmit their outlook, Lawrence's so-called blood philosophy, to the next generation.[14] Hence the importance of Connie's pregnancy. Occurring out of wedlock, it violates a third taboo. Separated at novel's end, Connie and Mellors plan to reunite "next year" after she secures a divorce (*LCL*, 282). They must keep Connie's child out of Sir Clifford's clutches. Whether these things will happen Lawrence seems uncertain. An additional irony remains possible: the novel's cure scene could prove to be transitory, its traducing of society's moral code a breakthrough best seen as an anomaly, if not a last gasp. I-330's frank sexuality discombobulates D-503 and a "pneumatic" Lenina Crowne (*BNW*, 40) unsettles John the Savage. Lawrence longs to invest the physical attraction between Mellors and Connie with utopic possibilities yet cannot be confident of having done so. Albeit the cure Mellors applies to Connie works, the need for it condemns the ethos of an anti-human industrialized system whose victims may still include Mellors and Connie.

In the lengthy cure scene from Huxley's *Ape and Essence* (1949), the Arch-Vicar of Belial fails to persuade an outsider, Dr. Alfred Poole, to enter the devilish priesthood that rules a post-nuclear society in Southern California. It is 2108, more than a century after atomic bombs pounded most of the world back into the Stone Age.[15] A simian community in and around Los Angeles is convinced that only diabolical possession—indeed, the devil himself—could have driven the twentieth century, especially "'between 1945 and the beginning of the Third World War'" (*AE*, 97), to the brink of universal self-destruction. Consequently, survivors worship Belial[16] and take orders from the Arch-Vicar, a shabbier version of "'his fordship'" (*BNW*, 37), Mustapha Mond in Huxley's previous dystopia.[17]

Alfred Poole is chief botanist for the New Zealand Re-Discovery Expedition. An isolated New Zealand was spared the "radioactive condition" prevalent everywhere else (*AE*, 28); its reconnaissance boat, a make-shift time machine, has reached Southern California in search of signs of life. A thirty-eight-year-old virgin whom his colleagues have nicknamed "Stagnant," Poole is captured by "villainous-looking" workers and taken to the Arch-Vicar (*AE*, 44). Once it becomes clear that Poole can help everyone get "'more to eat,'" the Arch-Vicar invites him to "'become one of us'" (*AE*, 55, 138). Joining the devil's priesthood, however, involves castration. All priests, Poole suddenly realizes, are beardless contraltos. The Arch-Vicar urges Poole to undergo "'physiological conversion,'" a cure which will free him from all temptations besetting "'an unmutated male'" (*AE*, 139).

Poole is subjected to a long history lesson reminiscent of Our Ford's lecture in Chapter III of *Brave New World*—except that it is too much a straight forward sermon to be nearly as effective. The Arch-Vicar reviews disasters that culminated in a third world war: overcrowding (i.e., the population explosion), hubristic misuse of technology, depletion of natural resources, heavy industrialization resulting in widespread pollution, etc. (see *AE*, 92–94). All the economic and political mistakes that Huxley's essays warned against throughout the 1940s have had predictably calamitous consequences. The lecture stands as Huxley's redoing of Mond's debate with the Savage in Chapter XVII of *Brave New World*, but Poole's infrequent and feeble objections are easily dismissed by the devil's advocate.

During Belial Day ceremonies in the Los Angeles Coliseum, deformed babies born during the past year are systematically slaughtered. Rounding up these victims of radioactivity is not difficult: all babies are conceived during the "'five weeks'" following Belial Day (*AE*, 102). When the Arch-Vicar's lecture and the slaughter of the innocents conclude simultaneously, Poole participates in the orgy that opens this dystopia's annual mating season. For the other forty-seven weeks, girls wear a patch saying "NO" over each breast (*AE*, 46) and on the seat of their trousers. Poole's shedding of inhibitions seems almost farcical compared with Connie Chatterley's. No longer restrained by "the conventions in which he was brought up" (*AE*, 109), he copulates repeatedly with Loola, a sexually precocious eighteen-year-old whose "'extra pair of nipples'" (*AE*, 63) did not merit extermination.

In Zamiatin's *We*, the One State removed D-503's soul; the dystopian society of twenty-second-century California wants to do likewise with

Alfred's testicles. Instead, Poole and Loola escape to a "'little community up north, near Fresno'" that is supposed to be "'[e]ighty-five per cent Hot'" (*AE*, 103), a sexually robust Lawrencian enclave in northern California instead of in New Mexico.[18] Ironically, Poole effects his own cure by avoiding the one Huxley's dystopia has in mind for him. Having discovered the joys of year-round sex, he and Loola become "'normal'" human beings with "'normal human feelings'" (*AE*, 145), a recovery akin to that of Connie and Mellors. But Huxley's couple will not settle for a Lawrencian fullness of bodily life. Once fully humanized, they are allegedly poised to take the next step towards spiritual enlightenment. As Huxley puts it, they are prepared to move from Shelley's *Epipsychidion*, which Poole quotes at novel's end, to the same poet's *Adonais* and then "beyond" to what the narrator calls "the wordless doctrine of the Pure in Heart" (*AE*, 149). Presumably, this is a state of mystical awareness vastly superior to the "purity" a sodomized Connie regains courtesy of Mellors (*LCL*, 232).

Poole and Loola pale in comparison with Mellors and Connie, but both couples find maintaining a healthy sexual relationship in a dystopian social environment risky business, as will Orwell's Winston and Julia, the even more depleted version of Connie and Mellors in *Nineteen Eighty-Four*. Indeed, a love affair's chances for success provide a reliable means of gauging a society's lack of utopic potential. Connie's blasphemous vision of her revivified physicality emerging Christ-like from "'the tomb'" has a certain gravity (*LCL*, 220). Its comical equivalent in *Ape and Essence* finds the pseudo-Lawrencian Poole, in search of Loola, "advancing from behind the tomb of Rudolph Valentino" (*AE*, 123).[19] Poole's is the weakest of Huxley's several cure scenes, but when Alfred is offered a choice between year-round sex and castration, he easily decides which cure to embrace.

Seated at his "speakwrite" machine in the Records Department of the Ministry of Truth,[20] Winston Smith is George Orwell's time traveler. He sends Winston back in time to rewrite historical events in light of the Party's current policies. "The past was brought up to date," says Orwell (O, 36); Winston, in effect, recreates it to suit the present. But his "'defective memory,'" as O'Brien calls it, his ability to remember things that the Party has decided never happened or should have happened differently, is one of several criminal acts (i.e., thought crimes) that lead to his and Julia's arrest for heresy by the Thought Police. Then commences the longest and one of the most painfully ironic cure scenes in modern utopian fiction: the "'drama'" involving O'Brien and Winston is "'played out'" in the misnamed Ministry of Love for "'seven years'" (O, 221), incredibly longer than Poole's lecture from the Arch-Vicar. "'Fortunately,'" claims O'Brien, Winston's "'heresies,'" more so than D-503's, are "'curable'" (O, 203, 221). "'I shall save you, I shall make you perfect'" (O, 201), Oceania's Inquisitor promises.

Combining brainwashing and physical torture, Oceania attempts to set to rights one of the few remaining relatively healthy intellects in its midst, thereby unmistakably revealing its fundamental wrongness. In a society which subscribes to the "mutability of the past" (O, 25) and thus continually revises it to please itself, only Winston clings to what T. S. Eliot calls "the historical sense"; this involves a perception of the continuing presence of an unchanging past.[21] The more abuse Winston suffers and the more debilitated he becomes, the sicker the social system professing to help him. Winston must be convinced that truth, at any given moment, is whatever the Party claims, even if it stipulates that "TWO AND TWO MAKE FIVE" (O, 228). If the Party can "'control the mind,'" it can determine what is real because, O'Brien argues, "'[r]eality'" is mental, only existing "'inside the skull'" (O, 218). After being attached to a "heavy piece of apparatus," Winston feels "as though a piece had been taken out of his brain" (O, 211–12). Similarly, D-503 underwent "the Great Operation," whereby a "splinter," allegedly his imagination, was removed from his head (Z, 232). But Orwell is more emphatic: the goal, O'Brien repeatedly informs Winston, is "'[t]o cure you! To make you sane!'" (O, 209) Sanity and insanity change places here, more disturbingly than crime and sickness do in *Erewhon*.

Regarding sex, Oceania is more restrictive than the simian society in *Ape and Essence*. The Party has determined "to kill the sex instinct" altogether (O, 57). Julia wears a "narrow scarlet sash, emblem of the Junior Anti-Sex League, […] around the waist of her overalls," the equivalent of the patches saying "NO" on women's breasts and trousers in Huxley's novel. Nevertheless, the rebel in her worships the sex instinct because "it created a world of its own which was outside the Party's control" (O, 110). Finding something the Party cannot control becomes the goal. Unfortunately, Winston and Julia are soon under surveillance even during their lovemaking. Nor does sex between them prove as liberating as intercourse outside the mating season is for Poole and Loola; nor does their behavior, perverse in the eyes of the state, rejuvenate Orwell's lovers as sodomy did Connie and Mellors.

Winston's "heart leapt" when Julia claims to have had illicit sexual encounters "'scores of times'" (O, 104). "Anything that hinted at corruption filled him with a wild hope," Orwell writes (O, 105). He has Winston ask, "'You like doing this?'" and Julia reply "'I adore it'" (O, 105). Thanks to this virtual but surely unintentional parody of a Lawrencian exchange, sexual intercourse, although "successfully performed," remains no more than "a political act" in *Nineteen Eighty-Four* (O, 105), never physically curative or a step towards enlightenment. Orwell either did not share, or perhaps could not mimic, Lawrence's confidence in a bodily path to redemption. Consequently, Charrington's shop, where Winston and Julia carry on, cannot rival the sacred wood where Connie and Mellors romp and she becomes pregnant. "Out of their bodies," Winston sadly realizes with respect to Julia and himself, "no child would ever come" (O, 181), no procreative consequences as in Lawrence to sanctify rebellion.

On the subject of freedom versus happiness, O'Brien disagrees vehemently with Huxley. Winston asks why the Party cherishes power. He expects to hear that "the choice for mankind lay between freedom and happiness" but that "for the great bulk of mankind, happiness was better" (O, 216), just as Mustapha Mond maintains. O'Brien rejects the suggestion that the Party rules "for the good of the majority" who are "not fit to govern themselves" (O, 216). "'The Party seeks power entirely for its own sake,'" O'Brien declares, because power is "'an end'" not a "'means'" (O, 217). What makes O'Brien more diabolical than Huxley's Mond and Zamiatin's Benefactor put together is the sadistic pleasure he takes in perverted cure scenes such as Winston's. Oceania in effect creates rebels and heretics, encouraging and nurturing the misfit's disobedience. Then it enjoys seizing and executing them, but only after they have been reformed, that is, once they have been made to renounce dissent and love Big Brother.

Zamiatin believed "'heretics'" keep the world alive; their recurrence allegedly frustrates totalitarianism by preventing ideals from hardening into "'official dogma.'"[22] Orwell found such confidence naïve. The truly authoritarian state of the future, he informed the Russian, will play devilish games; it will lure dissidents into the open with rumors of "vast underground conspiracies" against itself (O, 18). Winston is led to believe in a secret "Brotherhood" intent on overthrowing Big Brother. But its leader, Emmanuel Goldstein, is probably a myth. His book of heresies, *The Theory and Practice of Oligarchical Collectivism*, exposes how unscrupulously Oceania and its sister superstates operate. Most likely it is a fabrication by the Party to arouse false hopes in malcontents like Winston. O'Brien actually procures a copy for him. Mistaking O'Brien for a member of the Brotherhood, Winston and Julia are easily caught; they step forwards, eager to "incriminate" themselves as "enemies of the Party" (O, 140).

In other words, Oceania is the only modern utopia in which the sole outlets for rebels and dissidents are traps set up by the state. To justify itself, to prove itself to itself, a self-perpetuating Oceania is "'not content with negative obedience, nor even with the most abject submission'" (O, 210);

again and again, O'Brien explains, it must completely disabuse the heretic of disloyalty. If every "'erroneous thought'" can be eradicated, the Party's ideas will become as infallible as "'laws of nature'" (O, 210, 218). O'Brien tells Winston how cures in Oceania work:

> "When finally you surrender to us, it must be of your own free will. *We* do not destroy the heretic because he resists us; so long as he resists us *we* never destroy him. *We* convert him, *we* capture his inner mind, *we* reshape him. *We* burn all evil and all illusion out of him; *we* bring him over to our side, not in appearance, but genuinely, heart and soul. *We* make him one of ourselves before *we* kill him." (210; italics added)[23]

O'Brien, Winston decides, "is not a hypocrite; he believes every word he says" (O, 211). Yet he sounds like an agent of the Gestapo when he denigrates Zamiatin's confidence in the persistence of heresy and heretics. O'Brien concedes that both "'will live for ever'" but only because Oceania wants them to:

> "Every day, at every moment, they will be defeated, discredited, ridiculed, spat upon—and yet they will always survive. This drama that I have played out with you during seven years will be played out over and over again, generation after generation, always in subtler forms. Always we shall have the heretic here at our mercy, screaming with pain, broken up, contemptible—and in the end utterly penitent, saved from himself, crawling to our feet of his own accord." (O, 221)

In short, says Orwell, in the dystopia of the future, heretics will be cured over and over again to satisfy the state's hunger for power and gratify its need to demonstrate to itself its absolute authority. Thanks to Hitler and Stalin, Orwell could imagine horrific cure scenes beyond Zamiatin's ken and totally contrary to the pleasure-oriented brave new world.

The prolonged contest between Winston and O'Brien seems meant to trivialize Mond's debate with the Savage, in which no one wins. Orwell's is not an ironic cure scene just because the sick person is in charge; in addition, each side thinks it has triumphed when, possibly, neither has. Winston resolves to die "hating" the Party with one last "heretical thought" in his head, undetected and unpunished (O, 231). "'They can't get inside you,'" Julia counsels; the Party allegedly "had never mastered the secret of finding out what another human being was thinking" (O, 137, 138). But O'Brien denies that the heretic is ever able to "'carry rebellion locked up in his skull'" until the last minute when he is "'waiting for the bullet'" (O, 210). At first, O'Brien appears to be correct. The "final, indispensable, healing change" takes place after Winston's release from the Ministry of Love when he gazes up at "the enormous face" of Big Brother:

> Forty years it had taken him to learn what kind of smile was hidden beneath the dark mustache.[24] O cruel, needless misunderstanding! O stubborn self-willed exile from the loving breast! [...] He loved Big Brother. (O, 245)

Emblazoned with exclamation marks, the cure, a "healing change," involves a return to "the loving breast." This sounds maternal rather than fraternal.[25] Winston, one remembers, has always been ashamed of grabbing his sister's chocolate ration years ago and fleeing from his mother's admonitions. "He never saw his mother again," Orwell notes (O, 135). Behind Big Brother's "dark mustache," Winston discovers a mother surrogate with whom to reconcile, putting an end to his life-long guilt feelings. If so, he professes love for Big Brother due to reasons beyond the Party's grasp. Arguably, it has not gained control of his "inner heart" (O, 138). On the other hand, the Party remains unaware of its failure, as does everyone else except Winston, who is too befuddled on Victory Gin to capitalize on his breakthrough and is probably about to be shot. His victory, if it is one, goes unproclaimed. O'Brien observes that "'posterity'" will not "'vindicate'" Winston; it "'will never hear of you,'" he predicts (O, 210), just as Helmholtz Watson's influence seems likely to be confined to the Falklands. Orwell delivers an ironic cure scene in which no cure may have transpired although the Party believes its perverse idea of one has. Even if Winston has found a cure for his guilty conscience, it is more solipsistic than Connie's sexual liberation; nor does it include Julia the way Poole's does Loola.

Little Alex's crimes in Part One of Anthony Burgess's *A Clockwork Orange* (1962) are revolting. But one begins reluctantly to sympathize with the fifteen-year-old hooligan in Part Two because the state, when it cures Alex of anti-social tendencies, turns out to be worse. In the first of two ironic cure scenes, Alex is conditioned literally to throw up at the thought of committing violent acts. One sees him "heaving away" (*CO*, 104) when forced to watch film clips in which individuals are raped, viciously beaten, or burned alive. The state cures Alex by making him get sick whenever he witnesses violence or is tempted to behave badly. The Erewhonians viewed crime as a sickness. Alex's captors cure him by turning into a sickness his urge to commit crimes.

In the second cure scene (Part Three), public outcry compels the government to undo Alex's reclamation; he becomes well again once he recovers his appetite for criminal behavior. Sickness and wellness change places in

Burgess's modern satirical novel until it is uncertain which is which. So, too, with good and bad, right and wrong, sanity and insanity. Ironically, Alex seems better, healthier, saner as a victimizer in Part One, where his inclinations are detestable, than as a victim in Part Two, after he is rendered incapable of wrongdoing. The novel's tripartite structure takes Alex from bad to worse then back again to where something more terrible may yet await him. There can be no utopia for Burgess because whatever comes next always seems likely to be worse.[26]

"[B]adness is of the self," Alex theorizes; it is an inseparable part of the individual, indisposable if not essential. States "cannot allow the bad because they cannot allow the self," Alex decides (*CO*, 43). They want only docile individuals who have been "'deprived of the ability to make an ethical choice'" (*CO*, 95) and behave properly automatically. The real danger, Burgess contends, as he muddies conventional moral distinctions, stems not from sociopaths like Alex and his "droogs" (gang), but from the desire of the state, always inherently totalitarian, for model citizens, even if their obedience is involuntary. It may be "'horrible to be good,'" that is, to have to be good, the prison chaplain "Charlie" warns after little 6655321 (aka Alex) agrees to undergo the "'Reclamation Treatment'" (*CO*, 96, 95).[27] If it is bad to have to be good, it may be good to be bad, right to be wrong, healthier to be sick.

Individuals are kept human, Burgess claims, by their ability to choose, even to choose wrongly, thereby refusing to become automatically perfect. Retaining the individual's capacity to do wrong, the freedom to make bad choices, is more important to Burgess than attaining perfection, which he considers contrary to human nature. To achieve flawlessness, one would have to become what Alex indignantly protests against being made into: "'a clockwork orange,'" someone who is conditioned to "'ooze juicily,'" surrendering his or her "'sweetness'" (i.e., goodness) unnaturally like clockwork, without having to be squeezed by the state (*CO*, 27). "'Am I just to be like a clockwork orange?'" Alex shouts in Part Two after allegedly being cured (*CO*, 126). Without fully understanding it, he quotes the title of F. Alexander's book deploring the state's eagerness to turn everyone into a "'mechanical creation.'" Alex and his gang tore up this manuscript when they invaded the liberal author's home in Part One.

Burgess's constant theme is "the perpetual conflict between authority and the individual"; he foresees "the State [...] taking on more and more control [...] of the individual life" (Bunting, 511). In his opinion, only imperfection, one's determination to remain incurably less than perfect can preserve humankind's fundamental humanness. Consequently, an unlikely protagonist emerges: the despicable hero, a person like Alex who relishes making bad choices, becomes the last person likely to be reformed; he stands the best chance of thwarting the totalitarian state's plans to impose a uniform goodness. Ironically, Alex is good for humanity when bad, bad for it when good, saner and healthier as a criminal than as a citizen programmed for perfection. O'Brien calls a broken-down Winston Smith, who is literally "'falling to pieces,'" "'the last man,'" a kind of human being soon to be "'extinct'" (O, 222).[28] For Burgess, the final holdout is more likely to be Alex than Oliver Mellors or Helmholtz Watson. As the saint of reprehensibility, Alex is "a kind of martyr," says Burgess, "for man's power to choose" no matter how wrongly (Bunting, 523). Zamiatin and Huxley find certain types of utopia, Wells's scientific utopias in particular, highly objectionable; Burgess considers utopia *per se*, state-engineered perfection in any shape or form, undesirable.

As a general election nears, the anti-liberal incumbents need all the prison cells for political prisoners. In order safely to release the currently incarcerated, the Governor decides the state must "'[k]ill the criminal reflex'" (*CO*, 93) in malefactors like Alex. This reflex, not the sex instinct as in *Nineteen Eighty-Four*, is allegedly the state's real enemy. Imprisoned for bludgeoning an old lady to death, Alex can have his sentence commuted if he signs up for "'Reclamation Treatment'" (*CO*, 95). "'You are to be made into a good boy, 6655321,'" the chaplain explains. "'Never again will you have the desire to commit acts of violence or to offend in any way whatsoever against the State's Peace" (*CO*, 95–96). Foolishly confident in his incurable criminality, Alex laughs "at everybody's like innocence" (*CO*, 99) when only he is unaware of what can be done to him. Upon release, he expects to resume his old ways. Ironically, the gleeful rapist and willful murderer comes to seem more innocuous than the devious state that presumes to reform him. Burgess shakes the readers' confidence that one can readily tell guilt from innocence, just as he unsettles one's ability to distinguish sickness from health.

Doctors Brodsky and Branom sound like O'Brien when they assure Alex that, thanks to Ludovico's Technique, he is "'being made sane, […] being made healthy'" (*CO*, 109). Strapped to a table, prevented from closing his eyes, Alex receives injections that leave him trying to throw up as he watches film after film of people being savagely beaten. Formerly, he savored doing or watching vicious acts; now he finds himself "not feeling all that well" (*CO*, 103). His nausea, Dr. Branom insists, is a sure sign that he is behaving like "'any normal healthy human organism'" witnessing evil deeds (*CO*, 109).

More so than D-503's lobotomy or Winston Smith's, Alex's cure scene is extremely funny, the idea of illness as a cure, of vomiting as a healthy reaction, being as absurd as it is disgusting. "'What you've been doing,'" Alex objects, "'is to make me feel very very ill'" (*CO*, 109). The cure is not complete, Brodsky warns, until Alex, "'without medication,'" vomits at the mere suggestion of violence (*CO*, 116). Ludovico's Technique is crudely Pavlovian: at first, chemically induced sickness whenever Alex is exposed to violent behavior; eventually simple exposure makes him ill. Pavlov's dog salivated at the sound of a bell whether or not it signaled dinnertime. Alex sickens even without injections whenever he sees blood.

Alex, one realizes, is Burgess's portrait of an artist; his medium is violence. When he beats up an "old veck" (old man) or robs and assaults a female shopkeeper, he describes his actions and their physical consequences with a poet's zest; becoming a conductor, he orchestrates blows "that brought the red out like an old friend" (*CO*, 14, 17). Unfortunately, Ludovico's Technique robs Alex of this creativity, perverse though it is; it destroys his love of music, especially Beethoven's *Ninth Symphony*, which now makes him sick because all the violent films he watched contained musical scores. Ceasing "'to be a wrongdoer,'" laments the chaplain, Alex "'ceases also to be a creature capable of moral choice'" (*CO*, 126), i.e., a human being.

For Burgess, one must reiterate, good and bad in the individual are hopelessly intertwined; one cannot cure, that is, eliminate, the latter without hampering the former, hence no utopia. Dr. Brodsky boasts of creating in Alex "'your true Christian [...] ready to turn the other cheek'" (*CO*, 128), no matter how severely abused. In Burgess's opinion, only a patsy can be truly Christ-like, genuinely faultless, so Church and State want the same modified harmless person; they are equally enemies of one's real self. Burgess's ironic metaphor for both a genuine Christian and the model citizen is a mechanical orange, voluntarily yielding its juicy goodness without having to be squeezed. In future, says Burgess, there will be no need to lobotomize dissidents as in Zamiatin, or to dose them regularly with *soma* as in *Brave New World*, or for the "'boot stamping on a human face—for ever'" that O'Brien predicts (*O*, 220).

In Burgess's second ironic cure scene, Alex is cured of the cure Dr. Brodsky administered. In Part Three, having been released by the incumbents, Alex is victimized by nearly everyone towards whom he behaved badly in Part One; his insurmountable goodness renders him defenseless. The "old veck" Alex mugged in the first chapter incites a pack of "dirty old men" to beat him up until the police come (*CO*, 114). Led by Billyboy, Alex's "old enemy" (140), the "millicents" (i.e., police) give him a second beating.

Without realizing his whereabouts or being recognized, Alex finds refuge in the home of F. Alexander, the expert on clockwork oranges. Alexander and his fellow liberals decide to exploit the harm that was done to Alex in order to "'"dislodge"'" the incumbent Government (*CO*, 154). But when Alexander begins to recognize Alex as his wife's assailant, the latter escapes by jumping out a window. He lands back in the arms of the state. It cracks down on the liberals, imprisons F. Alexander for Alex's protection, then proceeds to undo Ludovico's Technique. Alex regains his love of "ultra-violence" and "the old in-out in-out" (rape); again he takes pleasure in "the glorious Ninth of Ludwig van" (172, 174). Without sensing a trace of the irony Burgess intends, one of the Government's "doctor vecks" observes: "'"You seem to be cured."'" He credits "'"[d]eep hypnopaedia,"'" apparently an improvement upon sleep-teaching techniques invented by the brave new world (*CO*, 172; see *BNW*, 21).

"I was cured all right"—these are Alex's last words and Burgess's, a scary declaration that makes *A Clockwork Orange* the only modern utopian novel with a second ironic cure scene to reverse the first. Alex has been cured wrongly—twice. He signs another mysterious document, "not knowing what [he] was signing and not [...] caring either" (*CO*, 175), just as earlier he signed up for reclamation. Part Three in the American edition has six chapters compared to seven apiece for One and Two.[29] The novel seems on the verge of a new cycle, ready for another swing of the pendulum. Unless readers are familiar with the British edition, in which, surprisingly, Alex settles down in the cancelled seventh chapter, they are left wondering what atrocities a twice-cured delinquent is capable of and doubtful whether the Government has really given up on mechanical oranges.

Conditions remain endlessly dystopian for Burgess because one's "capacity to choose"—he calls it "the only thing we have"—is unreliable, yet tampering with it only makes matters worse (Bunting, 523, 521). One is "always taking the wrong side," Burgess laments, because "by definition" the "right side" is "the other side" (Bunting, 520). That is, once one chooses, the choice not taken begins to look better.[30] Thus one sides against Alex in Part One, only to discover in Part Two that one has taken the wrong side. By the end of Part Three, the reader wonders if there is a right side. In Zamiatin and Orwell, sickness and health trade places but in *A Clockwork Orange*, one can no longer tell one from the other;[31] nor can one still believe in the individual's capacity to make good choices. For this loss of confidence in choosing, the ability Burgess considers one's only asset, *A Clockwork Orange* offers no cure.

The cure scene reaches its apotheosis in *Island* (1962), Huxley's last completed novel. A cynical Westerner is washed ashore on Pala after a freakish boating accident. Although Will Farnaby's physical injuries are minor, his outlook on life is sickeningly negative: a low opinion of humanity in general combined with a strong sense of personal guilt and consequent self-loathing. He cannot forgive himself for mistreating his wife, Molly, who died in a car crash shortly after their breakup. Nor can he forget the degrading death from breast cancer of his beloved Aunt Mary. As a journalist, Will has traveled "'[*f*]*rom* hell *to* hell,'" always covering the "'current horrors,'" which he feels make existence an "enormous joke."[32] *Island* extols the virtues of utopian Pala by telling the story of Will Farnaby's rehabilitation, the only eminently successful cure in modern utopian literature.

Butler's Erewhonians threaten to jail Higgs for getting sick. The Palanese, enlightened Mahayanist Buddhists who practice Vedanta's perennial philosophy, immediately put their unexpected visitor to bed and begin his therapy. Led by Dr. Robert MacPhail and Susila, his widowed daughter-in-law, a host of benign islanders recount Pala's history and praise its present workings. Nurse Appu, Ranga, Vijaya, Mrs. Rao, Shanta, Mr. Menon, and Mrs. Narayan extend the recovery process by lecturing Will at length even after he is up and around. Collectively, they persuade him that Pala is as utopic as life gets. "'The more I see of you people the better I like you,'" Will admits; "'I want to find out more about you'" (*I*, 111). Thus the process of Will's recovery and the unfolding of Huxley's positive utopia become one and the same. The more Will learns about Pala, the higher his revised estimate of human potentialities and the better he understands and accepts the good and bad in himself. Will's conversations with Pala's detractors—the Rani, Murugan, Mr. Bahu—are not so much setbacks in his recovery as counterpoints to be overcome in Huxley's final discussion novel of ideas.

Unlike the Savage, who grows increasingly disillusioned the more he sees of the brave new world, Will is delighted to learn about Mutual Adoption Clubs, the yoga of love, innovative methodologies for agriculture and education, "'DF and AI,'" etc. (*I*, 192). He studies the Old Raja's *Notes on What's What*, Pala's guide book to spiritual health. Having made sufficient progress, a rejuvenated Farnaby is given a pill to accelerate his cure. Susila asks Will if he is ready to take "'the *moksha*-medicine'" (*I*, 270). The novel's climax and the cure scene overlap in Chapter XV: Will swallows "'the reality-revealer, the truth-and-beauty pill'" that accomplishes the erstwhile cynic's "'mental transformation'" and makes him "'fully human'" (*I*, 138). While listening to Bach's *Fourth Brandenburg Concerto* more rewardingly than Alex savors Beethoven's *Ninth*, Will transcends his egotistic "selfhood," briefly becoming "blissfully one with Oneness" (*I*, 270). Huxley outdoes all previous cure scenes by granting a recuperating Will a glimpse of the Beatific Vision. Presumably, like most Palanese from the time of their initiation into adulthood, Farnaby will take a pill periodically as part of his spiritual regimen while also striving towards further enlightenment by means less pharmaceutical.

Island is unique among modern utopias in that it contains a cure scene within a cure scene. As part of Will's therapy, Dr. Robert relates how Pala came into being. A cure scene proved instrumental. In the 1850s, Dr. Andrew MacPhail, Dr. Robert's great-grandfather, was recruited to treat the island's Raja; a tumor "'had filled the nose, […] pushed up into the socket of the right eye, [and] had half-blocked the throat'" (*I*, 123). Using Professor Elliotson's technique for "'painless operations […] on patients in the mesmeric trance'" (*I*, 123), Dr. Andrew removed the tumor and saved the Raja's life. Dr. Robert's history lesson, a positive counter to Mustapha Mond's in Chapter III of *Brave New World*, goes on to tell how, together, the Scottish doctor, a "'Calvinist-turned-atheist,'" and the Palanese king, a "'pious Mahayana Buddhist'" (*I*, 129), made Pala into "'the best of both worlds, the Oriental and the European, the ancient and the modern'" (*I*, 130): Eastern spirituality married to Western know-how.

Pala began when an outsider cured its ruler. Ironically, it ends when its cure of an outsider, who behaves like a tumor or cancerous cell, has disastrous side effects for the body politic. It is as if the island's demise is the price it must pay for helping Farnaby. Modern utopists fear that oncoming oppressive societies will devise perverse cures to stifle non-conformists and muzzle dissent. Huxley fears that any utopia diligent enough to effect genuine rehabilitation will be exposed to fatal contamination, which is what happens to Pala thanks to Will.

Pala is called "the forbidden island, the place no journalist had ever visited" (*I*, 6). The island trusts to its isolationist policies to protect it from European imperialists and outside corporations anxious to gain access to its oil. "'No oil concessions to anyone'" is the rule; but a "'pro-oil minority'" (*I*, 21) consisting of Murugan Mailendra (Pala's future ruler), the Rani (his mother), and Mr. Bahu, the ambassador from neighboring war-like Rendang, hope to strike a deal with Joe Aldehyde's Southeast Asia Petroleum. Coincidentally, Farnaby is a journalist who works for Aldehyde and thus in effect penetrates Pala as Joe's "secret agent" (*I*, 111). Assurances he can offer of Aldehyde's support encourage the pro-oilers to invite Rendang's Colonel Dipa to overrun Pala. Murugan, his new ally, proclaims "'the United Kingdom of Rendang and Pala'" (*I*, 293), which undoubtedly will grant oil leases to Southeast Asia Petroleum on its way to becoming a westernized industrial state.

Dipa's invasion interrupts Will's cure, his *moksha*-medicine experience; the commotion outside turns inward bliss into chaos and nightmare. Asked earlier how he survived the boating accident and climbed a steep cliff from the shore, Will says: "'Remember the beginning of *Erewhon* […]. As luck would have it, Providence was on my side'" (*I*, 17). But providence is no longer on Pala's. As Huxley fashions the modern utopia's supremely ironic cure scene, Will acknowledges the novel in which the cure scene began.

Pala has managed to stay healthy (i.e., independent) by keeping aloof from a sick world, in effect quarantining itself. Rendang's "'magnificent harbor'" invited invasion by Arabs, Portuguese, Dutch and English; less accessible, Pala, as Ranga explains to Will, "'escaped'" all of these "'infestations'" (*I*, 81). "'So long as it remains out of touch with the rest of the world,'" Mr. Bahu lectures Will, "'an ideal society can be a viable society'" (*I*, 55). But he sees "'the outside world closing in on this little island of freedom and happiness. Closing in steadily and inexorably, coming nearer and nearer'" (*I*, 56).[33] Farnaby's arrival constitutes a loss of immunity, the next-to-last step in this unfortunate process. After it comes colonialization, commercial exploitation of its natural resources that Pala has resisted for a century.

As befits a novel that is practically one long cure scene, disease imagery abounds. Besides the Raja's "'tumor'" and Randang's "'infestations,'" there is oil itself. "'Pala's full of oil,'" Joe Aldehyde tells Will (*I*, 21), as if the island was infected by it. Murugan says "'the island is fairly oozing with the stuff'" (*I*, 41); he could be describing open sores. When the Rani insists that "'Pala's smooth bright skin concealed the most horrible rottenness'" (*I*, 51), her disapproval of its liberal attitudes makes it seem terminally ill, as indeed it is, for the healthier Will becomes thanks to the Palanese, the closer Pala is to expiring due to his promise to the pro-oil conspirators. The patient gets better as the caregiver declines. Will operates as a cancerous cell, sickening Pala and hastening its demise. Pala dies figuratively from cancer the way Will's Aunt Mary literally did: "'a little piece of her body'" started to work against the good of the whole (*I*, 242), just as the pro-oilers plot Pala's downfall.[34] The utopic island's symbol is Lakshmi, who perishes from incurable cancer. Throughout the novel, Dr. Robert's wife is "slowly wasting to extinction" (*I*, 25). The closer to death she comes, the less time Pala has left: her death is followed a chapter later by Will's *moksha*-medicine experience, which is interrupted by Colonel Dipa's invasion. Appropriately, Will attends Lakshmi's deathbed, underlining the ironic interconnections

Huxley establishes between her death, Will's cure, oil, and a doomed utopia.[35]

Utopias from *Erewhon* to *Island* regularly feature ironic cure scenes. Remedies imposed rarely display genuinely utopic qualities but reveal, instead, a society's fundamental malignancy. Supposedly utopian communities implement self-serving cures designed to neutralize deviants while safeguarding their own socio-political perversities. Thus the sick party administers what it regards as a cure; a rebel or heretic is allegedly straightened out by a benighted society. The cure is doubly ironic inasmuch as the so-called sickness being eradicated is usually a strength that society should profit from. A cure may transpire in spite of society, that is, without its assistance but contrary to its wishes. Ironically, such cures are too personal to change anything. A cure scene can have unwelcome consequences when a benign community actually rehabilitates an unwanted visitor only to succumb to forces from the insane outside world he represents. Cure scenes are often the funniest episodes in modern utopias, but always among the scariest.

In sum, as much as any other feature, a society's treatment of problem cases determines whether it merits consideration as the good place. An allegedly utopian community gives itself away by the manner in which it handles uninvited guests or responds to indigenous dissidents, be they rebels, heretics, or malcontents. Hence the preponderance of climactic cure scenes in modern British utopias. Beginning as a humble episode in *Erewhon*, the cure scene takes over increasingly larger portions of the narrative. Inability to imagine a non-ironic cure scene is one of the primary reasons few positive utopias appeared in the approximately hundred-year cycle from *Erewhon* to *Island*, heyday of the modern British literary utopia.[36] Nicolas Berdiaeff warned that utopias were not only realizable but rapidly approaching; he doubted the twentieth century would be able to avoid them.[37] The profusion of ironic cure scenes reveals an even more deep-seated anxiety, namely, that a negative utopia, once it materializes, will learn to prevent or defuse alternatives so that a genuine cure becomes impossible or unsustainable. No one manipulated cure scenes better or more often than Aldous Huxley, whose three utopias contain six of them: three in *Brave New World*, one in *Ape and Essence*, and two again in *Island*. The sixth and final cure, Will's, revalues the negative cure scenes in Zamiatin and Orwell. With Nurse Appu, Will discusses Pala's aptitude for finding the right "'cure'" for life's problems (*I*, 65). She contends "'there is no single cure'"; one must "'attack on all the fronts at once'"—diet, autosuggestion, meditation—the goal being a fully "'integrated man'" (*I*, 66). As the end of the cycle from *Erewhon* to *Island*, Higgs to Farnaby, only Huxley was able to produce one.

---

1 Although translated from the Russian, *We* must be considered a vital part of the modern British utopian tradition: Zamiatin warned readers of the totalitarian tendencies in H. G. Wells's scientific utopias; *We* strongly influenced *Brave New World* and *Nineteen Eighty-Four.*

2 The *Integral* is Wells's time machine retooled for nefarious purposes, a perfect example of misuse of science.

3 Mephi is short for Mephistopheles, the devil who tempts Goethe's Faust.

4 Huxley, one is reminded, used "negative utopia" instead of "dystopia," although its opposite, positive utopia, sounds redundant. See "Utopias," 1–5.

5 Aldous Huxley, *Brave New World* (London: Chatto & Windus, 1950), 171. [*BNW*]

6 William Shakespeare, *Julius Caesar*, III, ii, 78.

7 Huxley also parodies the cure scene in *The Time Machine*, although it was already ironic. H. G. Wells's Time Traveller journeys to the year Eight Hundred and Two Thousand Seven Hundred and One expecting to behold the triumph of evolution. Instead he discovers an Overworld of effete, cattle-like Eloi and an Underworld of cannibalistic Morlocks who prey on them. Desperate to escape these "'human rats,'" the Traveller sets forest and hillside ablaze, incinerating hundreds (*TM*, 107, 105). Instead of basking in the "'perfect world,'" Wells's Traveller lights up tomorrow like a pyromaniac Prometheus. As Huxley's time traveler, John journeys to Fordian London by Blue Pacific Rocket. This time machine carries him forwards from Malpais, a primitive Indian reservation where time stands still, to A. F. 632.

8 See "'My Hypothetical Islanders': The Role of Islands in *Brave New World* and *Island*," chapter 5 below.

9 See Huxley's epigraph to *Point Counter Point.*

10 This power could be unexpended evolutionary energy. Upon seeing listless Eloi and degenerate Morlocks, Wells's Time Traveller feared none was left.

11 Peter Firchow attributes resemblances between *We* and *Brave New World* to the "debt" both owed to H. G. Wells. See *End*, 40, note 5.

12 See Meckier, "Dickens and the Dystopian Novel," 51–58.

13 In his closing speech for the prosecution at the novel's obscenity trial in 1960, Griffith-Jones singled out this passage, saying it was "not very easy [...] to know what in fact [Lawrence] is driving at" (Rolph, 221). This was disingenuous innuendo designed to shock jurors without specifying sodomy. Brenda Maddox points out that "penetration per anum" was "a felony in English law" in 1960, but states wrongly that the "act of anal intercourse went unrecognized" during the trial (Maddox, 426, 425). Had the prosecution been more explicit, *Lady Chatterley* might have been convicted.

14 To Ernest Collins, in January 1913, Lawrence wrote: "'We can go wrong in our minds. But what our blood feels and believes and says, is always true.'" In

short, "'the blood, the flesh [is] wiser than the intellect'" (quoted in Worthen, 129).

15 Huxley saw *Ape and Essence* as an opportunity to correct a "vast and obvious failure of foresight" in *Brave New World*: in his 1946 "Foreword," he regrets the omission of any "reference to nuclear fission" (*BNW*, x).

16 According to A. C. Grayling, "evidence of the world is in fact more consistent with the existence of an evil deity than a good deity" (Grayling, 26).

17 Dominic Baker-Smith miscalls the Arch-Vicar, who wants to emasculate Poole, a "more engaging version of Mond" (Baker-Smith, 107).

18 In the 1946 "Foreword" to *Brave New World*, Huxley wishes he had afforded the Savage an escape to "a community of exiles and refugees from the Brave New World, living within the borders of the Reservation" (*BNW*, ix).

19 In *Aldous Huxley: Satire and Structure*, Jerome Meckier notes Poole's "failure to move convincingly from comic butt to mystic hero" (*SS*, 195).

20 Misnomers abound in Oceania, not just a Ministry of Truth where falsehoods prevail by a "speakwrite" apparatus that speaks wrong.

21 T. S. Eliot, *The Sacred Wood*, 49.

22 See "Afraid of Tomorrow," quoted in Ginsburg's introduction to Zamiatin's *We*, ix.

23 "'We'" appears nine times in this passage, a not-so-subtle allusion to Zamiatin, who allegedly underestimated the totalitarian state's coercive powers. "'[B]urn'" is a faint allusion to Lawrence's cure scene, in which Connie's deepest shames are burnt out of her.

24 If Winston is "thirty-nine" at the outset (O, 5) and forty when he embraces Big Brother, the length of his struggles with O'Brien becomes problematic. The latter's declaration that he has "'watched over'" the former for "'seven years'" (O, 201) could simply mean that Winston has been suspected since he was thirty-two, not that the cure scene *per se* runs nearly a decade. Yet O'Brien's subsequent statement that it has "'played out [...] during seven years'" (O, 221) surely suggests that it does. Perhaps "forty" refers to Winston's life prior to arrest and the commencement of his cure, in which case he is forty-six when earmarked for extermination.

25 Zamiatin's D-503 dreads the thought of being torn "away from the maternal breast of the One State" (Z, 197). He speculates that he might not have gone wrong "[i]f [he] had a mother, [...] *mine*—yes, precisely—my mother" (Z, 216). To Lenina, Bernard remarks: "'I often think one may have missed something in not having had a mother'" (*BNW*, 91). See Marcus Smith, "The Wall of Blackness," 422–23, for Winston's musings on being motherless.

26 In *The Long Day Wanes: The Malayan Trilogy* (1956–1959), Burgess has little sympathy with British rule in Malaya, which is coming to an end, but implications are that conditions in the new, independent country will be even less satisfactory.

27 An egregious play on words: "Charlie," the prison chaplain, the actor Charlie Chaplin.

28 In *Lady Chatterley's Lover*, Mellors is the last man, the only male who remains fully alive physically. When Watson joins the Savage in the fight to liberate the

Deltas from *soma*, the latter exclaims, "'Men at last!'" (*BNW*, 175) More directly than Huxley, Orwell may be alluding to Mary Shelley's *The Last Man* (1826), in which the narrator is the only person on earth to survive the plague.

[29] For Burgess's explanation of how his novel lost its final chapter in the American edition, see Bunting, 525. Omitting the last chapter, Michael Schmidt argues, "sacrificed [...] the symbolism of twenty-one chapters," which he equates with "coming of age" (Schmidt, 628). However, Alex is still only fifteen or sixteen at the end of a parodic *bildungsroman* in which a relapse substitutes for maturation.

[30] In Burgess's *The Wanting Seed* (1962), society alternates between a Pelagian phase of belief in human perfectibility and an Augustinian phase in which man is seen as inherently sinful. Different policies are put in place to accompany each phase. Gradually, the other phase, be it Pelagian or Augustinian, begins to look superior and a change is made.

[31] One can endorse Robert K. Morris's positive view of the novel's "triunal division" as "Alex damned, Alex purged, Alex resurrected" (Morris, 57), but he does not rebound into life as successfully as Mellors or Connie.

[32] Aldous Huxley, *Island* (New York: Bantam, 1963), 27, 15, 13. [*I*]

[33] Brave new worlders, one remembers, could not have freedom and happiness both; in 1932, these are one of life's counterpoints which it took Huxley thirty years to resolve.

[34] See Meckier, "Cancer in Utopia," *MSN*, 293–304.

[35] "Failure to convert [i.e., cure] Murugan to Palanese values," Peter Firchow objects, has "far greater and more immediate social consequences than Will's very private conversion." Success in curing Will is more than offset by Pala's apparent indifference to its failure with Murugan. See Firchow, "Brave at Last," 161.

[36] William Morris's *News from Nowhere* (1890) and Edward Bellamy's *Looking Backward* (1888), though optimistic, contradict each other. Both contain dreams about the future, not forecasts. Guest awakens in his own bed, doubtful if he can turn his "dream" of a return to pre-industrialized England into a "vision" (*NN*, 228). Julian West, having slept for a hundred years, has a nightmare in which he returns to the nineteenth century, then is relieved to awaken from it still in the twentieth, where, implausibly, he remains (see *LB*, 218). West's ideal society functions like a gigantic corporation, a machine-driven monopoly that disgusted Morris. In positive utopias such as *A Modern Utopia* (1905) and *Men Like Gods* (1923), H. G. Wells tried to ameliorate the pessimism in *The Time Machine* (1895) and *The First Men in the Moon* (1901); instead, he triggered negative responses from Zamiatin and Huxley.

[37] See Huxley's epigraph to *Brave New World*.

Chapter Three

GOLF IN *BRAVE NEW WORLD*

For holidays from reality, brave new worlders swallow a gramme of *soma* or go to the Feelies, talking movies (still a novelty to readers in 1932) that stimulate their sense of touch and smell. Always they golf. Huxley's funny yet frightening depiction of the dystopian future posits a community in which everyone is conditioned to play ridiculous games—Centrifugal Bumble-puppy, Escalator squash, Riemann-surface tennis, but primarily golf. The future, Huxley predicts, will resemble a factory during the workday, a gigantic golf course after hours.

In A. F. 632, six hundred and thirty-two years after Henry Ford marketed the first T-model, he has been deified as "Our Ford"—it rhymes with Our Lord.[1] World Controllers, his successors, run the World State. Mustapha Mond governs Western Europe from a London whose factories, tall as skyscrapers, make the city a cross between New York and Detroit. Lest inhabitants take "'a moment to sit down and think,'" the brave new world allows them "'no leisure from pleasure,'" says Mond (*BNW*, 65–66). Golf supplies the perfect distraction. A mindless pursuit in Huxley's opinion, golf is as compulsory as birth control. In Huxley's parody of the ideal future, one is obliged to practice both.

"'Two rounds of Obstacle Golf to get through before dark,'" Lenina Crowne apologizes, "'I must fly'" (*BNW*, 65). Hers is a tight schedule because sex begins after nightfall. "By eight o'clock," loudspeakers "announce the closing of the courses," and golfers abandon their games (*BNW*, 84). Mandatory golf fills the interval between work and sex. Lenina and Henry Foster, her partner for the evening, fly by helicopter from the Central London Hatchery and Conditioning Centre, where both work, to the Stoke Poges Golf Club. Huxley envisions London virtually surrounded by golf courses. "Every two and a half minutes," monorail trains bring "lower-caste golfers" to or from their "separate course" outside the metropolis (*BNW*, 84).

For upper castes, Stoke Poges offers a Club House; a "dividing wall" separates "smaller houses reserved for Alpha and Beta members" from the "huge lower-caste barracks" used by Deltas, Gammas, and Epsilons (*BNW*, 85). Golf still works as a great leveller because all are reduced to playing it. Every member of each caste must knock a small ball into a round hole every afternoon.

The "great advantage" that golf has over other sports, Herbert Warren Wind writes in *The Story of American Golf*, the reason it was hailed in the

1920s as "the great common denominator," is that one need not be "young, fast, [or] beautifully coordinated [...] to play acceptably" (Wind, 173, 4). Besides sex, golf is the one thing one can enjoy without being good at it. In the brave new world, golf helps to sanctify the status quo. Mustapha Mond extols "'the solid ground of daily labour and distraction'": "'Seven and a half hours of mild, unexhausting labour, and then the *soma* ration and games and unrestricted copulation'" (*BNW*, 264).

Huxley juxtaposes two bogus rituals: Henry and Lenina's golf date and Bernard Marx's bi-weekly Solidarity Service. Henry and Lenina join their fellow golfers; Bernard reluctantly bonds with a dozen worshippers of "'The Greater Being,'" presumably Our Ford (*BNW*, 98). In the future, playing golf is the equivalent of going to church, whereas actual church-going ends with an orgy. As Bernard and the other celebrants dance "round and round" (*BNW*, 98), Huxley links golf with spurious religion and recreational sex, two rounds on the links and "round and round" at the Solidarity Service.

Before festivities at the Fordson Community Singery commence, Morgana Rothschild ruins Bernard Marx's evening by asking, "'What were you playing this afternoon? [...] Obstacle or Electro-magnetic?'" (*BNW*, 92) Bernard prefers walking in the Lake District; he has shirked his obligatory rounds. "[B]lushingly," he admits that he has been playing "neither" (*BNW*, 93). After an "awkward silence," Morgana turns towards "the more sporting man on her left."

In the future, Huxley prophesies, oddballs, deviants, and malcontents reveal themselves as non-golfers. These misfits experience difficulty finding a partner even at orgies. They have trouble getting dates at other times as well. When Lenina announces that Bernard has invited her to visit the Savage Reservation, Fanny advises against it. "'They say he doesn't like Obstacle Golf,'" she objects (*BNW*, 51). Keeping their jobs is another problem for delinquent golfers. Bernard's boss, the Director of the Central London Hatchery and Conditioning Centre (the D.H.C.), yearns to banish him to Iceland on account of "'his heretical views on sport'" (*BNW*, 175).

When Bernard admires the sky on an exceptionally fine summer afternoon, Lenina's response is disappointing: "'Simply perfect for Obstacle Golf,' she answered rapturously" (*BNW*, 70). On their first date, Lenina is desperate for a diversion to occupy them until bedtime. "[W]hat about a round of Electro-magnetic Golf at St. Andrews?" she asks (*BNW*, 103). Bernard declines to visit the so-called cradle of golf; he denounces the game as "a waste of time." Lenina's astonished interrogatory reply — "'Then what's time for?'"—further incriminates golf. Huxley spent the rest of his life trying to answer Lenina's question.

At their hotel in Santa Fé, Lenina is pleased—Bernard dismayed—to discover "that Obstacle Golf and Electro-magnetic Golf could both be played in the park" (*BNW*, 116). In A. F. 632, vacationers still travel great distances to play the same games they are accustomed to at home. After a "'six and a half hour flight'" by rocket from London, Lenina and Bernard are encouraged to recreate on New Mexico's golf courses just as she and Henry Foster played at Stoke Poges.

The typical brave new worlder is "'a happy, hard-working, goods-consuming citizen,'" Mustapha Mond maintains (*BNW*, 278). By other standards, a society of fornicating, drug-ingesting golfers might appear "'degraded.'" But Mond insists that "'[y]ou can't play Electro-magnetic Golf according to the rules of Centrifugal Bumble-puppy.'" For a good sports metaphor to bolster a bad argument, namely, that standards for human excellence are relative, the Controller automatically turns to golf.

Huxley describes Centrifugal Bumble-puppy but remains silent about the rules for Electro-magnetic Golf. How it and Obstacle Golf are played is left to the reader's imagination. Were Huxley to elaborate, Obstacle Golf and Electro-magnetic Golf might turn out to be less absurd than they sound.

The earliest man-made golf courses were filled with obstacles to recreate the pastures and hillsides on which the game was invented. Besides incorporating trees, mounds, rocks—whatever lay in their path—course designers built stonewalls across a fairway, even laid down a railroad track. Brave new worlders probably drive through tunnels or putt under and around moving objects. For Electro-magnetic Golf, they may have to hit balls made of charged particles or contend with electric currents on fairways and greens that are actually magnetic fields.

While John Savage is growing up on the New Mexico Indian Reservation, his mother, a native brave new worlder, beguiles him with stories of the "Other Place" (*BNW*, 150). In particular, Linda recounts "all the nice games you could play." "Heaven and London," John concludes, are identical (*BNW*, 151). Brought to the brave new world, he is fatally disillusioned by its preference for "distractions." One cannot blame John's suicide on golf because he never plays. But he retreats to a heath as remote from golfers as possible. "Crowds that daily left London" in order to "play Electro-magnetic Golf" bypass his Surrey hideaway, John is relieved to discover; nearby Puttenham "possessed no links" (*BNW*, 289).

To "a troop of newly arrived students," Mustapha Mond explains "'the conscription of consumption'": "'Every man, woman and child [is] compelled to consume so much a year. In the interests of industry'" (*BNW*, 57). Obligatory golf best illustrates the beauty of consumption quotas. 2,000 million citizens conditioned to play two rounds of golf daily—think of the number of courses that the brave new world must construct and maintain. Calculate profits from the millions of clubs and balls its factories manufacture. Imagine the countless helicopters and monorail cars needed to bring players to the first tee. In the 1920s, notes golf historian Wind, 240 million golf balls kept two million golfers swinging away—not to mention 120 million dollars spent annually on mowers, seeds, and watering systems (see Wind, 165–66); this amounts to spare change in the brave new world.

"'[E]ven in Our Ford's day,'" the D.H.C. muses, "'most games were played without more apparatus than a ball or two and a few sticks'" (*BNW*, 33). Early golfers carried driver, putter, one or two irons, and a couple of balls. Obstacle Golf and Electro-magnetic Golf change all that. "'[E]laborate games'" that can only be played with expensive equipment, they boost the World State's economy. Golf maintains its ascendancy because World Controllers "'won't approve of any new game unless it can be shown that it requires at least as much apparatus as the most complicated of existing games'" (*BNW*, 34).

Utilitarian and consequently anti-Romantic, the brave new world uses golf "to abolish the love of nature" (*BNW*, 24). Nature-lovers "'consume transport,'" the D.H.C. complains, "'nothing else.'" Brave new worlders are conditioned to "'love all country sports'" but not the country itself. Because golf entails "'the use of elaborate apparatus,'" golfers "'consume manufactured articles as well as transport,'" the D.H.C. brags (*BNW*, 25). Compulsory golf provides "an economically sounder reason for consuming transport than a mere affection for primroses and landscapes."[2]

Bokanovsky Jones stands out among Huxley's oddly named characters (see *BNW*, 101). He commemorates Maurice Bokanovsky, a cabinet minister in Raymond Poincaré's Union National Government[3] and Bobby Jones, sensational American golfer. In 1930, Jones became the first player to win the United States and British amateur and open championships (four major tournaments) in the same year, a feat that landed him on the cover of *Time*. The brave new world links a champion golfer and an outstanding technocrat, because these unrelated personages showed the World State how to promote world-wide political stability: bokanovskification followed by prescribed golf.

Eager to reverse France's declining birth rate, the original Bokanovsky proposed that the state pay supplements to parents willing to raise large families. His goal was the rationalization of fecundity. In gratitude, the brave new world named "Bokanovsky's Process" after him. It "'consists of a series of arrests of development'" whereby a single bokanovskified egg divides into as many as "ninety-six buds," each of which "will grow into a perfectly formed embryo, and every embryo into a full-sized adult" (*BNW*, 5). Bokanovskification can yield "nearly eleven thousand brothers and sisters in a hundred and fifty batches of identical twins, all within two years of the same age" (*BNW*, 7). Never cloning too many drudges or too few, Bokanovsky's Process allows the brave new world "'to stabilize the population,'" just enough workers to turn out exactly the needed amount of goods as efficiently as possible.

Compulsory golf keeps cloned workers out of mischief when they are away from their machines but not copulating.[4] Golf, Huxley implies, administers additional arrests of development. Thanks to a complementariness that Bokanovsky Jones's names ironically commemorate, the World State achieves a reliable prosperity without precedent, something which Huxley's first readers probably despaired of after 1929. One of the brave new world's greatest accomplishments is the unthinking clone who hates nature, is addicted to sex, and consumes costly golfing equipment.

Huxley never asks whether "[m]aking ninety-six human beings grow where only one grew before" is advisable (*BNW*, 5). In his opinion, cloning became inevitable the day Henry Ford activated the first assembly line. As the novel's cynical narrator declares, cloning is "[t]he principle of mass production at last applied to biology" (*BNW*, 7). The real challenge facing the future is to determine how a technology-oriented, hedonistic society, in which everyone begins as a bottle baby and cloning is a fact of life for the lower orders, will keep its clones amused. The brave new world's answer is unlimited sex after mandatory golf.

Unfortunately, three castes out of five in the Fordian future are incapable of appreciating opera, ballet, classical music, art, museums, serious literature—none of which survives. Rather than cultivate Deltas, Gammas, and Epsilons, the brave new world retards its managerial classes. Alphas and Betas are proficient on the job but "'behave out of office hours like a babe in a bottle,'" to quote the D.H.C., who is citing Our Ford (*BNW*, 175). Upper-caste leisure activities are as infantile as those for the lower orders; this boils down to compulsory golf for both Alpha Plus and Epsilon-Minus semi-moron. To forestall the horrible utopia towards which life is marching, Huxley warned, one must tear up the world's golf courses. Eliminate this game and cloning will have to be postponed until an equivalent distraction can be found.

A 6'4" beanpole nearly blind from an attack of *keratitis punctata* at age sixteen, Huxley never took up golf. Nevertheless, he recognized this game as humanity's nemesis. Topical yet prescient, his remarkable satirical novel decried the spread of golf across the United States as one of the surest harbingers of an Americanized future.

Surveying his countrymen in an essay for *Vanity Fair* in 1925, Huxley asked: what "stop gap" fills up the "greater part of the vacuum of their existences?" "It is golf," he declared.[5] Two years later in the same magazine, Huxley regretted that the English "have more golf links per square mile than any other people in the world."[6] By 1932, however, there were more greens in the United States than savings banks and libraries combined. Between 1916 (when the Professional Golfers Association [PGA] staged its first championship) and 1930, the number of golf courses in America jumped from 742 to 5,700. According to Wind, these courses sat on real estate worth over one and a half billion dollars (see Wind, 172). In the early twenties, Wind asserts, "Americans played [golf] better than any other people in the world" (86). "Rampant golf consciousness" (3)—Wind's phrase makes it sound like an unintentional parody of enlightenment—emerged as the American state of mind.[7]

According to George Pepper, editor of *Golf in America: The First One Hundred Years*, golf came into its own in the 1920s, the golden age for course construction (see Pepper, 278–80). Municipal courses sprang up overnight; there were more than 500 by the end of the decade. In 1920, the all-wooden tee was invented. In 1927, the American team teed off against the British in the inaugural Ryder Cup Match. By 1929, steel shafts had improved club strength tremendously. A standard golf ball was adopted in the year *Brave New World* appeared.

Americans embraced golf. President Warren G. Harding (1921–23) golfed, as did movie stars Charlie Chaplin and Douglas Fairbanks and famous athletes Babe Ruth and Ty Cobb. America's "new religion," golf was part of the "national mania for sports" that took hold after World War One. Wind points without irony to this post-war exuberance as the start of "the brave new world" (Wind, 92, 106).

Having travelled across the continent in 1926, Huxley equated "the future of America [with] the future of the world." In the vulgar "Americanized" future, he predicted, amusement will become a way of life. People who "hate mental exercise" will demand "ready-made distraction," namely, golf (*America and the Future*, 1, 6).[8] *Brave New World* warned readers against the spread of golf and the Americanization of the future, which went hand in hand. Golf's ubiquity makes it Huxley's metaphor for global Americanization; the pervasiveness of this game certifies the advent of diversion as the modern lifestyle. To envision a materialistic, anti-intellectual society in which golf is a pseudo-religion, not to mention a multi-million-dollar leisure business, Huxley simply looked forward from 1920s America.

In "'the bad old days,'" old men used to "'retire, take to religion, spend their time reading, thinking,'" Mustapha Mond disgustedly recalls. "'Now—such is progress—'" old men are "'scampering from feely to feely, from girl to pneumatic girl, from Electro-magnetic Golf Course to …'" (*BNW*, 65–66). Here the Resident World Controller's panegyric is interrupted, but one gets the idea. In A. F. 632, everyone joins the Senior Tour. The brave new world having conquered aging, "'at sixty,'" one's "'powers and tastes'" remain "'what they were at seventeen'" *(BNW*, 65), another instance of retardation. Sexagenarians hasten from porno movies to copulation to Electro-magnetic Golf. In the brave new world, distractions such as golf impede expansion of the mind, that refinement of consciousness which Huxley was beginning to consider the point of existence.

"O brave new world / That has such people in it!" Miranda gushes in Shakespeare's *The Tempest* (V, i, 181–84) at first sight of Ferdinand's companions; "How beauteous mankind is!" Ruefully, John Savage repeats her exclamation once "the reality" of Fordian London contradicts the "paradise of goodness and loveliness" he anticipated (*BNW*, 188, 237). Instead of Shakespeare's world of courageous diversity, the Savage is discombobulated by a society of fornicating, drug-taking, golf-playing clones.[9]

---

1 Aldous Huxley, *Brave New World* (London: Chatto & Windus, 1932), 25. [*BNW*]

2 According to David Bradshaw, brave new world's requirement that "'elaborate'" games "'consume manufactured articles'" (*BNW*, 25) satirizes the economic theory of J. M. Keynes, who argued that the "problems which confronted Britain [in 1931] were caused by under-consumption." Keynes called for "a systematic programme of public works" to reduce unemployment and revive the economy. Bradshaw views the Obstacle Golf Course at Stoke Poges, the Centrifugal Bumble-puppy towers, and the double row of Escalator Five Courts as "bizarre manifestations of the Keynesian initiatives." See his "Introduction" to *Brave New World* (London: Flamingo, 1994), vi-vii. Note the difference between the simplicity of bumble-puppy when Minnie Beebe and Mrs. Honeychurch play in *A Room with a View* and the apparatus the game requires in *Brave New World.* "Playing bumble-puppy," writes E. M. Forster, is "an ancient and honorable game, which consists in striking tennis balls high into the air, so that they fall over the net and immoderately bounce" (*Room*, 128). In the garden outside the Central London Hatchery and Conditioning

Centre, "the Director and his students stood for a short time watching a game of Centrifugal Bumble-puppy. Twenty children were grouped in a circle round a chrome-steel tower. A ball thrown up so as to land on the platform at the top of the tower rolled down into the interior, fell on a rapidly revolving disk, was hurled through one or other of the numerous apertures pierced in the cylindrical casing, and had to be caught" (*BNW*, 33).

3 See James Sexton, "Aldous Huxley's Bokanovsky," 85–89.

4 Surely Huxley marked the following passage in H. G. Wells's *Anticipations of the Reaction of Mechanical and Scientific Progress Upon Human Life and Thought* (1902): "The essential aspect of all this wild and windy business of the sexual relations is, after all, births. Upon this plain fact the people of the emergent New Republic will unhesitatingly go. The pre-eminent value of sexual questions in morality lies in the fact that the lives which will constitute the future are involved. If they are not involved, if we can dissociate this relationship from this issue, then sexual questions become of no more importance than [...] the general morality of outdoor games. Indeed, then the question of sexual relationships would be entirely on all fours with, and probably very analogous to, the question of golf. [...] An able-bodied man continually addicted to love-making that had no result in offspring would be just as silly and morally objectionable as an able-bodied man who devoted his chief energies to hitting little balls over golf-links" (*Anticipations*, 171). Having separated sex from procreation, a proposition that Wells seems almost ready to entertain as a way of skirting the issue of sexual morality, the brave new world thinks of sex and golf as equivalent pastimes. Huxley finds the brave new world's addiction to both "silly and morally objectionable," to borrow Wells's phrase.

5 "The Horrors of Society," *Complete Essays*, I, 389.

6 "Recreations," *Complete Essays*, II, 84.

7 Having joined the Department of Public Health in Nautilus, Iowa, young Martin Arrowsmith is advised by Irving Watters on how to get ahead: "'Join the country club and take up golf'" (Lewis, 211). The year is 1912 but Sinclair Lewis's *Arrowsmith* appeared in 1925.

8 The essay was originally published as "The Outlook for American Culture: Some Reflections in a Machine Age," *Harper's Magazine* (August 1927), 265–70.

9 Prior to *Brave New World*, utopists paid little attention to games. The exception is Edward Bellamy's *Looking Backward: 2000–1887*, in which leisure has become a major concern because everyone is mustered out of the industrial army at age 45. In Chapter XVII, which Huxley doubtless noted, Doctor Leete broaches "the subject of popular sports and recreations at the present hour." It is 10 September 2000 in Boston. He informs Julian West, who was hypnotized in the nineteenth century and wakes up 113 years later, that "'the demand for *panem et circenses* [...] is recognized nowadays as a wholly reasonable one.'" Recreation ranks "'a close second'" to bread as a "'necessity of life.'" There are "'all sorts of games and matches by sea and land'" (*LB*, 137, 138). Lewis Mumford praised "the great interest in sport which characterizes Bellamy's utopia." One "should not be surprised," he added without irony, "if an infantile element predominated in the character of this happy republic" (Mumford, 166). In Huxley's parody, mindless diversions are not just crucial to

the maintenance of the rationalized state; they are inseparable from sustenance. Brave new worlders, Bernard Marx complains, are "'[i]nfants'" outside of working hours (*BNW*, 109), that is, at play. The ten generals of Bellamy's industrial army anticipate Huxley's ten World Controllers. Insanity and suicide have almost disappeared in 2000, Doctor Leete boasts, but John Savage, forced "to choose between insanity on the one hand and lunacy on the other" (Aldous Huxley, "Foreword" to *Brave New World* [London, 1950], viii), hangs himself. Perhaps Huxley had heard of Bellamy's *The Religion of Solidarity*, written in 1874 but unpublished in its author's lifetime. "'We have the World State now,'" Mustapha Mond lectures, "'[a]nd Ford's Day celebrations, and Community Sings, and Solidarity Services,'" like the one that Bernard Marx attends on "Alternate Thursdays" (*BNW*, 62, 91). Neil Postman overlooks golf when listing the constant distractions with which entertainment-crazed Americans are amusing themselves to death. America is a dystopia whose citizens have been "narcoticized" by technological diversions, such as TV, their *soma*. "Huxley, not Orwell, was right" (Postman, III, viii).

Chapter Four

Four Notes on *Brave New World*

1. Onomastic oversights

In *Brave New World*, the two characters responsible for John the Savage's birth and upbringing possess only a first name: Linda, his biological mother, and the Director of Hatcheries and Conditioning (the D.H.C.), his father, whom she calls "'Tomakin.'"[1] Presumably, John's parents both have surnames, as do the other Alphas and Betas in Aldous Huxley's signature novel, but the author never discloses them.[2] Inasmuch as satiric naming is pervasive,[3] one wonders if such reticence is deliberate or an oversight.

By the time Linda appears, her name has become a misnomer. It means "beautiful" in Spanish but no longer applies to a "very stout" squaw (*BNW*, 97). She is a far cry from the Beta-Minus blond who accompanied the D.H.C. on a visit to the New Mexico Reservation twenty-five years earlier. Having lost her way after a thunderstorm, she had a bad fall, got left behind, and had a baby.[4] Brave new worlders in "the Other Place" (i.e., London), never grow old physically; Linda has aged disastrously. When she comes forwards to be reunited with the D.H.C. in the Bloomsbury Centre, Huxley observes: "Bloated, sagging, and among those firm youthful bodies, those undistorted faces, a strange and terrifying monster of middle-agedness, Linda advanced into the room, coquettishly smiling her broken and discoloured smile, and rolling as she walked, with what was meant to be voluptuous undulation, her enormous haunches" (*BNW*, 123).

When John reveals that Linda came to the reservation with a man named "Tomakin," Bernard Marx recalls that the D.H.C.'s "first name" is "'Thomas'" (*BNW*, 97). Returning to the World State with Linda and John in tow, Marx embarrasses his boss and avoids being transferred to Iceland. In the Centre's Fertilizing Room, a perfectly ironic setting, he exposes the administrator in charge of producing and programming bottle babies as the father of a child by natural means. Linda exclaims "'Tomakin!'" and throws her arms around the Director's neck. The D.H.C., Huxley writes, "put his hands over his ears and rushed out of the room" (*BNW*, 124). Instead of sanctioning Marx for unorthodox behavior as he had planned, the D.H.C. resigns next day.

"Tomakin" has been misconstrued as a surname. One commentator states that Linda gets "pregnant by Tomakin," who is "stunned, humiliated, and ridiculed" upon her reappearance (Izzo, 5). Another refers to the "love affair between Linda [...] and Tomakin" (Combs, 164). Clearly, "Tomakin" can be neither surname nor first name; instead it is a pet name with a diminutive suffix, Linda's term of endearment for her lover. The D.H.C. is not Thomas Tomakin but his first name easily becomes "Tomakin," just as the dictionary, defining "-kin," gives "lambkin" for a young lamb.[5]

In early twentieth-century novels, the prospect or arrival of a child, even if illegitimate, gives the narrative a positive turn. In *Howards End*, Leonard Bast's bastard son by Helen Schlegel will inherit the house that symbolizes England. In *Lady Chatterley's Lover*, Connie is carrying Mellors's child, another bastard, who will personify their life-worshipper's philosophy into the next generation. However, when Linda and Tomakin present the brave new world progeny already fully grown, she is rejected, he is ruined, and their child eventually commits suicide.

Whether John possesses one name or two remains problematic. In the 1946 "Foreword" and throughout the text, Huxley refers to him as "the Savage" (*BNW*, vii and 127, for examples). The other characters call him "'John'" to his face or "'the Savage'" when discussing him (*BNW*, 126, 129). But "'Mr. Savage speaking'" is how John answers the phone in Chapter XII (*BNW*, 162). He is addressed as "'Mr. Savage'" by the reporter for *The Hourly Radio* and called for by that name when sightseers come to the Surrey lighthouse to find that he has hanged himself (*BNW*, 204, 212–13). In the preponderance of instances then, he has one name only, either "John" or "the Savage," but he may be Mr. John Savage, the only character in the brave new world to acquire a surname when already an adult.[6]

Absence of a last name for John the Savage's parents (and perhaps for John himself) may be accidental.[7] But onomastic satire is too prevalent in *Brave New World* for Huxley to have bypassed *two* opportunities to create ridiculous names. For instance, he delights in having Bernard Marx hunger for an indifferent Lenina when he does not know who Marx and Lenin were or that the latter was the former's disciple. Concealing John's parents' surnames, admittedly a minor stratagem, was an additional way of making the Savage an even greater anomaly in the World State. This refugee from D. H. Lawrence's beloved American southwest is the brave new world's principal misfit, a genuine bastard (i.e., born out of wedlock) in a future society wherein no one else has parents.

2. *Inconsistent historicism*

Throughout *Brave New World*, when Huxley alludes to the past—that is, refers to historical events, real or imaginary, and to historical personages actual or literary—he dispenses with consistency. The only common denominator is his compulsion to ridicule the conglomeration of ideas—

Fordian, Wellsian, Freudian, Pavlovian—upon which the World State rests. The brave new world is knowledgeable about the past when it abets Huxley's satire but remains ignorant of it when ignorance is more incriminating. The modern satirical novelist of ideas asks himself whether it is more disparaging, at a given moment, for brave new worlders to be aware of the past or unaware of it, for them to possess a historical sense or to make nonsense of history.

Fragments of the past survive in the unusual names of brave new worlders, none of whom, however, seems to comprehend who his (or her) namesakes were. Someone besides Huxley must be responsible for incongruities between most first names and surnames. Whose idea was the name Bernard Marx? Who came up with Benito Hoover or Calvin Stopes? Either the namers have a perverse sense of humor or, ignorant of the past themselves, they do not perceive the ironies in the incongruous first and last names they assign, merely recognizing them as once having belonged to famous persons. These names are a series of jokes at his characters' expense that Huxley shares with his readers.

Yet when Huxley pokes fun at H. G. Wells and George Bernard Shaw, their names are not rendered laughable by being used to form ludicrous combinations; each is satirized in his own right under his own name. The former's surname lives on as "'Dr. Wells,'" who prescribes Fanny's "'first Pregnancy Substitute'" (*BNW*, 30). Huxley may be remembering that in Wells's *A Modern Utopia* motherhood is a profession and mothers receive stipends (see *AMU*, 187–88). In the real future, Huxley implies, no one will take Wells's proposal seriously. Instead, motherhood will be abolished. Dr. Wells is unaware of the once-famous writer of scientific romances whose output *Brave New World* parodies. George Bernard Shaw, whom the D.H.C. praises as "'one of the few whose works have been permitted to come down to us,'" accidentally facilitated the development of *hypnopaedia* when giving a talk "about his own genius" (*BNW*, 18). Besides the D.H.C., no one alludes to this supposedly well-known playwright whose allegedly enduring qualities Huxley champions ironically.[8]

First names and surnames that contradict each other create a jumbled sense of the past. Perhaps, as Our Ford said, "'History is bunk'" (*BNW*, 26), little more than a disorderly array of personages whose conflicting lifestyles and diverse activities did not prevent the emergence of a brave new world. Bernard Marx is named for the father of Communism and either Bernard of Clairvaux, a twelfth-century saint, or Claude Bernard, a nineteenth-century French physiologist considered the father of experimental medicine. Either way, his first and last names, which he never thinks about, are as much a misfit as he is. Calvin Stopes's names commemorate John Calvin, Presbyterianism's founder, and Marie Charlotte Carmichael Stopes, who set up the first birth control clinic; neither of these historical figures would have more use for the other than did Herbert Hoover and Benito Mussolini, Benito Hoover's namesakes.

On the other hand, Mustapha Mond, a World Controller, is aptly named after the founder of modern Turkey, Mustapha Kemal, and England's most powerful industrial magnate, Sir Alfred Mond, the head of Imperial Chemical Industries Limited, though he seems unacquainted with either. In short, when it suits Huxley's satire to limit the brave new world's historical sense, he does so. At other times, the suitability of two names becomes cause for concern, if not alarm, as when Ford and Freud (Mond doubles as "Our Ford" and "Our Freud") are seen as spokespersons for the brave new world; the behavioristic world views of the American industrialist and the Viennese psychiatrist are dangerously complementary.[9]

Helmholtz Watson has never heard of Hermann von Helmholtz or John Broadus Watson, but the nineteenth-century scientist and the foremost American behaviorist go together more comfortably than do Darwin Bonaparte's first and last names. Capitalizing on von Helmholtz's theories about the conservation of energy, Huxley's Watson reconditions himself like a good behaviorist, redirecting his efforts from trivial pursuits towards a search for enlightenment. But consistency disappears when Watson, told by phone of the Savage's antics at the Park Lane Hospital, swears "'Ford in Flivver!'" (*BNW*, 174) He repeats as an oath a saying that also serves the brave new world as a bromide: "'Ford's in his flivver,' murmured the D.H.C. 'All's well with the world'" (*BNW*, 35). One doubts that either Watson or the Director of Hatcheries and Conditioning has memorized Robert Browning's poetry. Actually, the D.H.C. misquotes. Browning wrote "All's right with the world."[10] The brave new world, however, prefers wellness to rightness, a sense of purely physical comfort to moral or ethical rectitude. It seems inconsistent for Watson to cite "Pippa Passes," a minor Browning poem, and yet prove ignorant of Shakespeare's *Romeo and Juliet* when the Savage reads from it in Chapter XII (see *BNW*, 150–51). Huxley satirizes the D.H.C. for misquoting and criticizes both the Director and Watson for misappropriating a Victorian poet's attempt at ontological reassurance. Later, he ridicules a promiscuous brave new worlder's incredulous reaction to Juliet's sexual frustrations. Watson cannot comprehend the "smutty absurdity" of an "idiotic girl" not telling her parents that "for the moment, at any rate," she wanted "someone else" than the husband her parents have chosen (*BNW*, 151). Helmholtz ignores the fact that Juliet has parents and is being readied for nuptials, neither of which should be understandable in the brave new world.

No one catches the Savage's three allusions to *The Tempest* (see *BNW*, 114, 130, 172), from which comes Huxley's title. Asked to "'remember what Miranda says,'" Bernard asks John "'Who's Miranda?'" (*BNW*, 114), as if she were a brave new worlder he has not met. Yet the Controller mentions *Othello* and apparently can recall "'that bit in *King Lear*'" to which the Savage refers him as proof that there is "'a God managing things'" (*BNW*, 180, 193). All of John's allusions to *The Tempest* are ironical for the reader, but only with the last two, where John applies Miranda's exclamation of approval—"'O brave new world that has such people in it'" (V, i, 180–184)—to Deltas, Delta-Minuses, and Epsilon Semi-Morons, is the Savage actually being ironic.

Evidently, Mond also knows *The Tempest*, although he is not present any of the three times the Savage quotes from it. John expresses his delight with "'[a]ll that music in the air,'" one of the few "'nice things'" in the brave new world where a soundtrack apparently supplies a constant background. Mond recites Caliban's lines about hearing "'twangling instruments [...] and [...] voices'" (*BNW*, 179).[11] Pleasantly surprised, John says, "'I thought nobody knew that book here.'" Mond replies: "'I'm one of the very few.'" In short, Mond knows *Othello*, *Lear*, and *The Tempest.* Watson is ignorant of all three plus *Romeo and Juliet* and probably Shakespeare in general. When it pleases the satirist to have the memory of the greatest Elizabethan playwright survive until A. F. 632, it does; otherwise, no, and the loss is a major discredit for the World State.

How much of the past Mustapha Mond is allowed to know because of his exalted position as one of the brave new world's ten Controllers remains unclear. Does any of the other nine keep forbidden books in his study's safe, "'pornographic old books'" as Mond calls them, such as *The Holy Bible*, *The Imitation of Christ*, and William James's *The Varieties of Religious Experience* (*BNW*, 189)? Passages he reads to the Savage from Cardinal Newman and Maine de Biran effectively repudiate the brave new world's philosophy of life, especially its disregard for the individual's increasing spiritual needs as old age approaches (see *BNW*, 190–91).

Huxley injects two positive passages into his dystopian novel, but Mond prevents both Newman and Biran from exerting any influence on the World State. The Controller then compares the Savage to "'another of those old fellows called Bradley'" (*BNW*, 192). His explanation of Bradley's rationale for philosophizing—"'the finding of bad reason for what one believes by instinct'" (*BNW*, 192)—undercuts Newman and Biran about equally.

"'They're smut,'" Mond pronounces, because they prefer an imaginary God to the brave new world's belief in "'machinery and medicine and happiness'" (*BNW*, 192). F. H. Bradley was a fellow of Merton College, Oxford, whose prose style in *Essay on Truth and Reality* (1914) impressed T. S. Eliot. As a body of knowledge, a Catholic Cardinal, a nineteenth-century Frenchman, and a twentieth-century Oxford don form an oddly eclectic trio to salvage from the past.

Consistency in regard to the past becomes a major problem in Chapter III: the question arises whether history is a futile concern. Huxley answers affirmatively and negatively. The historical process may be as pointless as the World State contends, but nothing truly satisfying can be gained by obliterating the past. The choice between acknowledging it or disowning it seems as impossible as the choice between freedom and happiness.

Reverently, Mustapha Mond quotes "'that beautiful and inspired saying of Our Ford's: History is bunk'" (*BNW*, 26); it is supposedly irrelevant, meaningless. But the Controller immediately contradicts himself by delivering a history lecture of more than a dozen pages. His all-male audience is a "troop of newly arrived students, very young, pink and callow" (*BNW*, 1). Where they come from and why, at so late a date in their schooling, they need to have the history of the World State outlined for them is never spelled out. Surely it is the novel's readers who require orientation. Huxley supplies a lengthy disquisition that goes contrary to the brave new world's disdain for history.[12]

"'You all remember'" Our Ford's "'saying,'" says Mond, so the students are familiar with the industrialist's philistine philosophy. The historical places and personages that the unnamed narrator imagines the Controller's "invisible feather whisk" brushing aside like so much "dust"—Thebes, Babylon, Cnossus, Mycenae, Odysseus, Job, Jupiter, Gotama, Jesus, Athens, Rome, Jerusalem, King Lear, Pascal (*BNW*, 26–27)—have doubtless long since been swept into the dustbin. The students will never hear about them, except for Jesus, whom Mond credits as the individual responsible for "'a thing [...] called Christianity'" (*BNW*, 43), and for King Lear, whom the Savage discusses with Mond in Chapter XVII. Yet these people and places are clearly invaluable to the unnamed narrator, who satirizes Henry Ford and Mustapha Mond both. The unnamed narrator enumerates a series of people and places that Ford's precept ought to make it impossible for Mond to mention. The mentioning discredits Ford's pronouncement; the brave new world's arrogant stupidity leaves the reader with a profound sense of loss. On the other hand, Henry Ford (Our Ford), Sigmund Freud (Our Freud), and Ivan Petrovich Pavlov (Neo-Pavlovian Conditioning) have not been whisked away. Six centuries into the future, these figures from the past, along with Maurice Bokanovsky and Mr. Podsnap, are still influential.[13]

Mond's history lesson emphasizes horrendous events that led to the establishment of the brave new world: the Nine Years' War, the "'great Economic Collapse,'" the slaughter of Simple Lifers at Golders Green, "'the famous British Museum Massacre,'" in which "'two thousand culture fans [were] gassed,'" all culminating in "'a campaign against the Past,'" an anti-history movement that entailed "'closing'" museums and "'blowing up'" historical monuments (*BNW*, 38, 41).[14] Yet, Big Ben still stands. Named for Sir Benjamin Hall, commissioner of works in 1856 when the 13-ton bell was installed in the tower of the Houses of Parliament, this monument has been renamed "Big Henry" after Our Ford (*BNW*, 65). Now it functions as the clock for the Fordson Community Singery. Bernard Marx hears the bell tolling as he hastens to his Solidarity Service.

Eton was founded by Henry VI in 1440–41. Britain's most prestigious boys' school is still operating, although it has gone co-ed; it offers courses in "'elementary relativity'" and "'Malthusian'" birth control along with field trips to the "'Hospital for the Dying'" for death conditioning (*BNW*, 132, 133). The warnings of Thomas Robert Malthus (1766–1834) against overpopulation are still being heeded. Lupton's Tower, on Eton's campus, has not been destroyed either. Named for Roger Lupton, provost from 1503–1535, it has grown into a skyscraper of "fifty-two stories" (*BNW*, 131). When Bernard Marx and the Savage tour Eton, the former makes a dinner date with Miss Keate, the Head Mistress: "Eight o'clock at the Savoy" (*BNW*, 134). More than six centuries old in A. F. 632, this restaurant has to be the longest-running upscale eatery ever. Westminster Abbey also thrives as a nightclub.

Although they anger the Savage by shouting "with laughter," the "young Etonians" ought not to be able to view a clip of "the Penitentes of Acoma" beating themselves "with knotted whips" (*BNW*, 132). Evidently, Eton has a film archive. Given the anti-history campaign, Malpais should not exist. Yet, it has been carefully preserved as a tourist attraction. Linda and the D.H.C. visit it on holiday. Huxley needs Malpais to establish a mutually incriminating counterpoint: a primitive reservation that parodies D. H. Lawrence's fondness for the simple life against a Wellsian World State in which the invasion of society by machines is complete; they undercut each other. Far from being exploded or discontinued, some historical monuments and venerable cultural institutions flourish in A. F. 632 despite Our Ford's contempt for the past. They come into play whenever their continued existence helps Huxley to deplore the brave new world's allegedly utopic practices and procedures.

Mond exposes the brave new world's past (and history in general) as a record of pathological and psychotic behavior well worth forgetting—"'"fourteen thousand aeroplanes"'" dropping "'"anthrax bombs,"'" the Russians "'"infecting water supplies"'" *(BNW*, 38–39). But eliminating the past in favor of an eternal present, an unchanging and mindless "'"[s]tability,"'" allegedly "'"the primal and the ultimate need,"'" hardly seems a utopic alternative (*BNW*, 34). Things remain stable because there is no more past and no future; once the very idea of history has been annulled, reality has never been, and can never be any different. According to Mond, "'"there was a choice between World Control and destruction"'" (*BNW*, 39), which the satirist implies is really no choice at all. While Mond expounds on "'"the Caste System,"'" "'"conscription of consumption,"'" "'"hypnopaedia,"'" and "'"*soma*,"'" Huxley maintains an embarrassing counterpoint between these allegedly stellar features of the new order and the trivial concerns of brave new worlders that a spurious stability has led to, such as Fanny's desire for a "green morocco-surrogate cartridge belt" like Lenina's, which is "bulging [...] with the regulation supply of contraceptives" (*BNW*, 42).

Huxley's satire in *Brave New World* thrives on the inconsistency of its historicism. To debunk Henry Ford, Huxley demolishes his life story as the meretricious foundation text behind the World State's decision to run itself like a factory. "*My Life and Work, by Our Ford*" has replaced the Bible. The Savage finds this "massive volume" bound in black leather-surrogate, and stamped with large golden T's prominently displayed on a table in Mond's study (*BNW*, 178). After reading "a sentence here, a paragraph there," he decides that the book "didn't interest him" (*BNW*, 178). Were Huxley's satire consistent, Ford's autobiography should have been conscripted during "'"the suppression of all books published before A. F. 150"'" (*BNW*, 42).

Despite the brave new world's efforts, Peter Firchow notes, "remnants of the past stubbornly survive"; brave new worlders "are aware that once there were families and society was very differently organized" (*End*, 25–26). He points to the books in Mond's safe as proof that the past persists. For Firchow, surviving "remnants" are a positive sign. But several concealed texts and the ability to remember motherhood hardly constitute "a sort of subculture" (*End*, 25). A brave new worlder's knowledge of what a mother was or a father does not absolve Our Freud from elaborating on "the appalling dangers of family life" when "the world was full of fathers" and "mothers" (*BNW*, 30). It is not clear whether Mond is bent on instructing his young audience about parents or simply reminding them of what they already know, even if, strictly speaking, they ought not to know it if the past no longer exists. Whichever the case, Mond's actions are crucial for the satirist's indictment of the brave new world's parentless social order but inconsistent with its dismissal of the past.

3. Brotherly satire

Brave New World contains several positives, but the "amused, Pyrrhonic aesthete" (*BNW*, viii) in charge of the narrative makes certain no one benefits from them. Brave new worlders will never read Helmholtz Watson's heretical poem "'"about being alone"'"; despite countless administrative "'"warnings against solitude,"'" it dares to explore the attractions of contemplative silence (*BNW*, 148, 149). Nor will anyone peruse the collection of forbidden books in Mustapha Mond's office safe. Only to the Savage does Mond read passages from Cardinal Newman and Maine de Biran about fostering "the religious sentiment" (*BNW*, 191).

The severest deprivation results from the censoring of a "'"subversive"'" biology paper that challenges the brave new world's ridiculous conception of life's "'"purpose."'" A nobler idea of why human beings exist is lost when Mond scribbles "'"Not to be published"'" across "'"A New Theory of Biology"'" and orders its author "'"kept under supervision"'" (*BNW*, 145). Surprisingly, in a novel full of satirical names, the paper's author is left unnamed. Huxley may have expected readers to identify him on their own: it has been noted that the theory in this "'"highly ingenious, but heretical"'" paper "bears a striking resemblance to Julian Huxley's ideas"; Aldous takes a satirical look at "the biological musings of his elder brother" (*BNW*, 145; Deese, 64–65).

Julian's ideas, Huxley chides, would be disregarded in A. F. 632. They are irrelevant to what the future actually holds. Nevertheless, besides belittling Julian, the dystopian satirist damns the World State for ignoring the key to the human race's eventual salvation. A society in a novel set in the future is about to cancel its best chance for future development by siding with Henry Ford, H. G. Wells, and their ilk instead of heeding brother Julian.

Mond reads "A New Theory of Biology" in Chapter XII. In surrounding passages, the Savage declaims *Romeo and Juliet* and Lenina frolics with the Arch-Community-Songster. The counterpoint pits the Songster's lust and John's masturbatory "rapture" against Mond's hypocritical conclusion that the paper, though "quite possibly true," is "not [...] admissible," indeed, "'"dangerous"'" (*BNW*, 145). All three—Songster, Savage, and Mond—are up to no good, but the Controller's behavior is truly perverse. The unnamed biologist's "masterly" ideas, he decides, could

> easily decondition the more unsettled minds among the higher castes—make them lose their faith in happiness as the Sovereign Good, and take to believing, instead, that the goal was somewhere beyond, somewhere outside the present human sphere; that the purpose of life was not the maintenance of well-being, but some intensification and refining of consciousness, some enlargement of knowledge. (*BNW*, 145)

Aldous in 1932 sees no future for this theory. Foolishly, Mond dignifies "happiness" and "well-being" (i.e., simply feeling well) as a "faith," calling it "the purpose of life," its sole end or goal. Concern for "unsettled minds" among the Alphas and Betas amounts to an admission of the World State's fallibility.

The unnamed biologist's "New Theory" is indebted to the philosophy of "evolutionary humanism" that Julian Huxley began expounding in the 1920s. His landmark essay, titled "Evolutionary Humanism as a Developed Religion," emphasizes the mind's "intensification and increasing importance" as evolution continues ("EH," 191),[15] just as the brave new world's biologist calls for an "intensification [...] of consciousness." The "only avenue" still "open" for a human being's "further major advance," Julian continues, is "through the improvement of brain and mind" ("EH," 193). Similarly, the brave new world's biologist looks forwards to an "enlargement of knowledge."

In an essay on "Science, Natural and Social," Julian Huxley contends that the brain's evolution is the "one inexhaustible or at least unexhausted source" for "substantial evolutionary progress" ("SNS," 132). Humans have become "the trustees" of the evolutionary process ("ROP," 139). Their "sacred duty" ("EH," 194) is to guide the evolution of the human species in a desirable direction. Instead of letting brave new worlders do this, the "Resident Controller for Western Europe" (*BNW*, 26) sees to it that the paper similar to Julian's directive for evolution's "psycho-social phase" remains unpublished.[16] For Mond, "control" means censorship.

As was Julian Huxley, the unnamed biologist seems convinced that human beings are "the only organism" capable of "further evolutionary progress" ("EH," 194). They must "promote the maximum fulfillment of the evolutionary process" through the "fullest realization" of their "inherent possibilities" ("EH," 194).[17] The unnamed biologist would second Julian's call for the "realization of more possibilities by more, and more fully developed, individuals" ("EH," 194). Repeatedly throughout his career, including his introduction to Teilhard de Chardin's *The Phenomenon of Man*, he predicts "the evolution of progressively more conscious mind," the "intensification of mind, the raising of mental potential" (*Phenomenon*,

16), all things the "New Theory" advocates. As "awareness […] becomes increasingly important," mankind "as a whole will accordingly achieve more intense, more complex, and more integrated mental activity, which can guide the human species up the path of progress to higher levels of hominization" (*Phenomenon*, 17). Aldous finds this prospect unrealistic enough to receive his endorsement ironically as a satiric target; additional evolutionary advance for the species is an idea Aldous foresees his future society easily thwarting.

The only individual in Huxley's dystopian novel who might be capable of fulfilling the unnamed biologist's recommendations is Helmholtz Watson. Although he has never heard of the "New Theory," he starts to implement it. To Bernard Marx he talks of having "'[s]ome sort of extra power'" inside himself "'that was only waiting for […] a chance to come out'" (*BNW*, 57). This is surely a reservoir of unused evolutionary energy but, Watson complains, he "'can't make any use'" of it (*BNW*, 58). However, when he sublimates (i.e., redirects) his sexual energies and writes his first poem in which "'All silences rejoice'" and "'Slowly form a presence,'" he begins to utilize the "'extra, latent power'" inside himself (*BNW*, 148–49). Conceivably, he is about to take the next evolutionary step towards enlightenment by achieving an "intensification" and "refining" of his consciousness. The unnamed biologist equates this expansion of mind with mankind's advance towards the ever-greater awareness that is life's goal. Watson may be a prototype of the "more, and more fully developed" human beings Julian Huxley desired ("EH," 197). Should such a splendid being appear, Aldous tells Julian in 1932, he would most likely meet a fate similar to Watson's: rejection and exile. Nevertheless Huxley implies that the brave new world commits a grievous error in sending Helmholtz to the Falklands. It banishes a salvationary prototype, effectively derailing the evolutionary process that produced him.

Julian Huxley observes that "some regions of human potentiality"—such as "mysticism and Yoga"—"remain virtually unexplored, or at least unavailable to mankind as a whole" ("EH," 201). He states that artists have a "duty" to "experiment," that is, to investigate whatever may "raise the general level of innate human possibilities and capacities" ("EH," 206–7). Both observations reveal Watson to be a desirable poet-harbinger. He is an explorer of "regions" the brave new world's Controllers want to keep "unexplored" ("EH," 201). In 1932, however, the Huxley brothers disagree: although Julian acknowledges the desire for "a mystical sense of union with something greater than our ordinary lives," be believes all mental and spiritual forces are "not outside man but within him" ("Life," 146; "EH,"

195), the godless goal being "higher levels of hominization" (*Phenomenon*, 17), fuller and fuller self-realization; whereas Aldous, no matter if vaguely and satirically, places the ultimate goal "somewhere outside the present human sphere" (*BNW*, 145).

Ironically, ideas about what constitutes "the Sovereign Good" (*BNW*, 145) that Mond suppresses in Huxley's fifth novel acquire an increasingly respectful hearing in his later works. The reconsideration begins with the "Foreword" Huxley wrote in 1946 for a new American edition of *Brave New World*. Were he to rewrite *Brave New World*, Huxley divulged, the Savage would stumble upon a "third alternative" to Fordian London and primitive Malpais, a society devoted to "the conscious and intelligent pursuit of man's Final End, the unitive knowledge of the immanent Tao or Logos, the transcendent Godhead or Brahman" (*BNW*, ix). The unnamed biologist's "intensification," "refining," and "enlargement" (*BNW*, 145) are almost synonymous with a "unitive knowledge," full-blown mystical awareness. In the missing third society, the only question would be: "'How will this thought or action contribute to […] the achievement […] of man's Final End?'" (*BNW*, ix) In other words, will it help or hinder his further evolution.

In 1959, when Aldous writes the chapter on "Latent Human Potentialities" in *The Human Situation*, he urges readers "to grow to the limits of [their] capacities, to actualize [their] potentialities" (*HS*, 237).[18] Like Julian's "Evolutionary Humanism," Aldous's perennial philosophy seeks to preserve and extend the scientific process of evolution discovered by Darwin and championed by their grandfather, T. H. Huxley. "For the fully enlightened," Huxley contends in *The Perennial Philosophy* as if quoting the "New Theory," "there is a general enhancement and intensification of consciousness, and at the same time an extension and transfiguration" (*PP*, 342–43).[19] Refining one's consciousness (unnamed biologist), accelerating hominization (Julian), and maximizing one's spiritual potentialities (Aldous) have a common evolutionary denominator. Underlying brotherly satire one finds an intellectual allegiance.

4. *Iceland*

Is Bernard Marx really banished to Iceland? Maybe so. Evidence in the text seems to justify this conclusion. A recent essay consigns the miscreant from the brave new world's Psychology Bureau to this remote sub-station: Marx "is sent to a community of non-conformists and misfits" (Parkes, 185). Actually, no one maintains that Iceland is populated by undesirables; the sub-centre's isolation is hardship enough. Furthermore, Marx's demotion is not an absolute certainty. Possibly he is permitted to accompany his friend,

Helmholtz Watson, to the Falkland Islands, a punishment that, according to Mustapha Mond, boasts some advantages.

Misfit and malcontent, Marx stands "eight centimetres" shorter than the typical Alpha, due to a mistake in his decanting: too much alcohol in his blood-surrogate (*BNW*, 53). In a society dedicated to promiscuity—"'everyone belongs to everyone else'" (*BNW*, 34)—he enjoys minimal success with the ladies. He prefers being "'by himself'" to playing Obstacle Golf (*BNW*, 36). His eccentricities earn him "'fair warning'" from the Director of Hatcheries and Conditioning that he will be transferred "'to a Sub-Centre—preferably to Iceland'" if he persists in lapsing "'from a proper standard of infantile decorum'" (*BNW*, 80).

Initially, Bernard scoffs at Iceland as an idle "threat": "People simply weren't transferred for things like that," i.e., being thoughtful and solitary, he reassures himself (*BNW*, 81). Then he learns from Watson that the D.H.C. is looking for someone to replace him. "'I'm going to be sent to Iceland,'" he whines to Lenina, "Iceland, Iceland" (*BNW*, 85, 86).

This is the last one hears of reassignment until Marx, along with Watson and the Savage, is brought before Mustapha Mond in Chapter XVI, following the riot at the Park Lane Hospital. All three are in trouble for disrupting the distribution of *soma* tablets to the hospital's Delta work force. Groveling "in a paroxysm of abjection," Bernard pleads with Mond: "'Oh, please don't send me to Iceland'" (*BNW*, 185). Has the Controller heard of the D.H.C.'s intentions? (The Director departed in disgrace six chapters earlier when Bernard confronted him with John the Savage, his biological son from Malpais.)

Although Bernard is "carried out" "still shouting and sobbing," Mond never repeats the D.H.C.'s threats (*BNW*, 185). Instead, he tells Watson that Bernard's "'punishment is really a reward'": he is being sent to an island, Mond claims, where he will "'meet the most interesting set of men and women to be found anywhere in the world.'"[20] "'I almost envy you, Mr. Watson,'" Mond concludes. Whether the envy is sincere is debatable, but the focus has shifted from Marx to Watson with the implication that both are headed to a desirable place where non-conformists (i.e., individuals) thrive regardless of climate. Mond begins by praising Marx's transfer and ends by envying Watson. The Controller agrees to dispatch Helmholtz to "'the Falkland Islands,'" where he will supposedly wax more poetic in nasty weather. The matter having been settled, Watson goes off to comfort "'poor Bernard'" (*BNW*, 188).

In Chapter XVII, John, Bernard, and Helmholtz meet for the last time. Bernard and Helmholtz have "'come to say good-bye'"; "'we're off tomorrow,'" Bernard discloses (*BNW*, 198). This seems to indicate a joint departure, not separate destinations. "'Helmholtz was wonderful to me,'" Bernard adds. Huxley writes that, despite a society wherein love and happiness have become meaningless, "the three young men were happy" thanks to "their love for one another" (*BNW*, 199), the only example of true happiness in the novel.

John informs his friends that he asked the Controller if he "'mightn't go to the islands with you'" (*BNW*, 199). One wonders if "you" is singular or plural. Was John hoping to join Helmholtz with both of them leaving Bernard behind to accept his fate alone? Admittedly, Watson, not Bernard, asks the Savage for Mond's reply as if it concerned him only. But "the islands," such as the Falklands, is plural whereas Iceland is singular. Whatever John was planning, Marx is neither mentioned nor excluded; Iceland is not named. "The banishment of Watson and Marx to remote islands at opposite ends of the world" (Parkes, 185) may be what lies in store, yet such an outcome would prevent Huxley from preserving the only genuine friendship between two brave new worlders that his novel contains.[21]

---

1 Aldous Huxley, *Brave New World* (London: Chatto & Windus, 1950), 123. [*BNW*] John's surrogate fathers on the Malpais Indian reservation also have only one name: Popé, the promiscuous Linda's primary lover, and Mitsima, who instructs young John in the ways of the tribe.

2 Some brave new worlders have surnames only: Miss Keate, Eton's headmistress, and Dr. Gafney, its provost, for examples (see *BNW*, 216).

3 For a detailed analysis of satiric naming in *Brave New World*, see Jerome Meckier, "Onomastic Satire," *MSN*, 185–224. Alastair Fowler devotes an entire chapter to Joyce and Nabokov, "the two most eminent namers in our literature," but mentions Huxley only twice and not for *Brave New World*. See *Literary Names*, 8, 96.

4 Huxley does not explain why Linda and the D.H.C. neglected to use contraceptives while on holiday, an extraordinary lapse in a society where precaution is automatic: after an evening out with Henry Foster, Lenina does "not forget to take all the contraceptive precautions," having been conditioned to do so "three times a week" for six years (*BNW*, 64).

5 [–kin] is "a diminutive suffix for nouns: lambkin," according to *Webster's College Dictionary*, 745.

6 Like even worse abominations such as "Calvin Stopes" and "Darwin Bonaparte," John's names are a mix of the ironic and the comical. He is a voice "crying" in the wilderness (Matthew 3:31), as was the locust-eating Baptist, except that brave new worlders come to John's hideout "[l]ike locusts" and seduce him into participation in an orgy (*BNW*, 212). He has the intractable temper of the essayist, Walter Savage Landor (1775–1864): he punches the Deltas at the Park Lane Hospital and brutally whips the sightseer with a "peach-bright, doll-beautiful face," probably Lenina (*BNW*, 175, 211). A

caricature of the Noble Savage, he is not so noble. See Meckier, "Onomastic Satire," *MSN*, 217–20.

[7] Huxley confessed to two failures of "foresight": he made "no reference to nuclear fission" and ought to have offered the Savage an escape to "a community of exiles […] from the Brave New World, living within the borders of the Reservation" (*BNW*, x, ix). Such an escape would have ruined the novel's cynical ending.

[8] Shaw's surname also survives ignominiously in "Dr. Shaw," Linda's physician upon her return from the savage reservation. He agrees to administer the "ever larger, ever more frequent doses" of *soma* that kill her (*BNW*, 125–26).

[9] "For some inscrutable reason," says the unnamed narrator, Our Ford chose to call himself Our Freud "whenever he spoke of psychological matters" (*BNW*, 30). Huxley could not resist linking two similar sounding names as further proof that both were unwitting allies, two behaviorists in his opinion. Their ideas help to transform brave new worlders "into reliable and predictable mechanisms" (Baker, *Dark Historic Page*, 140). The "reason," therefore, is not "inscrutable," especially if Our Ford himself recognized his connection with Our Freud.

[10] Pippa sings "God's in his heaven—/All's right with the world," "Pippa Passes," ll. 227–28 (*The Selected Poetry of Robert Browning*, 15).

[11] See *The Tempest*, III, iii, 146–47.

[12] Peter Firchow excuses "the oddity of being given a history lesson when history has been officially abolished" on grounds that "rulers—especially when they are as powerful as Mond—can break the rules" (*MUF*, 68).

[13] Maurice Bokanovsky, a minister in Raymond Poincaré's cabinet in 1926, offered supplements to parents willing to raise large families. A bokanovskified egg will cause "ninety-six human beings [to] grow where only one grew before" (*BNW*, 5). In Dickens's *Our Mutual Friend*, Mr. Podsnap advocates sameness, routine, conformity, so naming after him a process for turning out "'batches of identicals'" (*BNW*, 5) makes a kind of sense.

[14] For a discussion of "the stable behaviorist present of the World State," see Baker, *BNWHSD*, 88–89. He argues that the brave new world has erased "the concept of history itself from human consciousness." Baker also considers "the futility of history" and the World State's determination to terminate the past in *The Dark Historic Page*, 135–45.

[15] "Evolutionary Humanism as a Developed Religion" appeared in 1928 in Julian Huxley's *Religion Without Revelation*, republished by Mentor in 1957.

[16] Julian sums up the "psycho-social phase" in the second volume of his autobiography; see *Memories II*, 245.

[17] According to R. S. Deese, Julian called upon his readers to become "managers" of evolution to determine earthly evolution's "future direction." See "Agnostic Gospels," 106. In "Philosophy in a World at War," from *Man in the Modern World*, Julian Huxley exalts "the fact of evolutionary progress" as "the most important single biological fact yet known" ("PWW," 160).

[18] Surely Aldous's emphasis on "human potentialities" is a variation on Julian's "human possibilities."

[19] For Julian Huxley, evolutionary humanism is the perfect substitute for the orthodox religions: bolstered by scientific evidence, it dispenses with revelation. For the argument that Darwin's theories amount to a secular religion, see Michael Ruse, *Darwinism as Religion.*

[20] For the complex function of islands in Huxley's utopias, see "'My Hypothetical Islanders,'" chapter 5 below.

[21] Lenina and Fanny Crowne may be another instance, but their relationship is confined to the workplace.

Chapter Five

"My Hypothetical Islanders": The Role of Islands in *Brave New World* and *Island*

Brave New World, Huxley's best-known satirical novel of ideas, appears at times to be the victim of insufficient thought. For example, in a society whose religio-economic basis is Fordism, the ever-more expedient mass production of people and goods, no one bothers to explain the absence of automobiles. None of the central characters—Bernard Marx, Helmholtz Watson, Lenina Crowne, and surely not John the Savage—has seen a "'flivver'"; only the D.H.C. mentions it.[1] Assembly lines remain for other purposes, but cars are inexplicably extinct. The Savage's ability to parse Shakespeare boggles the mind. The Complete Works is a strange birthday present from Popé, who is not plausible as a book lover. An autodidact just turned twelve, John instinctively knows that the "enseamed bed" and "nasty sty" in *Hamlet* are "about Linda and Popé" (*BNW*, 108). Huxley was too preoccupied with "the application to human beings of the results of future research in biology, physiology, and psychology" (*BNW*, x) to avoid small failures of the imagination. When the Savage disrupts the *soma* distribution at the Park Lane Hospital for the Dying and the Deputy Sub-Bursar decides to call Helmholtz Watson for help, he looks up a number "in the telephone book" (*BNW*, 173). In A. F. 632, the brave new world still relies on directories and rotary telephones.

Islands pose a bigger problem. Scattered throughout the novel, they are employed effectively but not consistently. Samoa, Trobriands, Iceland, Cyprus, St. Helena, Marquesas, Falklands are all variations on the theme of separation, but is island exile punishment or reward? Iceland is a threat to Bernard Marx as is St. Helena for an unnamed biologist, but for a special group of Alphas, Cyprus was a reward that turned sour; for Helmholtz Watson, the Falklands are a banishment that could be a blessing. Not until Pala in Huxley's last completed novel did he spell out once for all the role of an island in utopian fiction; it must be a necessarily isolated entity, as prescribed by Sir Thomas More, yet Huxley's perfect place cannot avoid an increasingly fatal inseparability.

Islands play a significant part in the history lesson that fills Chapter III. Mustapha Mond explains how "Our Ford—or Our Freud" first revealed "the appalling dangers of family life" (*BNW*, 30), the plethora of complexes and neuroses it generates. Ever since, the brave new world has abolished parenthood, decanting babies from bottles, and educating its youth in state-run conditioning centers. An unidentified voice interrupts, mentioning simpler, saner solutions that prevail "'among the savages of Samoa, in certain islands off the coast of New Guinea'" (30). The voice points out that for Samoan children "[h]ome was in any one of twenty palm-thatched houses." Able to move from family to family until comfortably situated, they are not subjected to "every kind of perversion" the way European youngsters were in pre-Freudian days.

Samoans have implemented something like the Mutual Adoption Clubs (MACs) that Huxley read about in Margaret Mead's *Coming of Age in Samoa.*[2] Susila MacPhail describes them for Will Farnaby in *Island*. On Pala, "'everybody'" in a club—fifteen to twenty-five couples—"'adopts everyone else.'"[3] In such an "'inclusive, unpredestined and voluntary family,'" each child has dozens of parents to choose from. Neglect ceases to be a problem; abuse, incest, lust for the mother and urges to kill the father disappear. To maintain a psychologically sound population, Samoans require only a few huts, not "fifteen racks" of bottles on conveyors that travel "[t]wo thousand one hundred and thirty-six metres" around galleries on three floors (*BNW*, 8). Instead of eliminating family, Samoan islanders have invented what Susila calls "'[a]n entirely different kind'" of it (*I*, 90).

Similarly, the voice continues, "[i]n the Trobriands conception was the work of ancestral ghosts; nobody had ever heard of a father" (*BNW*, 31). (The Trobriand Islands are in the Solomon Sea, east of New Guinea.) Thanks to a comical superstition, these islanders are as immune as brave new worlders from the Oedipus complex that torments John the Savage. To get rid of it, they need not apply "the principle of mass production" to biology (*BNW*, 5). But Huxley does not explain why primitive phenomena such as thatched houses and belief in ghosts are still tolerated in parts of what is supposedly a World State.

Islands again become a concern in Chapter VI when the D.H.C. threatens Bernard Marx with "'transference to a Sub-Centre—preferably to Iceland'" (*BNW*, 81), an island in the North Atlantic between Greenland and Scandinavia. Only about 14,000 square miles smaller than Great Britain, Iceland seems large for a "'Sub-Centre.'" Bad weather and involuntary isolation make a position there a terrible job. The D.H.C. warns Bernard against further failure to maintain "'a proper standard of infantile decorum'" after working hours (*BNW*, 81). Iceland is clearly a negative place, ideal only for exile. Too uncivilized to be Sub-Centres, Samoa and the Trobriands were nevertheless used as positive locales, twin embarrassments that make the technologically proficient brave new world seem primitive psychologically.

Initially "undismayed," Bernard dismisses the D.H.C.'s warning as "just a threat"; no one gets "transferred for things like that," he rationalizes

(*BNW*, 81). Yet when he learns that the D.H.C. has been "'looking out for someone to take [his] place'" (85), Bernard wails to Lenina, "'I'm going to be sent to Iceland.'" Huxley elaborates upon the D.H.C.'s warning in order to shatter Bernard's fragile bravado and expose his fundamental cowardice. Unlike Samoa and the Trobriands, however, Iceland reappears prominently: in Chapter XVI, Bernard pleads with Mustapha Mond not to be sent there.

Chapter XII reinforces the idea of using islands for exile when the World Controller bans a paper titled "'A New Theory of Biology'" (*BNW*, 145). Its author posited "some intensification and refining of consciousness" as the "purpose" of earthly existence, a position that foreshadows the later Huxley's. By comparison, the brave new world's *summum bonum*, "maintenance of well-being," seems shallow. Lest the biologist's heretical ideas unsettle brave new worlders, his "'transference to the Biological Station of St. Helena may become necessary,'" Mond writes across the censored pages. Marx's potential exile sounded like a casual threat, no thought having been given to a society's systematic use of islands as a dumping ground for misfits and malcontents. Here that comic stroke has developed into an administrative policy for dealing with undesirables. But when Huxley increased the role of islands, they had to accept gifted overachievers like the biologist, not just slackers like Bernard, while still remaining strictly punitive.

A British island of forty-seven square miles in the South Atlantic, St. Helena was Napoleon's place of exile from 1815 until his death in 1821. For all its technological wizardry, the World State still falls back on a centuries-old method of isolating disruptive individuals. Although humane compared to solitary confinement or outright liquidation, island exile is hardly foolproof. Napoleon escaped from Elba, an Italian island in the Mediterranean, his first place of exile (1814–1815). That Mond bypasses Elba and selects St. Helena straight off indicates a willingness to learn from past mistakes, even if Henry Ford maintained that history is bunk.

In Chapter XVI, prior to confessing that, as a young man, he narrowly avoided banishment to an island, Mustapha Mond gives Marx, Watson, and the Savage an account of "'the Cyprus Experiment'" (*BNW*, 182). (An island in the Mediterranean south of Turkey, Cyprus was a British colony in 1932.) On it, the Controller recalls, the brave new world set up "'the only society of Alphas'" in history (183) in the only utopian experiment ever conducted by a dystopia. The role that Cyprus plays in *Brave New World* differs substantially from the roles assigned to Samoa, the Trobriands, Iceland, and St. Helena. Samoa and the Trobriands make the brave new world's resort to elaborate mechanization look foolish. Iceland and St. Helena both emphasize exile as punishment, but the latter specializes in ostracizing brave new worlders whose excellence is unwanted, while the former appears to be reserved strictly for delinquents. Cyprus may have implanted in Huxley's mind the idea that an isolated island might be the perfect spot for utopia.

John inquires why the brave new world does not "'make everybody an Alpha Double Plus'" (*BNW*, 182). "'A society of Alphas,'" Mond responds, "'couldn't fail to be unstable and miserable.'" On this point, he says, the Cyprus Experiment, a resounding failure, "'was convincing'":

> "It began in A. F. 473. The Controllers had the island of Cyprus cleared of all its existing inhabitants and re-colonized with a specially prepared batch of twenty-two thousand Alphas. All agricultural and industrial equipment was handed over to them and they were left to manage their own affairs. The result exactly fulfilled all the theoretical predictions. The land wasn't properly worked, there were strikes in all the factories; the laws were set at naught, orders disobeyed; all the people detailed for a spell of low-grade work were perpetually intriguing for high-grade jobs, and all the people with high-grade jobs were counter-intriguing at all cost to stay where they were. Within six years they were having a first-class civil war. When nineteen out of the twenty-two thousand had been killed, the survivors unanimously petitioned the World Controllers to resume the government of the island." (182–83)

Although the long paragraph on the Cyprus fiasco seems pertinent to the discussion about islands in Chapter XVI, it remains a tour de force. Huxley takes a moment to ridicule implausible distributions of effort in the Wellsian utopia. In "A Note on Eugenics," Huxley asked:

> [Where] every individual is capable of playing the superior part, who will consent or be content to do the dirty work and obey? The inhabitants of one of Mr. Wells's numerous utopias solve this problem by ruling and being ruled, doing high-brow and low-brow work in turns. While Jones plays the piano, Smith spreads the manure. At the end of the shift they change places; Jones trudges out to the dung-heap and Smith practices the A minor Etude of Chopin. (*PS*, 281)

"An admirable state of affairs if it could be arranged" (*PS*, 281), Huxley decided. But "a state [...] of chronic civil war" (*PS*, 281) is more likely, he predicted, because a "state with a population consisting of nothing but these superior people could not hope to last for a year" (*PS*, 282), an ominous forecast for any society of superiors such as Pala. The brave new world's experiment on Cyprus confirmed anti-Wellsian prophesies Huxley delivered five years earlier in *Proper Studies*. Huxley's choice of details—"dung-heap" versus "Chopin"—makes the idea of job rotation ludicrous.

Which is more credible, Huxley asked Wells's admirers in 1932, cooperation between Jones and Smith or the Cyprus debacle?[4]

The failed experiment on Cyprus, Mond argues, justifies keeping "'eight-ninths'" of brave new worlders "'below the water-line'" (*BNW*, 183). A kind of floating island made of ice, Mond's "'iceberg'" becomes Huxley's anti-Wellsian model for a perfectly organized society. The Cyprus community ridicules Wellsian job rotation within a World State that is already a complex refutation of Wells's. Nearly five centuries into its existence, the brave new world implausibly considered abolishing its caste system with a universal upgrade on Cyprus. An all-Alpha society seems like a high-minded experiment in eugenics, an instance of benevolent social engineering: the twenty-two thousand Alphas were "'specially prepared'" (*BNW*, 183). But one suspects that this experiment's failure was so predictable that the project was conducted to rule out alternatives to the status quo. In 1932, "'the Cyprus Experiment'" was excellent satire that raised more questions about the role of islands in utopia than Huxley was prepared to answer. If Iceland and St. Helena exist respectively for misfits like Bernard and overachievers like the marine biologist, who does what Huxley called "the dirty work" (*PS*, 281) on either?

When the Palanese address the problem of high-brow, low-brow work, the solution is deceptively Wellsian. "'Changing jobs,'" Dr. Robert MacPhail emphasizes for Will Farnaby's edification, holds the key (*I*, 148). "'[M]ost people like it better than doing one kind of job all their lives,'" he adds, which would be news to the Cyprians. The crucial difference is that the Palanese switch occupations willingly because they find changes therapeutic. "'Maximum efficiency'" suffers in that everyone is always "'part-time,'" Dr. Robert admits, but "'human satisfaction,'" all realize, takes precedence. Vijaya testifies that he enjoyed doing "'four months'" in a "'cement plant,'" followed by "'six months in the jungle, as a lumberjack'" (*I*, 148). In his younger days, Dr. Robert recalls, he "'did a stint at the copper smelters,'" then worked on "'a fishing boat. Sampling all kinds of work—it's part of everybody's education,'" he maintains (*I*, 148); "'[o]ne learns an enormous amount […] about all kinds of people and their ways of thinking,'" provided, of course, this is society's agreed-upon goal. Evidently, the Controllers never thought to condition Cyprian Alphas to enjoy spells of menial labor. Vijaya and Dr. Robert concur that physical toil benefits Pala's intelligentsia. Both have been out doing "'muscular work'" in the fields (142). "'In Pala,'" explains Dr. MacPhail, "'even a professor, even a government official, generally puts in two hours of digging'" every day (143). This sounds absurd until one compares diurnal digging with "'two rounds of Obstacle Golf,'" the compulsory daily distraction for brave new worlders (*BNW*, 46).

When Mond tells Marx, Watson, and the Savage that in his youth, having conducted unauthorized physics experiments, he was "'on the point of being sent to an island'" (*BNW*, 185), Huxley confirmed the role of islands as a destination for the inconveniently talented. Bernard, in trouble for his part in the *soma* riot at the Park Lane Hospital, feels his old fears revive at the mention of islands. "'You can't send *me*. [...] Oh, please don't send me to Iceland,'" he sobs, as if his Fordship knew the details of the D.H.C.'s earlier warning. Iceland remains for Bernard a geographical bugbear. But in Chapter XVI, the kind of island to which Mond was nearly sent sounds more exciting than the dead-end demotion proposed by the Director of Hatcheries and Conditioning. Because one can be dispatched to an island for displaying initiative and originality, the question again arises: which is island exile after all—reward or punishment?

"'But *you* didn't go to an island,'" the Savage reminds Mond in Chapter XVI. The Controller admits that he regretfully sacrificed "'pure science'" in exile for a position on the Controllers' Council (*BNW*, 186). He makes transference sound more attractive than duty. Indeed, when Mond sentences Marx and Watson, being consigned to an island begins to seem like a blessing. Huxley alters banishment from the worst possible fate to a prize in disguise: "'punishment,'" says Mond, that is "'really a reward'" (186). Watson will be "'sent to an island'" the Controller decrees:

> "That's to say, he's being sent to a place where he'll meet the most interesting set of men and women to be found anywhere in the world. All the people who, for one reason or another, have got too self-consciously individual to fit into community-life. All the people who aren't satisfied with orthodoxy, who've got independent ideas of their own. Everyone, in a word, who's anyone. I almost envy you, Mr. Watson." (186)

Were it not for the "'almost,'" the reader might take Mond at his word and be envious also. Watson, he implies, is a privileged misfit. Earlier, he wasted no such sentiments on the marine biologist slated for St. Helena. "'It's lucky,'" Mond now muses, "'that there are such a lot of islands in the world. I don't know what we should do without them'" (*BNW*, 187). Huxley, it seems, did not know exactly what to do with them; their role diversified as they multiplied.[5]

Mond offers Watson a choice of destinations: "'[t]he Marquesas, for example, or Samoa,'" both renowned for "'a tropical climate'" (*BNW*, 187). (The Marquesas are a group of French islands in the South Pacific, where one also finds Samoa, another island group.) Conceivably, Helmholtz is being awarded a vacation in paradise. He surprises Mond by choosing the equivalent of Iceland. When Mond asks, "'What about the Falkland Islands?'" Watson decides, "'Yes, I think that will do'" (188). He believes that he will "'write better'" in bad weather. (A group of islands in the southwest Atlantic to the east of Argentina, the Falklands were a British colony in 1932.) "'[O]fficially'" Mond disapproves of Watson's choice but admires his "'spirit'" (188). John the Savage is not so lucky. Mond denies his request to "'to go to the islands'" with Marx and Watson. When John's efforts to isolate himself in a Surrey lighthouse, in effect creating an island on land, fail dismally, the would-be islander commits suicide, the sole instance in *Brave New World* where *not* being sent to an island proves worse than being sentenced to one.

From the first, Huxley conceived of the novel's climax in Chapter XVII as a debate between opposing value systems: Mond represents the ideas of H. G. Wells, Henry Ford, Freud, Pavlov, and Mond's namesake, the industrial magnate, Sir Alfred Mond; whereas John speaks for Shakespeare's conception of art and the life-worshipper's philosophy of D. H. Lawrence. However, in spring and summer 1931, between 27 May and 24 August (see Meckier, "Americanization," *MSN*, 180), late in an extensive revision process, Huxley decided to bolster Watson's role as a potential third alternative[6] to the "insanity" of a Fordian utopia, on the one hand, and the "lunacy" of an Indian village in Lawrence's beloved American southwest on the other (*BNW*, vii-viii). Thanks most likely to this revision, an island holds out to Watson a liberating opportunity for mental and spiritual advancement much as Pala in *Island* will prove rehabilitative for Will Farnaby.

In Chapter XVI, as it stands, Watson, Marx, and John are present at the start of the conversation with Mond. Then only Mond and the Savage talk in a section probably written *before* the chapter's opening pages. Huxley brought Watson and Marx back into the discussion for the chapter's third section, breaking up the talk with Bernard's hysterical collapse at the mention of islands (see "Americanization," *MSN*, 182). Originally, on pages written earlier, Mond may have outlined "'the Cyprus Experiment'" for the Savage's benefit only. That would explain why the account of this disaster jars against Mond's subsequent praise for Watson's upcoming destination. If a batch of specially prepared Alphas fared miserably on Cyprus, one wonders how a unit composed of disgruntled Alphas like Watson can do better on the Falklands. Possibly, Huxley wrote about Cyprus when parodying Wells was his top priority, that is, before Watson's prospects for enlightenment improved and the Falklands became more sanctuary than punishment.

The point to underline is that Huxley seems to have expanded the positive role of islands as Helmholtz Watson's importance to the novel increased. His burgeoning poetic urge presages spiritual growth. When Watson writes his first poem in Chapter XII, he embarks on the expansion of consciousness called for by the marine biologist.[7] The spectacle of Marx "on his knees before the Controller," begging for "'another chance'" (*BNW*, 185), completed a key aspect of Huxley's revision process. Originally, the plot called for a rebellious Bernard, prompted by the Savage, to pose a real threat to the World State (see "Americanization," 435). Now Marx collapses, the Savage and Mond will argue to a standstill; only Watson still shows promise. In short, when Huxley proceeded to devastate Bernard and heroicize Helmholtz, he found island exile a useful vehicle for embarrassing the former and exalting the latter.

The narrative voice in *A Modern Utopia*, presumably that of Wells's utopic alter ego, justifies his model society's reliance on "islands of exiles" to dispose of criminals and failures (*AMU*, 174). He maintains that a modern utopia must "purge itself." But Wells's alter ego reluctantly acknowledges that "there is much dissatisfaction with our isolation of criminals on islands" (278). When Huxley improved upon Wells's idea, he foresaw additional possibilities for islands depending on whether the malcontent was a scapegrace like Marx or, like Watson, a poet and nascent mystic. Inability to envision island exile as a complicated issue, Huxley implied, negated Wells as a practitioner of the discussion novel of ideas.[8]

When Huxley imagined Pala as an island, he resolved the separation issue posed by islands, the question of rewards versus punishment left unsettled in *Brave New World*. As the World State's opposite or "reverse,"[9] Pala's policies systematically correct the former's mistakes. Pala stands out as an alternative to the brave new world's negative usage of Iceland and St. Helena. Bypassing the Falklands, Huxley did not hesitate to choose a tropical setting for his ideal society. His final island depends for its appeal on a meticulous working out of the Controller's guilty admiration for the "'most interesting'" islanders whom the soon-to-be exiled Watson is scheduled to meet (*BNW*, 186). That is how the utopist wanted readers to regard the Palanese. To them, Miranda's outburst about "beauteous mankind" applies straightforwardly.[10] In *Island*, Huxley changed the role of islands from that of a virtual penal colony into what Mond hints the Falklands may prove to be: the exceptional individual's only intellectual and spiritual haven in a mad world.

Pala resolves the counterpoint between primitivism and civilization that lies at the heart of *Brave New World*: Malpais versus Fordian London, a

Lawrentian simple-lifer like the Savage versus a Wellsian *samurai* such as Mond, native psychologists such as Samoans and Trobrianders versus Our Freud. In *Beyond the Mexique Bay* (1934), Huxley wished one could combine "the virtues of primitives with those of the civilized," while exhibiting "the vices of neither" (*BMB*, 208, 211). The Palanese do this; they are Huxley's idea of noble savages. Only these islanders can be as rational and scientific as Wells's modern utopians, yet as natural and ritualistic as Trobrianders and Samoans. Thus Dr. Robert MacPhail holds forth like a good technocrat on Pala's "'"population policy,'" which combines the latest techniques in experimental farming with universal birth control to produce better foods for a "'"stable population'" (*I*, 83). At the same time, the initiation ceremony in Chapter X, where Palanese youth climb a mountain before ingesting the mind-expanding *moksha*-medicine, is the ideal community ritual. As a foretaste of enlightenment, it surpasses both the snake dance at Malpais (see *BNW*, 93) and the Solidarity Service that Bernard Marx suffers through in Chapter V. As spiritually enlightened, technologically proficient primitives, Palanese islanders outstrip Wells's *samurai*. They are not only Huxley's improvement on Lawrence's Indians of the North American southwest but also upon Samoans and Trobrianders; mentioned once and then mostly forgotten, both receive their due in *Island* when Huxley ties up a loose end from *Brave New World*.[11]

Huxley strove throughout *Island* to be more consistent in his thinking about islands than he had been in *Brave New World*. With Pala, he scolded Wells for dealing in monolithic utopias[12]; yet he also scoffed at Austin Tappan Wright's cult classic, *Islandia*, for overestimating an island utopia's chances for survival. The challenge was to disown Wells's brand of utopia without seeming complicit with him when also parodying Wright—in effect cancelling both the World-state and the island utopia. Huxley's solution was to present *Island* as a modification of Sir Thomas More's eponymous *Utopia*: Pala is modern enough to offer a third alternative to Wells's scientific propaganda, on the one hand, and realistic enough to counter Wright's romantic fantasy on the other.

"No less than a planet," Wells pontificated, "will serve the purpose of a modern Utopia. Time was when a mountain valley or an *island* seemed to promise sufficient isolation for a polity to maintain itself intact from outward force" (*AMU*, 11; italics added). Worldwide utopia, Huxley countered, almost certainly entails some measure of totalitarianism.[13] Authorities define perfection crudely and impose it on their charges. A small island, Pala is made up of even smaller constituencies.[14] In "'a federation of self-governing units,'" Dr. MacPhail explains, there is "'no place for any kind of dictator at the head of a centralized government'" (*I*, 146).

Ranga, one of several islanders to engage Will Farnaby in expository conversations more like lectures, admits that Pala "'has been extraordinarily lucky.'" Next-door neighbor Rendang was overrun in turn by Arabs, Portuguese, Dutch, and English, but the Palanese escaped these "'infestations'" (*I*, 82) because their island was more difficult to reach. Consequently, Pala has not been victimized by planters and "'foreign administrators'"; her soil has not been subjected to "'systematic exhaustion.'" Still, Huxley's preference for an island utopia is compromised by Ranga's suspicion that Pala's survival has been a fluke. Huxley contends that Wells's demand for "a planet" is dangerous to human liberty, yet he must attribute his ideal society's continued existence, her non-absorption into the so-called community of nations, mostly to luck. Nor, to recall Wells's words, can he "promise sufficient isolation […] to maintain [Pala itself] intact" from outsiders (*AMU*, 11). In the closing chapter, when Rendang annexes Pala, Wells's warnings turn out to be accurate. His World-state is the best choice in *A Modern Utopia*, Huxley chided, because it is the only choice; in *Island*, however, the best choice does not remain viable for long. The novel reads like a requiem, a parody of the planetary World-state that could also serve as a post-mortem for the island utopia.

Although Mr. Bahu's lecture-like talk with Will about Pala's status precedes Ranga's, it is the bleaker of two assessments. Rendang's "Voltairean" ambassador argues that Pala "'is out of context, […] completely irrelevant to the present situation of the world in general'" (*I*, 58). As long as it stayed "'completely off the map,'" Pala could survive. That is, Bahu resumes, "'[s]o long as it remains out of touch with the rest of the world, an ideal society can be a viable society. Pala was completely viable, I'd say, until about 1905. Then in less than a single generation, the world completely changed,'" thanks to movies, cars, airplanes, radio. "'By 1930 any clear-sighted observer could have seen that for three quarters of the human race, freedom and happiness were almost out of the question. […] What was once a viable ideal is now no longer viable,'" Bahu concludes (58).

The ambassador sums up viability the way Wells did: as a synonym for isolation. His choice of "'1905'" as the last time an island utopia stood a chance seems to validate the World-state in *A Modern Utopia*, which was published that year. Picking "'1930'" as the cut-off date for the human race to be simultaneously free and happy, Bahu endorses *Brave New World*; published two years later, it presented "'freedom and happiness'" as one of life's fundamental counterpoints. In the novel's climactic debate, Mond champions happiness while John is willing to be unhappy if free. In *Island*, Huxley rejected Wells's call for global utopia only to appear to allow Pala to crumble in apparent accord with his rival's forecast.

Actually, Huxley's use of an island for utopia amounts to the conscientious revival of an anachronism whose time, he believed, had come again—in the real world Pala must be overcome, but in the realm of the imagination, in the genre of the utopia, an island could still function as the *hypothetical* alternative that utopia originally was meant to be. In 1962, Huxley returned utopian thinking to what it had been before 1905, when Wells got his hands on it. He charged Wells with replacing open-minded intellectual discussion with self-interested predictions: the future not only foreseen by H. G. Wells but also designed by him. *Brave New World* parodies the sort of utopia Wells wanted; *Island* attacks Wells's kind of utopian thinking.

To re-orient twentieth-century literary utopianism, Huxley measured Austin Tappan Wright as well as H. G. Wells against Sir Thomas More. He contended that *Island* satisfies More's criteria in ways that Wells's *A Modern Utopia* and Wright's *Islandia* do not. Huxley parodied the plot governing Wright's first five hundred pages by darkening the success for Islandia in remaining un-Westernized into catastrophe for Pala. When the latter is overrun by neighboring militaristic Rendang at the instigation of the West's oil companies, Huxley exposed to ridicule Wright's naiveté much as he had done with Wells's unacknowledged totalitarianism earlier. Wells overlooked authoritarian propensities in planet-wide utopia; Wright seemed oblivious to an island utopia's fragility in an age of imperialism. At the start of the twentieth century, Islandia is threatened by imperialistic nations but survives; when multi-national corporations endanger Pala in the 1950s, Rendang engulfs her.

Huxley risked seeming even less consistent about islands than he had been in *Brave New World*: first he preferred an island utopia to a planetary one, then he collapsed his island utopia for being vulnerable, just as Wells said anything smaller than a planet would be. Huxley was not contradicting himself, however. Although planet-wide utopia would be a genuine nightmare, a disaster that had to be forestalled, a utopia such as Pala had to remain imaginary, indeed, a daydream, because Huxley believed that ideals ought not to be presented as enduring entities. To Huxley's way of thinking, "negative" utopia, thanks largely to Wells, had become a distinct possibility by 1932, whereas, thirty years later, "positive" utopia was as impractical as ever.[15] The modern utopist's task, therefore, was to ridicule "negative" utopias without deluding readers into expecting impossibly "positive" ones.

Unfortunately, no hard evidence exists for Huxley having read *Islandia*, Wright's life's work. For its 1942 publication, eleven years after the author's death, his daughter slenderized a manuscript of 600,000 words into a volume that still runs over 900 pages. The similarity in the titles cannot be coincidental. Surely Huxley was calling attention to a source that presented a target for *Island* just as *Men Like Gods* did for *Brave New World*. Lawrence C. Powell, librarian at UCLA, provides a tenuous link. One of Wright's strongest admirers, Powell praised *Islandia* for its telling "critique of our industrial civilization, Puritan morality, and business ethics" (Powell, 701). Huxley liked Powell and relied upon his services. In July 1956 he wrote "Dear Larry" asking for help in locating several books for a "literary project" he had "just begun," presumably *Island* (*L*, 799). Huxley does not specify *Islandia* but Powell may have recommended Wright's novel once he learned the nature of Huxley's project.

In 1907, John Lang, recently graduated from Harvard, secures an appointment as American Consul to Islandia, vaguely described as being situated on the northern portion of the Karain subcontinent in the southern hemisphere. For two years, the longest an outsider is allowed to visit, Lang will also operate as "agent" for his uncle Joseph's company and for American "commercial" interests in general (Wright, 25). They desire to sell the non-industrialized Islandians labor-saving equipment, such as agricultural implements and sewing machines. In return, American and European companies hope to investigate "the possibilities of oil" (Wright, 300). Islandia has been given an ultimatum by the West: she must either ratify the Mora Treaty granting concessions to outside interests, as Lord Mora's pro-Western party wishes, or decide to keep her exclusionist laws in place, as Lord Dorn's followers recommend. If they do the latter, disappointed French and German concessionaires may goad their governments into invading.

At the start of *Island*, a freakish sailing accident washes Will Farnaby ashore on Pala so that he can infiltrate "the Forbidden Island" closed to all Westerners (*I*, 122). Considerably older than Lang, the jaded, cynical Farnaby, ostensibly a journalist, is also a "secret agent" (*I*, 111)[16] for Joe Aldehyde's Southeast Asia Petroleum, which covets the rights to Pala's rich oil deposits. If Will can assist Pala's "'pro-oil minority'" to reverse the island's policy of granting "'[n]o oil concessions to anyone,'" "'Uncle Joe,'" as he calls his employer, will give him a year's sabbatical in which he can return to serious literature (*I*, 26, 105).

Lang and Farnaby both work for an avuncular businessman variously named Uncle Joseph, Joe Aldehyde, and "'Uncle Joe,'" the nickname

Churchill and Roosevelt coined for Stalin. Thanks to Islandia, Lang begins to develop into the high-minded writer-journalist Farnaby once was; he supplies American newspapers with even-handed articles about deliberations over the Mora Treaty. Joe Aldehyde is greedier and less scrupulous than Lang's uncle, a not especially virulent caricature of America's burgeoning materialism at the start of the twentieth century. Farnaby and Lang both feel increasingly guilty about betraying their hosts. However, the latter's decision to resign as consul and his uncle's representative comes easier than Will's "twinge of conscience" for "plotting" to "subvert" Pala (*I*, 85). Wright has Lang choose the right side: Lord Dorn's policy triumphs without repercussions. Farnaby helps to destroy Pala against the dictates of his conscience. Although he secedes from the pro-oil conspiracy he at first abetted, it succeeds despite his change of heart; his conversion cannot alter anything. Unlike Lang, Farnaby ultimately chooses the losing side, which—Huxley implies, contrary to Wright—is what the right side often is.

Initially, Lang feels that "a country so civilized as Islandia in a world growing so small could not avoid commercial contacts" (Wright, 155). His point of view resembles Bahu's and Wells's. Before long, however, Lang, a would-be Islandian, finally declares: "'I want Islandia unchanged'" (Wright, 459), that is, pre-industrial, non-commercial. There are no real villains in Wright's island. In the climactic debate at the novel's mid-point, civility reigns. Lord Mora insists that Islandia must immerse herself in "'the stream of progress'" or be destroyed by it (Wright, 445); Lord Dorn warns against letting in syndicates because he fears a take-over. After the exclusionists win by a narrow vote, both sides cooperate peacefully. Islandia will continue without outside interference as it has for centuries, an outcome Huxley considered preposterous.

In short, by an orderly vote of 23–11, Islandia's councilors turn down concession-seekers from France, Germany, and America. Islandia is allowed to remain isolated, unmolested. The island trades with no one; it accepts a maximum of one hundred immigrants a year. In contrast, Mr. Bahu—Rendang's ambassador is also a member of the pro-oil conspiracy—describes Pala as "'a small island completely surrounded by twenty-nine hundred million mental cases'" (*I*, 68). It is a doomed anomaly by the 1950s, fated to fall victim to the West's imperialist greed. Which scenario, Huxley asked, is more likely, peaceful prosperity for Islandia or Rendang's annexation of Pala?

The remaining five hundred pages of *Islandia* did not interest Huxley. Lang has an affair with Nattana and distinguishes himself in a skirmish with the Bants, a band of marauding savages less dangerous than Rendang. In

1909, his visa having expired, Lang leaves Islandia for America where he goes to work in his uncle's New York office. Although he likes the taste of success, even purchasing an automobile, he comes to his senses in time to turn down Uncle Joseph's offer of a partnership in order to go back to Islandia, in his words "'to live the rest of my life'" (Wright, 801). With him, he takes Gladys Hunter, a not especially interesting American girl whom he corresponded with during his stay in Islandia. In the last hundred pages, Lang buys Lay River Farm from Lord Dorn's son, his best friend since they were undergraduates at Harvard. He settles down to an uneventful existence. His marriage begins to work smoothly. Johnlang and Gladysa, as they are now known, resolve to have a child.

In the closing pages of *Island*, Dr. Robert MacPhail, a Prospero figure who epitomizes Palanese values, is summarily shot by soldiers from Rendang. Will's future with Susila, Dr. Robert's widowed daughter-in-law, the Miranda figure in Huxley's novel, remains uncertain. Wright's ending shows an American couple beginning a new life, Adam and Eve in the uncommercialized garden of Islandia. Anti-Miltonic to the core, Huxley depicts Will and Susila stranded in a lost paradise which Farnaby has helped to destroy. When *Island* was still a work-in-progress, Huxley knew that a utopia in the actual world could never succeed as well as Wright's: "I'm afraid," he told the *Paris Review*, "it must end with paradise lost—if one is to be realistic" (W/F, 199).

Huxley felt that Wright allowed romantic fantasy to prevail in the face of harsh fact. Admittedly, Johnlang and Gladysa fall in love not just with each other but also with all things Islandian. Huxley doubtless admired Wright's anti-consumerism and the sexual freedom he grants Islandians. But Pala, says Huxley, is what really would happen to some place like Islandia. Pro-oilers take over by force, disrupting the spiritual progress Will is making with Susila's help. Rendang's Colonel Dipa stages a coup with the approval of Murugan, Pala's teen-age Raja. Seizing power before coming legally of age, the dangerously immature Murugan dreams of transforming the island into "'a Modern State'" (*I*, 75). This sounds Wellsian but is actually worse: seventy-five percent of the oil royalties will finance an "'intensive programme of industrialization'" (*I*, 46) that will emphasize the production of weapons of mass destruction.

While Islandia will flourish forever, the island of Pala, from being the best place, turns into one of the worst. Pala submits to a faction that caters to the imperialist West's politicians, tycoons, generals, and moneylenders, whom Farnaby damns collectively as "'the cyanide of the earth'" (*I*, 81). Unlike Wright, Huxley realized that an island utopia can never be blameless;

its goodness is an affront that neighbors will not abide. "*Too* good—that was their crime," Will decides about the Palanese, using "crime" ironically but not inadvisedly. Though entirely commendable, Pala nevertheless resembles the unsustainable private worlds that Huxley's eccentric characters are always setting up in order to reconfigure reality to suit themselves (see Meckier, *SS*, 12–26). Where Lang becomes a staunch defender of Islandia, Farnaby, states Huxley, is "the serpent in the garden" (W/F, 199). Poisonous imperialists, goodness as a reproach or insult, a remorseful, formerly serpentine protagonist—these are grave matters beyond Wright's ken, Huxley's parodic reworking seems to say.

Speaking against the Mora Treaty, Lord Dorn argues that "'the inner life of Islandia'" would be ruined by the "'disease of commercialization and industrialization,'" each a "'contamination'" (Wright, 462). Compared to the internal life of the Palanese, a society of mystics well versed in Buddhism and Vedanta, the religio-philosophical attitudes of Islandians seem superficial. But Huxley elaborated upon Lord Dorn's disease metaphor. Farnaby "can be seen as a diseased cell which the body of the Palanese state neutralizes too late. By then some of its other cells have been seriously infected; Will gives Murugan and the Rani [his mother] badly needed assurances of Western financial backing" (Meckier, "Cancer in Utopia," *MSN*, 295). A cancerous agent encourages the island's internal enemies to join forces with their allies in Rendang. *Island* is full of cancer imagery: Lakshmi, Dr. Robert's wife, dies of the disease, as did Will's Aunt Mary. Oil itself seems a cancerous pollutant: "'the island is fairly oozing with the stuff,'" says Murugan (*I*, 45). Ironically, the Palanese cure Will, transforming him from a cynical, self-loathing Manichean into a potential contemplative with a hunger for enlightenment, but not before he has fatally infected their island.

On 11 June 1908, with Theodore Roosevelt in the White House and America the epitome of big business, John Lang records "the most important event in Islandia's history" (Wright, 437). The vote pitting exclusionists, calling themselves Utopians, against the forces for change boils down to what Lang calls a

> test of a nation's right to be individualistic, to work out alone her own way of living, to refuse to yield to the new Western civilization, commercial and industrial, and to hold for itself material things, which other countries coveted, because the touch of the foreigner upon these things would endanger what she believed to be good. (Wright, 437)

Pala fails this test in the 1950s because Huxley believed that Islandia should not have passed it so easily in 1908. Although vastly superior to

Islandians intellectually and spiritually, the Palanese yield to "Western civilization" and their island loses control of its materials. Bahu, one remembers, conceded Pala's viability "'until about 1905'" (*I*, 58). Wright grants Islandia three additional years before she is seriously threatened; then he extends her viability indefinitely. Pala lasts fifty years longer than Bahu's cut-off date and for half a century after Wells predicted the advent of planet-wide utopia; but Pala's demise in the 1950s made Islandia's good fortune in 1908 seem like a stay of execution.

Huxley invented Pala, one must reiterate, simultaneously to resist Wells's idea of planetary utopia and to redo Wright's island utopia more realistically. Wells and Wright had both sinned against the cardinal rules for utopian fiction as exemplified in Sir Thomas More's *Utopia*. They wrote utopias that the inventor of the genre would not have condoned: the former insisted on a planet instead of an island, whereas the latter posited an actual island instead of a purely conjectural one. Formerly called Abraxa, More's Utopia became an island because King Utopus, who gave the place its new name, dug up fifteen miles of territory so that the sea could surround the land (see *U*, 56). Apparently, the king thought Utopia would be more secure reconfigured as an island. Following More, Huxley insisted that his last novel is really about "the precariousness of happiness, the perilous position of any utopian island in the context of the modern world."[17]

Island utopias become more secure in proportion to the difficulty in finding them. Not even More knew exactly where Utopia is located, most likely because it is a figment of his imagination. Raphael Hythloday, a seasoned mariner, told More about his journey to the island of Utopia in the New World, where he lived "'five years and more'" (*U*, 52). But Hythloday is even harder to find than his fabulous island because he, too, may be imaginary. More neglected to obtain latitude and longitude. Now it is rumored that Hythloday, whose name translates as "expert in nonsense" (*U*, xxii), has perished at sea.

Wells dodged the topography issue by presenting modern utopia as his better self's dream-vision. Nevertheless, the locus is clearly England in a future that Wells implies will materialize shortly. In her "Afterword," Sylvia Wright tried to align John Lang with More's Hythloday, but the joke falls flat. Lang, she observes, assumed "that everyone knows where [Islandia] is," so he never mentions "latitude and longitude" (Wright, 944). Presumably, Pala lies somewhere in the vicinity of the Samoan and Trobriand islands mentioned favorably in *Brave New World*.[18] Of these three, only Huxley—not Wells or Wright—stressed his utopia's inaccessibility in More-like fashion. Pala's "rock-bound coast" has only one "sandy beach" surrounded by steep cliffs (*I*, 12). This is both the "forbidden island" (*I*, 11) and a very forbidding place. Swept ashore when his boat overturns, Will jokes that "'Providence was on [his] side'" (*I*, 22)[19] but, as it turns out, not on Pala's.

More's Utopia is nowhere to be found because he implied that the imagination is the ideal place for it. Though written in Latin, *Utopia* is famously founded on a Greek pun: if one spells the *u* in u-topus (place) as *ou*, it means "no place"; if the *u* is *eu*, it means "the good place." More wished to suggest that "the good place" must always be "no place," a mental construct impossible, perhaps inadvisable, to attain. Huxley gave More's pun a cynical twist when he modeled the conclusion of *Island* after *Paradise Lost*. He confirmed More in that by novel's end, "the good place" is "no place" again. The more Will Farnaby and the reader learn to appreciate Pala, the closer the novel inches towards the island's extinction. Indeed for the reader, Pala is becoming "the good place" and "no place" at the same time.

In *A Modern Utopia*, Huxley objected, the World-state violates More's practice and intention twice over. Seen correctly, it is not a fine place but an awful one as the parodist revealed in *Brave New World*; moreover, instead of being nowhere, it was everywhere, not far off in time or space but proximate and imminent.[20] Wells had the audacity to call attention to its ubiquity by scornfully dismissing the More-like "Nowheres"—Butler's *Erewhon*, William Morris's *News From Nowhere*—on which pre-modern utopists wasted time and effort before Darwin "quickened the thought of the world" (*AMU*, 5). In short, complained Huxley, Wells made utopia the inevitable product of a strictly scientific evolution that he was speeding up. As for Wright, he pretended Islandia actually existed; real countries—Germany, France, America—have consulates there. Islandia allegedly will continue to be a somewhere, a prospect Huxley considered escapist.[21]

Transforming "no place" into every place or presuming that a romanticized best place could persevere indefinitely were, to Huxley's way of thinking, equally fatuous undertakings. "From More to Bellamy," he lectured, "from the Republic to the Phalansteries and the world of 1984, there is no utopian blue-print for a better world or an organized hell upon earth that could ever be fully actualized" ("Utopias," 3).[22] This sweeping generalization implies two things: first, fabricating a perfect society should remain a literary exercise, an intellectual pastime, as it was for More, and not become a matter of community planning; secondly, human nature may be too complex to be fully subjected to any utopic scheme, whether agreeable or diabolical, despite Berdiaeff's warning in the epigraph to *Brave New World* that "Utopias are realizable" and that twentieth-century "Life marches towards them." Contrary to Wright and Wells, Huxley urged a return to a type of utopian speculation more in accordance with More's.

His classic island utopia, a forum for the discussion of ideas, may be regarded as "a humorous, even satirical critique of European society" (*U*, xxi). A playful venue, More's *Utopia* is best read as a series of suggestions rather than a warning, prediction, manifesto, or blueprint.[23] Yet no one did more than H. G. Wells to convert the literary utopia into a prophecy. More's communism, for example, sounds highly theoretical, but the Professor of Foresight, as Huxley disdainfully christened Wells, stands squarely behind the scientifically planned archetype of the welfare state outlined in *A Modern Utopia*.[24] Wellsian proposals are "a soap-bubble" (*AMU*, 352) that eventually bursts, leaving him—i.e., his real self, not his utopian double—back in the England of 1905. But Wells's advocacy of his predictions and his confidence in their accuracy are never in doubt. Huxley described *Brave New World* "as a parody" that "got out of hand" (W/F, 198) once he began playing Wells's game by making predictions of his own. Following many of the criteria for a perfect society set down in the opening pages of *A Modern Utopia*, he produced a "negative Nowhere, a Utopia in reverse" ("Utopias," 1) very different from Wells's allegedly perfect society. Huxley's return in *Island* to an island utopia amounts not just to a preference for island over planet, but also for More before Wells, classical utopia more than modern and, above all, *hypothesis* over prediction. These preferences did not stop Huxley from issuing *Brave New World Revisited* in 1958 to show that his predictions from 1932 were unfortunately coming true daily. Nor was Huxley deterred from telling George Orwell that "the nightmare" of *Brave New World* was more likely in the long run than that of *Nineteen Eighty-Four* (*L*, 605). But *Island* is always an hypothesis, never a forecast except of Pala's inevitable demise.

Huxley knew the real problem facing the utopist: to develop just enough story to avoid seeming "'"exceedingly didactic and expository."'"[25] The first half of *Islandia*, the tale of an island's struggle to remain independent of outside interests, supplied a plot Huxley could parody. He could dismiss Wright as a pseudo-Lawrentian reactionary. Not only fantastic, Islandia is also anti-progressive. In everything from agriculture to human relationships, the Palanese champion enlightened progress, indeed, progress towards enlightenment. They can do so because Huxley, like More but not Wright and more so than Wells, was a genuine polymath, a man for all seasons, a wide-ranging thinker equally well versed in philosophy, politics, economics, and the sciences, not to mention world literature and oriental religions. In *Island*, Huxley wonders what a society would look like that adopted the lovemaking techniques of the Oneida community, applied W. H. Sheldon's science of human natures, practiced universal, state-supported birth control, made eugenic use of artificial insemination to upgrade the gene pool, revolutionized methods for teaching and farming, and subscribed to Vedanta's perennial philosophy with some Buddhist supplements. Compared with this eclectic recipe, its ingredients drawn from diverse fields, Wells's heavily scientific approach seems narrow and one-pointed, whereas Wright's emphasis on simplicity is revealed to be over-simplification.

In Huxley's final role for an island, Pala may be considered a kind of *hybrid*.[26] Clearly a good place, it abruptly ceases to be a place when Murugan and Colonel Dipa replace it with the "'United Kingdom of Rendang and Pala'" (*I*, 284). Utopia is nowhere not everywhere, no place not everyplace, Huxley tells Wells. It is imaginary, not real and definitely not indestructible, he cautions Wright. Yet Pala, as a synthesis of classical and modern, remains a blueprint of sorts: the Palanese are what human beings might be capable of becoming if they endeavored to live up to their potentialities and were permitted to do so, two unlikelihoods in Huxley's estimation.

Writing to Dr. Humphry Osmond on 14 December 1960, Huxley referred to the Palanese as "my hypothetical islanders" (*L*, 899), a term one may also apply retrospectively to prospective islanders, malcontents such as Bernard Marx and Helmholtz Watson. Throughout *Brave New World*, Huxley pondered the usefulness of islands in utopian speculations. Finally, he settled on an island as his perfect place, provided it was imaginary or at least virtually inaccessible. Utopia, he decided, cannot be everywhere; nor can it ever be far enough from everywhere else. "Hypothetical" remains the key word for the Palanese; they and not Wells's *samurai* or Wright's Islandians are the true successors to More's elusive Utopians.[27]

---

1 Aldous Huxley, *Brave New World* (London: Chatto & Windus, 1950; with Huxley's 1946 "Foreword"), 35. [*BNW*] "Flivver" is slang for a small, old, and inexpensive auto.

2 See Mead, 44–45, and Jerome Meckier, "Coming of Age in Pala," *MSN*, 74.

3 Aldous Huxley, *Island* (London: Chatto & Windus, 1962), 90. [*I*]

4 Here the Controller, a caricature of Wells's idealized technocrats such as the *samurai* in *A Modern Utopia*, seems to side with Huxley against Wells.

5 Islands for dissidents are "powerful utopian elements" in Huxley's dystopia, Peter Firchow argues ("Brave at Last," 157), but does not elaborate.

6 See "Helmholtz Watson's 'Mental Excess': A Third Alternative," Section III of Meckier, "Our Ford, Our Freud," *MSN*, 149–64.

[7] See Meckier, "Poetry in the Future," *PM*, 236–42.

[8] In his introduction to *A Modern Utopia*, Mark R. Hillegas points out that Wells claimed to be combining the utopia with "the discussion novel" developed by Peacock and Mallock (*AMU*, xxxiii).

[9] Huxley told interviewers that Pala was "a kind of reverse brave new world" (W/F, 198). For a discussion of the reversals, see Meckier, *SS*, 199–205.

[10] See Shakespeare's *The Tempest*, V, i, 184–87.

[11] See Meckier, "*Brave New World* and the Anthropologists," *MSN*, 225–40, and "Coming of Age in Pala," *MSN*, 259–73.

[12] According to Warren Wagar, whom Mark R. Hillegas quotes in his introduction, Wells's "'great contribution'" to the utopian tradition was "'the concept of the World State'" (*AMU*, xi).

[13] Robert S. Baker credited Huxley with detecting "the political dystopia hidden within Wells's scientific utopia" (*BNWHSD*, 45).

[14] For Donald Watt, "an island" is one of the richest symbols in Huxley's last novel (Watt, 155). It symbolizes the isolation of the individual and of the Palanese as a society; but it also signifies a potential unity in that islands are connected beneath the sea.

[15] According to Erik Reece, "close to two hundred utopian communities sprang to life [in America alone] from 1820 to 1850" (Reece, 4). Little more than communes, most appear to have misunderstood More.

[16] The allusion to *The Secret Agent* is one of many to Conrad that add a sinister note not found in Wright; see Meckier, "Conradian Reminders in Aldous Huxley's *Island*," *MSN*, 274–92.

[17] See Huxley's letter for 19 January 1962 to Ian Parsons at Chatto & Windus (*L*, 928).

[18] Peter Firchow positioned Pala near the Andaman Islands in the Indian Ocean close to Sumatra but suggested that Huxley actually had Bali in mind as a model ("Brave at Last," 172). Bali is an island in Indonesia, to the east of Java. Huxley told the *Paris Review* that Pala is "an imaginary island between Ceylon and Sumatra" (W/F, 198).

[19] Will's allusion to Samuel Butler's *Erewhon*—"'Remember the beginning of Erewhon,'" says Farnaby: "'As luck would have it, Providence was on my side'" (*I*, 22)—deepens the irony. For the Erewhonians, Higgs's advent, which he considers providential for him, is a mixed blessing, not the misfortune Farnaby's brings to Pala.

[20] Peter Firchow pointed out that classical utopias are set in "no time" as well as in "no place" (*End*, 84). Starting with Wells, however, dates became increasingly important. His Time Traveller reaches 802,701 A. D.; the World-state occurs by 2100, the brave new world by A. F. 632, Orwell's Oceania by 1984. Modern utopists presumed to tell readers not only *where* utopia would materialize but *when*.

[21] The reviewer for *Time* underlined Wright's "desire for complete escape from the actual world" (Little, 86). In the *New York Times*, *Islandia* was called "a dream-compensation" for shortcomings in the American way of life (Strauss, 1, 22).

[22] In the lecture on "Utopias Positive and Negative," Huxley adopted a sarcastic tone towards both Wells and More. He ridiculed the World-state in *A Modern Utopia* as a "totalitarian" mistake ruled by "a cross between the Boy Scouts and the Society of Jesus." More's Utopia, he continued, "is administered like an old-fashioned boarding school" ("Utopias," 4).

[23] In his introduction, however, Richard Marius disparages critics who separate More's views from Hythloday's (*U*, xxi).

[24] Robert S. Baker called the Wellsian utopia "a form of prophetic history" (*BNWHSD*, 25).

[25] See Aldous's letter to his son, Matthew, quoted in Bedford, II, 248.

[26] Wells was fond of this term. In *A Modern Utopia*, he aimed for a "hybrid" of fiction and essay (*AMU*, 2). Michael Szczekalla called Pala "the hybrid civilization" of Huxley's "literary imagination" (Szczekalla, 159); from its founding, it combined the fruits of two enlightenments: that of eighteenth-century Scotland thanks to Dr. Andrew MacPhail and the Raja's Buddhist-Vedantic mysticism.

[27] Huxley would have deplored J. W. Johnson's description of Islandians as an "updated version of More's Utopians" (Johnson, 269). Naomi Jacobs considers *Islandia* an "anticipation" of plotting strategies in subsequent utopias (Jacobs, 80).

Chapter Six

Enemies of Utopia: Young Krishnamurti and Madame Blavatsky in *Island*

The impression persists that Aldous Huxley's unsparing caricatures of friends and family occurred mostly in his *romans à clef* prior to 1940.[1] Supposedly, the satirical novelist grew more charitable after abandoning the philosophy of meaninglessness to pursue fuller knowledge of man's Final End. Instead of positing pointlessness as the point of everything, Huxley sympathized with Vedanta's perennial philosophy, which teaches that unitive knowledge of the divine Ground is our common goal.[2] Unnoticed, however, is the vicious portrait in *Island* of young Krishnamurti as the obnoxious Murugan, future ruler of Pala. The attack includes a debunking of Madame Blavatsky, who appears in Huxley's last completed novel as Murugan's mother, the despicable Rani. The Raja's widow promotes a bogus religious movement, "'the World-Wide Crusade of the Spirit'"[3]; this is Huxley's derogatory version of the Theosophical Society, which Blavatsky founded, and of its offshoot, the Order of the Star in the East, which was sponsored by the Society and spearheaded by the youthful Krishnamurti.

Despite not having become of age, Murugan Mailendra seizes control of Pala in the novel's closing pages and immediately unites the utopic island with Rendang, its militaristic neighbor. With Murugan as Raja and Colonel Dipa, Rendang's strongman, as prime minister, "'the United Kingdom of Rendang and Pala'" (*I*, 284) will trade rights to its rich oil deposits for the latest Western technologies in hopes of becoming an increasingly industrial, consumer-oriented modern state. Murugan hopes to manufacture biological weapons, such as "'nerve gas,'" in order "'to make Pala strong'" (*I*, 46). Twenty-five per cent of oil royalties will go towards "'World Reconstruction'" through the Rani's "'Crusade of the Spirit,'" the "'great world movement'" that Murugan calls "'man's only hope'" (*I*, 46).[4]

Krishnamurti's career as a god-in-waiting began in 1909 when Charles Webster Leadbeater, a sort of talent scout for the Theosophical Society, spotted him playing on a beach at Adyar in India. The boy's spiritual potential, his remarkable aura, impressed the former Anglican curate. Under Madame Blavatsky's leadership, the society had charged itself with discovering the next reincarnation of the Buddha; he would return to syncretize the world's religions and thereby establish the universal brotherhood of man. Eighteen years after Blavatsky's death, Annie Besant, the new president of the Theosophical Society, acted on Leadbeater's recommendation and proclaimed the fourteen-year-old Krishnamurti the next *jagadguru* or World Teacher—the bodily vessel for Lord Maitreya's reincarnation and thus the twentieth century's Buddha.[5]

Premature Raja, impending godly reincarnation—Murugan and Krishnamurti are both tools of power-hungry fakers. No friend to peace-loving Pala, Colonel Dipa aspires to rule the entire region. The alliance with Murugan legitimizes his first power grab. Similarly, Leadbeater hoped to eclipse Mrs. Besant by usurping what had been Blavatsky's unique role. Until her death in 1891, she claimed to receive directions on running the Society and redeeming the world by psychic connection on the astral plane with the "ascended [i.e., immortal] masters," Lord Morya and Koot Hoomi, fully evolved holy men whose earthly base was located somewhere in the Tibetan Himalayas (Sawyer, 116–17). Through Krishnamurti, Leadbeater laid claim to his own pipeline to the infinite. Madame Blavatsky maintained that her book, *Isis Unveiled* (1875), had been composed for her by the Tibetan Mahatmas while she slept. Similarly, Leadbeater claimed that *At the Feet of the Masters* (1910) contained Koot Hoomi's teachings as transmitted through Krishnamurti. Leadbeater tutored the boy in worldly subjects by day, but at night Koot Hoomi allegedly instructed him in spiritual matters on the astral plane. Next morning, Leadbeater's semi-literate pupil wrote down the lessons he had been given.[6]

To deflate the take-over in the late 1950s of a pacifist island utopia by a rogue state of potential terrorists, Huxley compared Rendang's annexation of Pala to squabbles between the frauds in the Theosophical Society during the early 1900s. Simultaneously, he discredited Madame Blavatsky, Leadbeater, Annie Besant, and young Krishnamurti by magnifying their absurd activities into offences against reason and religion serious enough to destroy the perfect place. Pala's enemies are as ludicrous as Theosophists; Theosophists are supposedly as dangerous as Pala's enemies. Satire in *Island* cuts both ways: similarities with Leadbeater's tutelage of Krishnamurti undermine the gravity of Colonel Dipa's manipulation of Murugan as effectively as Dipa's manipulation of Murugan brings out the perversity in Leadbeater's tutoring.

Ragged and unpresentable when Leadbeater first saw him, Krishnamurti grew into an extremely good-looking boy, as handsome as Murugan. Having been washed ashore on Pala after a boating accident, a convalescing Will Farnaby is visited by a dark-skinned boy "[d]ressed only in white sandals, white shorts and a platinum wrist watch" (*I*, 40). He is struck by Murugan's comeliness. Nurse Radha, who once tried to seduce Murugan, tells Will: "'You've no idea how beautiful [Murugan] looks in white satin pajamas'" (*I*, 71).[7] Farnaby realizes that he met Murugan five days earlier in Rendang-Lobo, Rendang's capital, where Murugan drove Colonel Dipa's Mercedes like a "maniac." Will suspects that "'[m]y young friend Muru,'" as Dipa calls him, has been "playing Antinous" to the dictator's Hadrian (*I*, 42).[8] Leadbeater, Krishnamurti's guardian-tutor, was a notorious pederast, accused, though never convicted, of molesting young boys. He admitted teaching them to masturbate lest they commit more grievous impure acts (see Washington, 121–23).

In 1912, J. Naryaniah, Krishnamurti's father, filed suit to regain custody of his sons, Krishna and Nitya, from Mrs. Besant, to whom he had consigned them. He charged that Leadbeater had committed "unnatural" acts with Krishnamurti from 1910 onwards (Nethercot, 184). There were two sensational trials: Naryaniah won his case in India in 1913, but Mrs. Besant appealed successfully in England a year later. At the first trial, several witnesses claimed to have witnessed Leadbeater misusing young boys (see Nethercot, 173, note 1). During the second trial, both boys declared their wish to remain under Besant's supervision (see Nethercot, 200). The blatant Murugan-Dipa sexual partnership is Huxley's nasty rendition of the homosexuality implicit in the Krishnamurti-Leadbeater relationship. In an interview in 1975, Christopher Isherwood told me that he once remonstrated with Huxley over Murugan's homosexuality, which he considered gratuitous. Seen as part of an attack on Krishnamurti, it becomes relevant.

Women, especially older and rich Theosophists, loved to mother Krishnamurti when Leadbeater brought him to London. There Annie Besant formally adopted him after gaining full custody over his father's objections, in May 1914 when Krishnamurti was nineteen (see Campbell, 122). To tighten his satire, Huxley makes the Rani, the novel's Blavatsky figure, Murugan's biological mother. He is clearly a mama's boy. He chooses the Rani's idiotic religion over the mixture of Buddhism and Vedanta that serves the rest of the Palanese. Farnaby wonders if Murugan's "clutching and devouring mother" knows the extent of her son's tie to Dipa; perhaps she prefers it to a wife or girlfriend, who might "supplant her," he reasons (*I*, 57). Huxley implies that Besant may have entrusted Krishnamurti to Leadbeater for similar reasons.

When the sexually uninhibited Palanese tried to interest Murugan in girls, the Rani whisked him off to Switzerland. This hegira, the equivalent of Krishnamurti's eight-year sojourn in England (1912–1920), detrimentally westernized Murugan; he became a confirmed materialist as, to a surprising extent, was young Krishnamurti. Farnaby condemns the Rani as "a grotesque monster of a woman" for "egging […] on" her son "in the name of God and an assortment of Ascended Masters, to become a bomb-dropping spiritual crusader" (*I*, 249). Ironically, Murugan is the only Palanese adolescent never to have had a taste of enlightenment; he refuses to ingest the *moksha*-medicine, "'the reality revealer, the truth-and-beauty pill,'" because he insists it only provides a "'lot of illusions,'" nothing but "'false *samadhi*'" (*I*, 136).[9] Nevertheless, creating a war-mongering religious zealot was never Madame Blavatsky's intention with Krishnamurti. Fairly or not, Huxley insinuates that Theosophy is the sort of religion best spread by crusade or jihad.

Leadbeater brought Krishnamurti to England so that the next Buddha could attend university. Unfortunately, despite extensive cramming, the sixteen-year-old made little progress. Eventually, he failed the entrance examinations. In 1914, Cambridge and Oxford—Huxley's college, Balliol, in particular—both denied him admittance. London University subsequently followed suit in 1920 (see Nethercot, 229). Mary Lutyens, Krishnamurti's official biographer, describes the young man of 1914 unflatteringly as having been "quite vacant, childish, almost moronic, interested in nothing really except golf and motor bicycles" (Lutyens, *The Life and Death of Krishnamurti*, 160–61). She marvels that such an unpromising youth developed into an acclaimed teacher.[10] Murugan seems to have been created directly from Lutyens's description, but Huxley came first by several decades. To Maria Huxley, meeting Krishnamurti in the late 1930s, he seemed too "simple" ever to have been "treated as a prophet" (Jayakar, 88).

Murugan is said to be as self-centered as the golf-playing, motor-bicycling young Krishnamurti. He seems "too whole-heartedly concerned with himself to be able even to simulate the slightest interest in anyone else" (*I*, 40). Farnaby surprises the future raja reading the Spring and Summer Catalog of Sears, Roebuck & Co. instead of *Elementary Ecology*, the book he is supposed to be studying. The consumer's bible was a gift from Colonel Dipa. Murugan is particularly fascinated by the picture of an "'Italian Style Motor Scooter'" (*I*, 134), the match for Krishnamurti's motor bikes. In 1914, while cramming for Oxford, he was permitted to have a motor bicycle and became a first-rate mechanic (see Nethercot, 229). While Farnaby and Dr. Robert MacPhail observe a Palanese initiation ceremony, in which a party of young people climbs a mountain to mark their transition from children to adults, the ineducable Murugan peruses "a gaudily bound American magazine" titled "'Science Fiction'" (*I*, 159).

Helena Petrovna Blavatsky has been dubbed the archetypal "fraudulent guru" (Washington, 45). Huxley calls the Rani "a female tycoon" bent on cornering the market "in Pure Spirituality and the Ascended Masters" (*I*, 58). The Rani bears a strong physical resemblance to the Russian occultist.[11] The co-founder of the Theosophical Society was short, stout, forceful "with strong arms, several chins, unruly hair, a determined mouth, and large, liquid, slightly bulging eyes" (Washington, 26). When the Rani enters, Will Farnaby is struck by her "large, bulging eyes" (*I*, 49). He beholds "a large florid woman swathed […] in clouds of white muslin" and notes her "thick bejewelled fingers" (*I*, 48). Drastically overweight, Madame Blavatsky, an incessant talker like the Rani, took to wearing loose, badly fitting robes. Her hands were always covered with rings (see Washington, 41). Eventually, she tipped the scales at 17 ½ stone (nearly 250 lbs.). Murugan's mother seats herself "with all the majestic emphasis of her hundred kilograms" (roughly 220 lbs.) (*I*, 49).[12]

The daughter of the late Sultan of Rendang, the Rani was sent to Switzerland to complete her education. Mme Buloz, wife of Professor Buloz and an "intensely ardent Theosophist," introduced her husband's pupil to "the Master Koot Hoomi" (*I*, 52). His "Presence" instructed them both in the Oratory atop the Professor's house. On 23 November 1953, recalls the Rani, "'the Master came to me […] in Person'" and proclaimed "'a World Movement to save Humanity from self-destruction'" (*I*, 53). As "'the Appointed Instrument,'" the Rani has been raising money for "'the World Crusade of the Spirit'" for eight years.[13]

Madame Blavatsky's favorite ascended master, Koot Hoomi, supposedly assisted Lord Maitreya in supervising such matters as Religion, Education, and Art the world over (see Washington, 35). In Huxley's version, the Theosophical Society's world-wide mission is blatantly hypocritical and far more insidious. As a member of Pala's pro-oil minority, the Rani supports ceding mineral rights to Joe Aldehyde's South-East Asia Petroleum conglomerate. Although some of the profits will aid her "'great world movement,'" most will be spent in producing what Murugan, "with relish," calls "'absolute weapons'" (*I*, 46). His speech upon seizing power incriminates the Rani's brand of theosophy by celebrating "'Progress, Values, Oil, True Spirituality'" (*I*, 286), a bizarre confluence that Blavatsky never imagined.

A ludicrous experience in itself, the Rani's spiritual awakening conflates those of Blavatsky and Leadbeater, who claimed to have travelled, separately, for tutoring by the Ascended Masters on the astral plane. The difference is that the Master comes to the Rani in Switzerland instead of having her astral body visit him in Tibet. But the Rani's awakening also parodically resembles Krishnamurti's account of his own enlightenment. It allegedly took place on the evening of 20 August 1922 in Ojai, California, where he would later settle and teach. Krishnamurti described this momentous occurrence in a letter to Annie Besant. Seated cross-legged beneath a pepper tree, he was transported:

> I saw the Star bright and clear. Then I could feel the vibration of the Lord Buddha; I beheld Lord Maitreya and Master K[oot] H[oomi]. I was so happy, calm and at peace. [...] The presence of the mighty Beings was with me for some time and then They were gone. I was supremely happy for I had seen [...] the glorious and healing Light. The fountain of Truth has been revealed to me [...]. I have drunk at the fountain of joy and eternal Beauty. I am God-intoxicated! (Jayakar, 48)

Like the Rani, Krishnamurti specifies an exact date in an attempt to give his epiphanic moment of divine intoxication a precise, matter-of-fact basis. He realized that he had been blessed, much as the Rani considers herself to have been anointed. When he "saw the Star bright and clear," he felt vindicated for having adopted this storied supernatural sign in 1911 as his personal symbol when instituting the Order of the Star in the East.[14] However, Krishnamurti's enlightenment is a transfiguration, the Rani's more of an annunciation. Intoxicated, he manifests himself in all his glory; she is told of her future course. Also, the suddenness of Krishnamurti's breakthrough places it at odds with the testimonials from Blavatsky, Leadbeater, and Besant, all of whom claimed, as does the Rani, to have been patiently conducted into greater awareness through several stages of initiation. Nightly, the Rani undergoes "a course of instruction" in Mme Buloz's Oratory (*I*, 52). Even Murugan, whose spiritual potentiality is almost nil, refers to "'the Fourth Initiation'" (i.e., stage) along the Path (*I*, 51).

The common denominator in Blavatsky's teachings, Leadbeater's tutoring of Krishnamurti in India, the Rani's conversion in *Island*, and Krishnamurti's enlightenment is Koot Hoomi. Inasmuch as this ascended master seems to be fictitious, entirely Blavatsky's fabrication, Krishnamurti's encounters with him both in India on the astral plane and under the pepper tree at Ojai, must be judged as worthless as the Rani's. "[F]or the greater glory of Koot Hoomi" (*I*, 61), the Rani's shibboleth, is just baloney. Krishnamurti's enlightenment in California in 1922 remains a spiritual curiosity. It would be seven years before Krishnamurti, increasingly uncertain of his claims to divinity, dissolved the Order of the Star and forsook his Messianic role in the Theosophical Society. Perhaps the twenty-seven-year-old was still deluded in 1922; or, already doubtful, he attempted to reassure himself that he had been rightly chosen. Possibly, he was telling his adopted mother what she yearned to hear: a long-awaited confirmation of Leadbeater's selection, thirteen years earlier, of Krishnamurti as the next Buddha. As one observer has concluded, something had to happen "to erase [Krishnamurti's] doubts and inspire him with confidence in his mission which Mrs Besant and Leadbeater had so long assigned him" (Nethercot, 343).

Refusing to condemn young Krishnamurti as "an opportunistic fraud," another commentator has contended that the pepper-tree epiphany may have been "an ineffable *samadhi* experience" (Poller, 127). Having sensed a presence, possibly the Buddha's, Krishnamurti simply called it Koot Hoomi, a name Besant was familiar with. Perhaps he had been doing this all along, that is, having mystical experiences and using a nomenclature supplied by Leadbeater and Besant. But if the genuine mystic employed the fakers' terminology, how could the latter accept the former's experience as genuine? Besides, the pepper-tree epiphany seems to be a first, an alleged broadening of awareness rather than an astral journey. One wonders, then, what to make of the nightly trips to Koot Hoomi on the astral plane that Krishnamurti supposedly took with Leadbeater's help ten years previously. If they, too, are genuine, though different, it is difficult to explain the time gap between them and Ojai, a decade of non-communication with the ascended masters followed by a sudden resumption.

Madame Blavatsky, Leadbeater, Annie Besant, and Krishnamurti all profess to see someone they identified as Koot Hoomi. So does the Rani. All seem to be referring to the same personage, whose existence no one but a few Theosophists credit. Illustration no. 3 in a recent study of Theosophy shows a sketch of Koot Hoomi as he allegedly appeared to Blavatsky: in the person of "a fair Kashmiri Brahmin with blue eyes" (Washington, 35).[15] To the Rani, he simply appears "'in Person'" (*I*, 53). Krishnamurti also states that he beheld Lord Maitreya, another product of Blavatsky's imagination. This compounds the problem of borrowed terminology. It makes the intent to please Besant seem the strongest motivation behind Krishnamurti's report. After Krishnamurti renounced the Order of the Star and abandoned Theosophy, Koot Hoomi disappeared from his discourse forever.

Huxley shifted his novel's bogus enlightenment from its Krishnamurti figure to the Rani, its stand-in for Blavatsky, who was synonymous with Theosophy. Murugan is a potentially dangerous spoiled brat, not the "complete phony" at least one of Huxley's Hollywood acquaintances considered Krishnamurti.[16] Yet one fails to see how this shift, which works well for the satire, was much of a kindness on Huxley's part. He may have felt that Krishnamurti should have no hard feelings about the caricature of his younger self in *Island* because he had turned out very differently from Murugan. No matter how compliant Krishnamurti may originally have been with the plans of Leadbeater and Besant, he eventually declined to continue as a Buddha-in-waiting and chose a different path. The mature Krishnamurti's disdain for gurus, his insistence that one find the way oneself, was a blanket rejection of Blavatsky's system, which was predicated on receiving constant direction from her spiritual guides, just as the Rani maintains that she does.

Krishnamurti first met Huxley and Gerald Heard in April 1938; Huxley was 44, a year older than Krishnamurti. Between the two, there was an "immediate rapport" (Lutyens, *The Life and Death of Krishnamurti*, 92). In 1946, Krishnamurti started Happy Valley School in Ojai, California; Huxley delivered the commencement address in 1951 (see Murray, 387). Three years later, he supplied a "Foreword" to a series of Krishnamurti's talks published as *The First and Last Freedom*.[17] By the early 1950s, Krishnamurti had become a "significant spiritual ally"; as the "third friend" in Huxley's life, he succeeded Heard, who had replaced D. H. Lawrence (Sawyer, 116–17). As Huxley's relationship with "Krishnaji," as he called his friend, steadily "deepened" (Sawyer, 142–43), the latter exerted a strong influence on the final stage of the former's philosophical development.[18] No one else, Huxley is said to have remarked, reminded him so much of the Buddha (see Washington, 356).[19] In short, there was nothing in the Huxley-Krishnamurti relationship to provoke the satire in *Island*. Huxley's comparison of the adult Krishnamurti with the Buddha is clearly sincere, despite the Theosophical Society's misguided attempts to deify Krishnamurti's younger self. Everywhere but in *Island*, Huxley expressed nothing but "great affection and respect."[20]

Krishnamurti dissolved the Order of the Star in 1929, and severed his ties with the Theosophical Society a year later, but he never withdrew his claim to have been enlightened in 1922. By 1962, when *Island* appeared, he had been for many years a respected sage who traveled the globe conducting religious seminars. Yet Huxley resurrected this holy man's problematic past, choosing to emphasize his association with a Society that has been called religion's "greatest imposture."[21] He depicted his friend's younger self as a detestable young person who helps to ruin utopia. Along with Colonel Dipa, Murugan destroys "[t]he work of a hundred years [...] in a single night" (*I*, 285). In the person of the Rani, Huxley treated Madame Blavatsky as harshly as he maligned Henry Ford, one of the models for Mustapha Mond in *Brave New World*. The calumniating of Krishnamurti's younger self as Murugan rivals the disrespectful portrayal, also in *Brave New World*, of D. H. Lawrence as John Savage.[22]

No authorized biographies of Krishnamurti appeared in Huxley's lifetime. He had to rely on recollections, his own and those of his Hollywood inner circle, several of whom, Christopher Isherwood, for example, knew Krishnamurti intimately. The doings of the Theosophists were constantly in the news during the nineteen twenties and thirties when Huxley was making a name for himself as a writer. In August 1926, shortly after Huxley completed his round-the-world journey, the *New York Times* covered Krishnamurti's arrival in America on the front page. Earlier, in February, after Krishnamurti's body was said to have been taken over by the World Teacher, newspapers everywhere proclaimed the coming of the so-called new Messiah (see Nethercot, 373–76).

By the late 1920s, the amount of literature being written by or about Theosophists had become "prodigious" (Gomes, 425). Doubtless, Huxley was familiar with Madame Blavatsky's *Isis Unveiled* and *The Secret Doctrine*. He may have known *The Lives of Alcyone*, Leadbeater's fanciful account of Krishnamurti's past lives. Surely he would not have overlooked the countless exposés, such as John N. Maskelyne's vitriolic pamphlet on "Madame Blavatsky and her accomplice or dupe, Colonel Olcott," the Theosophical Society's co-founder (Maskelyne, 7). The Society for Psychical Research played a key role in discrediting several of Blavatsky's claims. Huxley considered the founder of the Society, F. W. H. Myers, a psychologist superior to Freud and would have relished the attacks on Blavatsky, whom the society considered "one of the most accomplished [...] imposters of history" (Washington, 83).[23] Instruction on the astral plane, messages to and from the Masters only through Madame Blavatsky—it was all "bunkum," Huxley assured his father in a letter from Eton for 12 November 1917 (*L*, 136–37). He told Leonard how much he enjoyed pointing out to his pupils Mrs. Besant's "errors in science and history, which thickly encrust her books."[24] For attire, Besant favored flowing white robes; she was Krishnamurti's mother by adoption (he always called her "Mama"). So the Rani may be a scathingly satiric composite mostly of Blavatsky but including Huxley's life-long disdain for Besant.

Huxley's most reliable source could well have been Krishnamurti himself. During "conversations" more valuable than books, Huxley wrote in 1942, Krishnamurti spoke "of some of his experiences in a most interesting and illuminating way" (*L*, 475; see note 19 above). These talks may have included autobiographical material that the novelist capitalized on twenty years later in ways that Krishnamurti never anticipated. Between 1929 and 1932, Krishnamurti apparently recounted his life story willingly to numerous confidants. Later, however, he "begged" interlocutors "to believe that all he knew of his own life before 1929 he knew only because his friends had told him of it"; he had "lost his memory of everything that had happened to him before the year 1929," when he broke off relations with the Theosophical Society (Nethercot, 449). One wonders if Huxley managed to overcome Krishnamurti's selective amnesia. Conceivably, Huxley tapped some of the same sources that Krishnamurti's biographers eventually used.

Not until 1959, when Mary Lutyens revealed Krishnamurti's letter to Lady Emily (her mother) for 22 September 1922, did the general public learn the details of Krishnamurti's "mystical apocalypse" beneath the pepper tree at Ojai (Nethercot, 343). The letter told "how he had undergone a tremendous spiritual awakening" and "regained touch with his Master [Koot Hoomi] and with the Lord Maitreya." The Lutyens letter resembles the missive Krishnamurti sent Mrs. Besant about being intoxicated by God. Huxley had begun *Island* in 1956 (see *L*, 18); the Lutyens letter may have come in handy once he decided to make one of Pala's internal enemies a Theosophist.

A nobler motive emerges here than lurked behind the satirizing of D. H. Lawrence as John Savage. In *Brave New World*, Huxley was separating himself from the life-worshipping noble savagery of an erstwhile mentor, whose views he felt he had outgrown. In *Island*, Huxley reaffirmed Krishnamurti's separation from Theosophy lest his youthful involvement with its teachings be confused with the Hindu doctrine of Advaita Vedanta, a form of the perennial philosophy that Huxley's Palanese find congenial and that the mature Krishnamurti's system "closely parallels" (Sawyer, 188).[25] One of the cruelest counterpoints in *Island* pits the Buddhist practices of peace-loving Pala against the militant "Crusade of the Spirit" poised to engulf it.

One can readily understand Huxley's eagerness to distance his novel and the grown-up Krishnamurti from the latter's boyhood stint with Theosophy. In the 1917 letter to his father dismissing "astral bodies, spiritual hierarchies, reincarnation and so forth," Huxley conceded that "theosophy seems to be a good enough religion" otherwise (*L*, 137). He was pleased with "its main principles," especially the contention that "all religions contain some truth." Readers of *Island* were not to repeat this error. To rectify an earlier mistake, Huxley distinguished a spurious philosophy that saw some legitimacy in every religion from Vedanta; the latter extracts from all religion the highest common denominator, the factor that constitutes their shared essence, namely, the belief that the "Atman" or God inside us is identical with, and capable of union with, "Brahman," the God outside.[26] In short, Huxley warned, Madame Blavatsky's Theosophy, its makeshift synthesis of science, religion, and philosophy, must never be misconstrued as the British version of the perennial philosophy in vogue at the turn of the twentieth century. He believed that he had given the Vedantic outlook its definitive Anglo-American formulation in *The Perennial Philosophy* nearer the century's midpoint.

Unfortunately, commentators continue to repeat the blunder that Huxley seemed over-anxious to redress. In chapter 17 of a study of Western gurus, Peter Washington hears "strong echoes of Theosophy" in Huxley's religious position (Washington, 318). He considers the perennial philosophy "ironically close to the theosophical ideal of a synthetic wisdom of religion, combining the common doctrines and best aspects of all faiths" (Washington, 318). *The Perennial Philosophy*, Washington alleges, "includes paragraphs that might be lifted from the works of Blavatsky or Besant," despite the fact that neither appears in Huxley's text or bibliography.[27]

More distillation than synthesis, Huxley's version of the perennial philosophy strives towards the isolation of the key aspect in all religions, rather than a combination of every religion's best features (i.e., syncretism). As Ranga explains to Will Farnaby: "'*Tat tvam asi*, 'Thou art that'—[is] the heart of all our philosophy'" (*I*, 76). That is, Vedanta emphasizes the "heart" or core, which is certainly not a synthesis. That the god or Atman within us is identical with the god or Brahman without boils down to Sebastian Barnack's "minimum working hypothesis" in *Time Must Have a Stop* (see *TMHS*, 289), again a condensation instead of a combination. Because the Godhead or divine Ground is both "transcendent and immanent," Barnack maintains, it is possible, indeed, imperative, for all to achieve "unitive knowledge" of it (*TMHS*, 289). To do so, one does not require the assistance of intermediaries such as the ascended masters or Madame Blavatsky; their claims to exclusivity of access or intercessional necessity are clearly fraudulent.

Manner and method in *The Perennial Philosophy* seem deliberately anti-theosophical. Madame Blavatsky set herself up as sole mediatrix between theosophists and the ascended masters. Messages went back and forth through her alone. But the masters were figments of her imagination. In contrast, Huxley functions as transmitter, editor, and exegete; he anthologizes, then discusses, the similar pronouncements of numerous enlightened individuals, actual mystics not in far-off Tibet yet widely separated in time, space, and social position. The similar conclusions they reached about participatory knowledge of the divine Ground as man's Final End resemble scientific experiments insofar as they duplicate, and therefore corroborate, each other. "Apart from the statements of Madame Blavatsky and Mrs. Besant," it has been pointed out, "no atom of reliable evidence has ever been adduced to prove the existence of Morya and Koot Hoomi, the mythical Mahatmas of Tibet who prompted Blavatsky to found the Theosophical Society" (Maskelyne, 7). To the highly suspect testimonies of Blavatsky, Leadbeater, and young Krishnamurti, Huxley added the Rani's.

Madame Blavatsky insisted that one of the Theosophical Society's paramount goals was "'to unite the philosophic Orient and the practical West.'"[28] Throughout his career, Huxley dreamed of converting the counterpoint of East against West into a collaboration between the former's wisdom and the latter's know-how. But he wanted to preserve only the best of the Orient and Occident, not simply to "'unite'" them. He fabricated Pala to expose the shallowness of Blavatsky's conception of an East-West synthesis. In contrast to Besant's error-riddled prescriptions and Theosophy's chicanery, Pala combines the finest ideas that Huxley had culled from art, science, and theology in the thirty years since he wrote *Brave New World*, for which *Island* is the antidote point by point.[29] Blinded by egotism and greed, Murugan and the Rani fail to notice how well the Palanese have already achieved Blavatsky's objective. They have done so in accord with Huxley's ideas, which were drawn from Vedanta, Mahayana Buddhism, Dr. William Sheldon, Margaret Mead, the Oneida community, and a number of other sources, some quite esoteric, but not from Blavatsky, Besant, or Theosophy.

In *Ape and Essence*, the diabolical Arch-Vicar explains to Dr. Poole how the devil precipitated an apocalyptic World War III by persuading "'each side to take only the worst the other had to offer'" (*AE*, 184). Western nationalism, its armaments, movies, and Marxism for the East; despotism, superstition, and "'indifference to individual life'" for the West—in short, "'the worst of both worlds.'" The Arch-Vicar shudders to imagine "'if they'd made the best'": "'Eastern mysticism making sure that Western science should be properly used; the Eastern art of living refining Western energy; Western individualism tempering Eastern totalitarianism. [...] It would have been the kingdom of heaven,'" the devil-worshipper reluctantly concedes (*AE*, 185). Part blueprint, part prophecy, plus a good deal of wishful thinking, *Island* is Huxley's recipe for a temporal version of the heavenly kingdom. Outstripping Theosophy, it depicts the first-ever society that unifies East and West to nurture a truly enlightened populace.

Ultimately, Huxley's satire against Blavatsky and Besant may be topical, indeed, prescient, not just retroactive. Given its interest in such matters as mysticism, mind-expanding drugs, and decentralization, *Island* supposedly stakes "a good claim to be one of the first New Age texts" (Deery, 155). But through the anti-Theosophical satire, Huxley seems to have been expressing reservations about pseudo-religious thinking in the late 1950s and early 60s that "builds on nineteenth-century spiritualism," in particular, "Theosophy" (Deery, 152), or that considers such movements as authentic as Vedanta. Ironically, the list of New Age thinkers, or of figures whom New Agers admire, generally includes Huxley along with ostensible income-patibles such as Jung, Hesse, Ram Das, Timothy Leary, Alan Watts, the Beat poets, the Beatles, Pierre Teilhard de Chardin and, of course, Krishnamurti. Huxley is frequently embraced as either "an important forerunner" or as a "respectable fellow traveler" (Deery, 152). This may not have suited him.

In *Island*, as has been shown, Huxley tried to distinguish his friend Krishnaji from the young Krishnamurti, the pawn of the Theosophists. Also, he wanted to make clearer how his involvement with Vedantic mysticism and Oriental religion in general differed as fundamentally from the Theosophy he once spoke well of as his notion of an East-West partnership did from Madame Blavatsky's. Theosophy was incapable of reconciling East and West because neither Besant nor Blavatsky was the polymath such a task required. Similarly, Huxley may have hoped not to be grouped indiscriminately with a new batch of intellectuals—New Age scientists, philosophers, and theologians—many of whom shared one or two of his concerns, but none of whom could match his range as both an original thinker and a master distiller-synthesizer. Individually, most New Agers, no matter how creative, were as limited and one-pointed as Besant and Blavatsky. That is, none of them could sift through a host of ideas and then put together a full-fledged utopian society in which believable characters thrive and solutions to the major issues—religious, scientific, sexual, and psychological—not only make sense *per se* but dovetail.

The Rani is said to be "'what the Germans call *eine grosse Seele*,'" a large soul (*I*, 64). Unfortunately, this compliment comes from Mr. Bahu, Rendang's unscrupulous ambassador, a cynic of Voltairean proportions who supports Colonel Dipa's plan to annex Pala. In sum, lest readers confuse the beliefs and behavior of Theosophists with Vedanta, Huxley patterned the Rani and Murugan on Madame Blavatsky and young Krishnamurti. He made their fictional counterparts reprehensible sponsors of a nascent military-industrial complex, thereby satirizing mother and son not just as false prophets, but also as enemies of utopia.[30]

---

[1] In a *roman à clef*, i.e., a novel with a key, one unlocks additional meaning if one knows the personages on whom its characters are based and the events the author has borrowed from real life. Lady Ottoline Morrell, chatelaine of Garsington, the country home Huxley began visiting while at Oxford, was chagrined to be caricatured in *Crome Yellow* as the orange-haired Priscilla

Wimbush, an eccentric horoscopy addict. Nancy Cunard, with whom the married Huxley fell unhappily in love in 1922, supplied the original for Myra Viveash, the *femme fatale* in *Antic Hay*, and for Lucy Tantamount, an even crueler siren, in *Point Counter Point*. Mark Rampion serves as Huxley's spokesperson in that novel, but D. H. Lawrence, his real-life model, found him boring. John Beavis, Anthony's pater in *Eyeless in Gaza*, is an unsympathetic depiction of Leonard Huxley, Aldous's pedantic father. Brian Foxe's suicide resembles that of Trevenen, the novelist's elder brother. Even short-term acquaintances could find themselves victims. Dr. Remsen D. Bird showed Huxley around Occidental College only to become one of the models for the sycophantic Dr. Mulge in *After Many a Summer*, in which his college appears as Tarzana.

2 Nevertheless, "Huxley's sensitivity to the human condition constantly drove him toward pessimism" even during his association with the Vedanta Society (Sawyer, 128).

3 Aldous Huxley, *Island* (London, 1962), 53. [*I*]

4 Although the Theosophical Society boasted 45,000 members in the 1920s and built its London headquarters at a cost of $50,000, it was never that powerful financially; see Campbell, 128, and Maskelyne, 9.

5 For the story of Krishnamurti's involvement with the Theosophical Society, I have conflated accounts in Sawyer; Poller; Lutyens, *Krishnamurti: The Open Door* and *The Life and Death of Krishnamurti*; and Jayakar.

6 Experts agree that Leadbeater wrote *At the Feet of the Masters*, not Krishnamurti, who spoke Telega better than English (see Lutyens, *The Life and Death of Krishnamurti*, 9).

7 The seduction ended when Murugan jumped out of bed "'and locked himself into the bathroom.'" He did not come out until Radha "'passed his pajamas through the transom'" (*I*, 71). In *Brave New World*, when Lenina attempts to seduce John, his violent reaction drives *her* into the bathroom; he pushes her clothes "'through the ventilator over the door'" (Aldous Huxley, *Brave New World* [London, 1932], 231). [*BNW*]

8 Hadrian was Roman emperor from 117 to 138 A. D. Antinous was his favorite boy-lover.

9 Sanskrit for "putting together," *samadhi* is the final stage of meditation, in which we attain superconsciousness, the unqualified bliss called *moksha*. See Gaynor, 161.

10 In an interview with his biographer, Krishnamurti countered that a vacant mind was a truly receptive one (see *The Life and Death of Krishnamurti*, 160–61). Perhaps he was endorsing "wise passiveness" (see Wordsworth's "Expostulation and Reply," l. 24). The overly intellectual Huxley allegedly envied Krishnamurti for having "a mind born of perceptions untainted by knowledge" (Jayakar, 88).

11 "It seems likely [...] that [Huxley] was thinking of Blavatsky when, in *Island*, he created the character of the Rani," Jake Poller has observed (Poller, 13, note 6). Paul Fussell argued that E. M. Forster infused Mrs. Moore in *A Passage to India* with "certain elements of the character of Helena Petrovna Blavatsky" (Fussell, 388).

[12] Madame Blavatsky had grown so obese by 1884 that when she took ship for Madras, "she had to be hauled on board in a chair attached to a rope and pulley" (Washington, 86).

[13] *Island* is therefore set in 1961.

[14] The Order of the Star in the East was designed to smooth the way for the coming of the Buddha/Messiah (see Poller, 116). Compare the star over Bethlehem which guided the Wise Men to the infant Jesus.

[15] Koot Hoomi is sometimes "Kuthumi," which sounds less ridiculous (see Lutyens, *The Life and Death of Krishnamurti*, 2). An ascended master is supposedly a fully evolved, transcendent human being who uses his god-like stature to aid humanity in its quest to become like him. Blavatsky may have borrowed the idea from the Buddhists. A bodhisattva—it means "existence in wisdom" in Sanskrit—is one who has qualified to enter Nirvana but elects to continue as a Buddha-to-be in order to work for universal salvation (see Gaynor, 27). Blavatsky claimed to have studied with Koot Hoomi on three separate visits to Tibet (see Leonard; also see Cranston). Marion Meade opined that Koot Hoomi and Lord Morya are "copies of Zanoni," a mysterious, ageless Indian in Bulwer Lytton's 1842 novel *Zanoni* (Meade, 470).

[16] This observation allegedly comes from Krister Kuylenstiernan, a member of the "Krishnamurti-Rajagopal-Huxley-Isherwood-Heard-Kirsh group in California" (Nethercot, 450, note 8). But there is no mention of Kuylenstiernan in Huxley's letters or Bedford's biography.

[17] According to Mary Lutyens, Huxley encouraged Krishnamurti to start writing down his talks for publication (see *The Open Door*, 14).

[18] For the remarkable congruence between Huxley's thoughts and Krishnamurti's pronouncements on such subjects as pacifism, nationalism, and meditation practices, see Poller, 20–22.

[19] Huxley's letters always speak highly of Krishnamurti. To Christopher Isherwood, a fellow Vedantist, Huxley reported that conversations with Krishnamurti were "[b]etter than books." See the letter for 7 February 1942 (*L*, 475). Huxley informed Hubert Benoit that he found Krishnamurti's method of meditation less "mechanical" than that taught by the swamis of the Ramakrishna Mission. See the letter for 5 November 1949 (*L*, 608, note). To Humphry Osmond, Huxley lauded Krishnamurti's *Commentaries on Living* and *The First and Last Freedom* for their "amazingly subtle diagnosis of our psychological delinquencies." See the letter for 22 February 1957 (*L*, 818). Again to Osmond, this time from Gstaad in Switzerland, Huxley praised a series of Krishnamurti's lectures he was attending: "It was like listening to a discourse of the Buddha." See the letter for 4 August 1961 (*L*, 917). Also see *L*, 851, and *L*, 963.

[20] See the letter to Reid Gardner for 18 September 1962 (*L*, 938).

[21] This phrase appears in the lengthy subtitle of John N. Maskelyne's 1913 exposé (see Maskelyne).

[22] The portrait of Lawrence as the doomed savage amounts to Huxley's coldhearted dismissal of a former guru whom he had lionized in *Point Counter Point*. Huxley praised Krishnamurti's disdain for gurus in a third letter to Osmond on 15 October 1963, just five weeks before he died (see *L*, 963).

[23] For one of Huxley's many elevations of F. W. H. Myers over Freud, see *HS*, 152–53. For the argument that the Hodgson Report of 1885, i.e., the Report of the Committee to Investigate Phenomena Connected with the Theosophical Society, the committee on which Myers served, was flawed and biased, see Harrison, vii.

[24] Ten years later, Huxley felt the same way; he dismissed "the lucubrations of the theosophists and their kind," which were "full of mysteries, 'rays,' 'vibrations,' 'ethers,' 'magnetic currents,' and the like" (*PS*, 81).

[25] To Claire Nicolas, Huxley wrote in Spring 1947: "Krishnamurti is not a Vedantist, nor is Gerald Heard—tho' both have affinities with Vedanta" (*L*, 569).

[26] Huxley thought "this teaching is expressed most succinctly in the Sanskrit formula, *tat tvam asi* ('That art thou'); the Atman, or immanent eternal Self, is one with Brahman, the Absolute Principle of all existence; and the last end of every human being is to discover the fact for himself" (*PP*, 8).

[27] Washington claimed to hear the "echoes" as early as 1925 when Calamy begins to formulate his ideas at the end of *Those Barren Leaves*. Actually, Calamy previews the perennial philosophy when he asserts that "'the axes chosen by the best observers have always been startlingly like one another, Gotama, Jesus and Lao-tze, for example; they lived sufficiently far from one another in space, time, and social position. But their pictures of reality resemble one another very closely'" (*TBL*, 377). The list of "'best observers'" does not include Madame Blavatsky or Annie Besant, who lifted some of the observers' ideas.

[28] This and other objectives of the Society are quoted from Blavatsky by Fussell (392).

[29] See Chapter VII, "Utopian Counterpoint," in Meckier, *SS*, especially 196–205.

[30] Ironically, when Annie Besant visited Ojai in 1925, she waxed utopist: it would be the place where Blavatsky's "more perfect people" congregate (Taylor, *Annie Besant*, 324)—a Theosophical Garsington.

Chapter Seven

THANATOPSIS / THANATOLOGY IN *BRAVE NEW WORLD* AND *ISLAND*

"At any given period," Aldous Huxley opined, "preoccupation with death is in inverse ratio to the prevalence of a belief in man's perfectibility through and in a properly organized society."[1] In other words, the more utopian one's situation, the less concern with death. Yet *Brave New World* and *Island*, though published thirty years apart under very different circumstances,[2] seem equally preoccupied with mortality. According to one commentator, "no other writer is so much concerned with death" as Huxley, who allegedly saw it "as the final proof of the absurdity of both men and the universe."[3]

Reminding readers of death's inevitability has long been one of the satirist's favorite pastimes, a foolproof means of subverting vanity and pretension. However, most modern utopias, inherently non-metaphysical, do not worry overmuch about death. Its inevitability poses little or no threat to social arrangements in the imaginary societies of Butler, Morris, Bellamy, and Zamiatin, to name only four. Huxley seems to be telling his immediate predecessors that nothing enhances or damages a community's claims to perfection more than its manner of handling death, both the idea of it and the event itself.

Thanatopsis is an invented Greek word meaning 'viewing death' or the contemplation of death. William Cullen Bryant used it as the title for his famous 1814 poem (see "Thanatopsis," Pockell, 18–21). In *Island*, Dr. Robert MacPhail prefers "'thanatology,'" the study of death and its circumstances, which he calls "'the ultimate science […] that sooner or later we shall all have to be examined in.'"[4] One can compare John the Savage's disastrous visit to the brave new world with Will Farnaby's redemptive sojourn in Pala by isolating what each learns about death and dying. In both *Brave New World* and *Island*, Huxley introduces an outsider to a supposedly model society. He gives the Savage and Farnaby a crash course in thanatology, which only the latter passes; the former perishes. Ironically, the brave new world survives even though John does not. Even more ironically, Pala's demise, its involuntary absorption into war-mongering Rendang, coincides with the conclusion to Will's rehabilitation. Nevertheless, Will and Pala do right what John and the brave new world get all wrong. Pala has formulated a commendable thanatopsis, whereas the World State's outlook is despicable. How each society contemplates death is one of the surest ways of distinguishing Huxley's genuinely good place from a bogus utopia.

The counterpoint involving John's and Will's responses to death—dissimilars facing a similar problem differently—extends to their respective societies.[5]

Before the Savage's arrival, Lenina Crowne, distracted by Henry Foster, whom she no longer wishes to date, momentarily neglects her embryos: "'[H]ave I given this one its sleeping-sickness injection, or haven't I?'" she asks herself (*BNW*, 153). "Twenty-two years, eight months, and four days" later, "a promising young Alpha-Minus administrator at Mwanza-Mwanza" dies "of trypanosomiasis—the first case for over half a century" (*BNW*, 154). By A. F. 654, Lenina may be long since dead. No one investigates the administrator's death. Her negligence may not be an isolated incident. The counterpart in *Island* is Dugald MacPhail's mountain-climbing accident. Dr. MacPhail's eldest son, Susila's late husband, "'died four months'" before Will's arrival (*I*, 16), but is still being mourned by wife and father. Both societies accept accidental death. The brave new world indifferently nullifies its impact in that there are no fathers or husbands to grieve.

The brave new world's response to death, its attempt at thanatopsis, is an insidious mix of concealment and denial. A "properly organized society" (*TV*, 167), utopia to Huxley's way of thinking, does not conceal their mortality from its citizens as long as possible. The World State is satirized for doing so, its policy not humane in this regard but a sham designed to keep a populace of pleasure-seeking, mindless consumers docile and worry-free. "'All the physiological stigmata of old age have been abolished,'" Mustapha Mond boasts (*BNW*, 46). As Bernard Marx tells Lenina, brave new worlders never even look old: thanks to biological engineering, all are kept youthful in appearance and disease-free; "'[y]outh almost unimpaired till sixty, and then, crack! the end'" (91). How brave new worlders cope with this fact of life when they get into their late fifties is unclear. The lower castes seem blissfully ignorant of Marx's deadline or are constantly distracted from it.

Huxley seems not to have worked out the implications of an orchestrated "'crack!'" of doom. Gammas, Deltas, and Epsilons are decanted in "uniform batches," as many as "ninety-six" to a batch, until "[m]illions of identical twins" have been produced (*BNW*, 4, 3, 5). During any given period, with everyone suddenly mortal at sixty, large numbers of the lower castes must be expiring all the time virtually in unison. The warrantees of each "Bokanovsky Group" staffing the Electrical Equipment Corporation that John visits, for example, should expire almost simultaneously: "eighty-three" Deltas, "fifty-six" Gammas, "one hundred seven" Epsilons, "[t]hirty-three Delta females," "two sets of Gamma-Plus dwarfs" (forty-seven in each), "eighteen identical" Gammas, "thirty-four short-legged, left-handed" Delta-Minuses, "sixty-three" Epsilon Semi-Morons (*BNW*, 130). With groups of the lower castes passing on in such numbers, it might be difficult for the crematoriums to handle the rush and even harder to hide the inevitability of death.

Brave new worlders are "'never ill,'" claims Mustapha Mond: "'they're not afraid of death'" (*BNW*, 180). This is not strictly accurate. The reader knows that, due to Lenina's carelessness, at least one brave new worlder will sicken and die from sleeping-sickness. Nor is it true that no one fears death. Henry Foster's aversion to Slough Crematorium hints at a continuing deep-seated anxiety. As Henry and Lenina fly over Slough, he crows that "'over ninety-eight percent'" of the phosphorus in every corpse is now "'re-covered'" every time someone is cremated (*BNW*, 61). Even when dead, Foster rejoices, brave new worlders "'go on being socially useful'" by "'making plants grow.'"[6] Huxley ridicules the exalting of fertilizer as man's "final end."[7] Then Henry's helicopter shoots upwards on a column of air from the crematorium's chimneys. He is disconcerted by the thought of "'some human being [...] [g]oing up in a squirt of hot gas'" (*BNW*, 62). To dispel the ignominy, he recites the reassuring hypnopaedic proverb "'Every-body's happy now'" in "a resolutely cheerful voice" (*BNW*, 62). For Henry and hundreds like him, thanatopsis equals phosphorus.

Miss Keate, headmistress at Eton, insists that death in the World State has been made to seem "'like any other physiological process'" (*BNW*, 134). This comes about, Dr. Gaffney points out to the Savage, because every brave new worlder's "'[d]eath-conditioning begins at eighteen months. Every tot spends two mornings a week in a Hospital for the Dying'" where it learns "'to take dying as a matter of course'" (*BNW*, 133). "'All the best toys are kept there,'" Gaffney says of the death wards, and the tots "'get chocolate cream on death days,'" which must occur often given the frequent simultaneous deaths of batches of Gammas, Deltas, and Epsilons.

"'Death-conditioning'" is thoroughly Pavlovian. Huxley despised Pav-lov's attempt to elicit automatic, hence dishonest, responses from irrelevant stimuli, in effect creating a false connection, a sort of non-sequitur. Just as a bell caused dogs to salivate, having been taught to confuse the signal with dinnertime, brave new worlders, from infancy onwards, are trained to link death with splendid toys and special dessert. Hospitals for the dying become child-care centers, combinations of playground and sweet shop. At Park Lane, Pavlov's behavioristic techniques have been easily perverted to disguise a basic shortcoming of existence, its unavoidable termination. No society that cannot honestly prepare its citizens for death should be considered flawless, Huxley contended. "'Death-conditioning'" in the brave new world is a perfidious obfuscation.[8]

It breaks down when the Savage's mother is admitted to the Park Lane Hospital for the Dying before anyone realizes how unorthodox her death will be. Her son has never been death-conditioned. Linda, not Slough Crematorium, becomes the novel's *memento mori*. To palliate her impending demise from drug abuse, her "ever larger, ever more frequent doses" of *soma*, the brave new world lays on "all the modern conveniences" for her to die "in company [...] with" (*BNW*, 163): synthetic music, television, a new perfume pervading the room every fifteen minutes, but no real consolation beyond "the Semi-finals of the South American Riemann-Surface Tennis Championship," the diversion Linda watches until she expires.

Huxley underscores Linda's embarrassing grotesqueness: her "pale, bloated face" makes her "a monster of flaccid and distorted senility," despite a *soma*-induced "expression of imbecile happiness" (*BNW*, 164, 166). Old, fat, and ugly, she "astonished and rather alarmed" the "interminable stream" of khaki-clad "identical eight-year-old male twins" who are brought in to be "'death-conditioned'" (*BNW*, 165, 166). The Deltas crawl and clamber over her like maggots until John begins thrashing them. When Linda confuses her son with Popé, her former lover, John shakes her, hastening her end. As she asphyxiates, "the terror of her staring eyes revealed what she was suffering" (*BNW*, 169). Nurses quickly pacify the twins with chocolate éclairs lest "the shocking scene" undo their allegedly "wholesome death-conditioning" (*BNW*, 165). Their "pale goggling eyes" might see death for what it is: "something terrible," as if the dying person "mattered" (*BNW*, 170). For Huxley thereafter, death-conditioning oneself, learning how to assert the importance of the individual in response to the awfulness of death, became a career-long concern. In the last line he penned of his unfinished thirteenth novel, Edward Darley, the protagonist, asks and answers the all-important question, "What *was* I? I was someone who was going to die."[9]

The Savage is left to ponder "Death": "Why had Linda died?" he asks himself (*BNW*, 208). Why had the Delta twins "swarmed defilingly over the mystery of Linda's death"? (*BNW*, 171) Because the brave new world offers no answers, John falls back on Macbeth's nihilistic summation: "And all our yesterdays," the Thane of Cawdor declares, "have lighted fools the way to dusty death."[10] John's grief and anger lead to two additional fatalities. After inciting a riot at the Park Lane, he retreats to a Surrey lighthouse where he subsequently kills a sight-seeing Lenina and then hangs himself, a pair of deaths the brave new world's perverse thanatopsis is powerless to prevent or explain.

Worse than the maggoty Deltas, scores of excursionists from London come like "locusts" to watch John whip himself for desiring "white, warm, scented, infamous Lenina," whom he imagines himself "flogging" (*BNW*, 209, 207). Spotting her among the curious, John begins "slashing at her with his whip of small cords" (*BNW*, 211).[11] An orgy ensues as the excited crowd joins in, all "beating one another." Next morning, revolted by his "long-drawn frenzy of sensuality," John hangs himself (*BNW*, 212). A caricature of natives of the American southwest, whose culture D. H. Lawrence admired, John travels from a primitive environment to a Fordian, Pavlovian, Wellsian future so disappointing that suicide is his only recourse.[12] As his body turns "like two unhurried compass needles," first "towards the right," then "back towards the left" (*BNW*, 213), *Brave New World* literally comes to a dead end. Unable to locate true north, to which all compasses point, John is left with no direction to take except death. Linda's gruesome demise, the senseless murder of Lenina,[13] and a despairing John's ignoble act of self-destruction expose the World State's failed thanatopsis. One can only wonder what the next morning's "swarm" of death-conditioned sightseers, entering John's lighthouse, will make of his dangling "pair of feet" (*BNW*, 213).[14]

Island begins with a cynical Will Farnaby badly in need of both physical and spiritual resuscitation, being washed ashore on Pala, the "forbidden" (i.e., inaccessible) island (*I*, 6), after a freakish boating accident. He lies "there like a corpse" (*I*, 1), a sign that death will be the major obstacle to his enlightenment. A jaded journalist, Will has covered nothing but wars and atrocities as one of life's "special correspondents on the trail of death" (43). Eventually, he reads crucial passages from the Old Raja's *Notes on What's What*, the foundation text and spiritual guidebook for the Palanese much as Henry Ford's *My Life and Work* was to the brave new world. The *Notes* acknowledge that all life leads to "'the certainty of death'" (85), but is not cowed by this admission. When Will reminds Susila that "'people still die. Even in Pala,'" he fails to shake her conviction that an enlightened person, presumably having digested the *Notes*, "'dies with a difference'" (245, 243). Having discovered his or her "'Buddha Nature,'" every enlightened Palanese remains "'aware, even in the final agony,'" of who he or she really is (244), namely, someone whose Atman (God-within) is capable of knowing and uniting with Brahman (God-without). This union can be maintained, indeed, strengthened, during one's last moments, as Lakshmi's death-bed scene demonstrates.

Farnaby has been disillusioned by the deaths of his dog, Tiger, his Aunt Mary, and his wife, Molly. Pala's worth as a candidate for utopia can be gauged by its ability to recondition Farnaby, to instill in him a workable thanatopsis denied to brave new worlders. Tiger, a "beautiful red setter," came down with "distemper"; Will remembers his "'sticky'" fur and "'bad smell'" (*I*, 240). The animal died while he was holding him. Only four, Will was "confronted by the awful, inexplicable fact of death" (240). When he was just sixteen, his aunt Mary's death from cancer proved even more traumatic. To Susila MacPhail, Dugald's widow and Dr. Robert's daughter-in-law, he graphically recounts the loss of "'the only person [he] ever loved'" (100): "'Off with the right breast; then, a year later, off with the left. And after that nine months of X-rays and radiation sickness. Then it got into the liver, and that was the end'" (100). For Aunt Mary, it meant "'degradation.'"

"'Here,'" says Will, "'was a soul that radiated goodness and love and heroic charity. Then, for no known reason, something went wrong [...], a little piece of her body started to obey the second law of thermodynamics. And as the body broke down, the soul began to lose its virtue, its very identity'" (*I*, 242). No longer loveable and admirable, just as Tiger smelled bad, Aunt Mary whined continually as she "'was slowly [...] put to death in solitude'" (242). Her demise may be based in part on the death in November 1908 of Aldous's beloved mother, Julia Huxley, when he was just fourteen. Julia died swiftly from an inoperable cancer but, like Aunt Mary, she was only forty-five and deeply resented her fate (see Bedford, I, 24–26). "'Why do I have to die, and so young!'" she reportedly exclaimed (Murray, 26). "'Why to me? Why should this thing have happened to me?'" Aunt Mary wails (262).

Immediately upon regaining consciousness after a fall while climbing up from Pala's rocky shore, Will relives his breakup with Molly. Less than an hour after their final argument, his wife, having walked out on him, was killed in a traffic accident: Molly, he recalls, "was in the ambulance, dying" (*I*, 2), leaving him, an adulterer, feeling responsible. After Will tells the sad stories of Tiger, Molly, and Aunt Mary to Susila, she, along with her father-in-law, undertakes Will's therapy much as Bernard Marx shows the Savage around the brave new world. "'It's death itself, death as such, that you find so terrible,'" is Susila's diagnosis (*I*, 239). To authenticate itself, Pala must assuage Farnaby's fear of death, the disaster he has learned to regard as proof positive of life's "'Pure and Applied Pointlessness'" (100). That the point of it all was that there is no point was Huxley's attitude towards life well into the 1930s,[15] so Will's fears and the problems associated with them are obliquely autobiographical as is Will's eventual change of outlook.

What may be called Farnaby's cure, his reconditioning, requires long, lecture-like conversations in which Dr. Robert, Susila, Vijaya, nurse Radha and several other Palanese take turns relating Pala's history and pointing out the island's numerous advantages. No discussion novel of ideas has ever held so many discussions or expounded this many ideas.[16] There are, however, two key incidents, both involving death. First, Will witnesses the Palanese version of death-conditioning, participating vicariously. Then, at Lakshmi's bedside as she dies, he passes his thanatology exam by proxy. In a clear case of utopian counterpoint, Huxley reworks the Park Lane Hospital episode in which khaki-clad Deltas frolic while Linda expires. In sharp contrast to the Savage's mother, Susila's mother-in-law dies what Huxley considers a perfect death in his idea of the perfect society.

Along with Dr. MacPhail, Farnaby watches young Palanese ascend a mountain to mark their transition from childhood into adolescence. Inasmuch as this initiation ordeal is quite dangerous, Dr. MacPhail observes, it "'helps them to realize the omnipresence of death, the essential precariousness of all existence'" (*I*, 162). As opposites of brave new worlders, who are conditioned to ignore death, Palanese are taught to be ever mindful of it. Mountain climbing, says Vijaya, is "'life at its highest pitch of bodily and mental tension, life more abundant, more intensely precious, because of the ever-present fear of death'" (169). For the Palanese, life at every moment must be "'reconciled with the perpetual imminence of death'" (169), a procedure that demands, in short, constant thanatopsis and that helps to determine one's every act.

Deltas in the Park Lane Hospital's death ward receive chocolate éclairs as a pleasant distraction. Atop the mountains, climbers are given their first taste of *moksha*, the wonder drug that facilitates mystical awareness. The lesson Pala's youth learns is that transcendence is always possible despite the inevitability and omnipresence of death. Will's vicarious participation in the ascent reverses his "climbing" and "falling" in the novel's opening chapter (*I*, 7). Dr. MacPhail explains how, thanks to *moksha*, one has "'a succession of beatific glimpses'" culminating in "'Liberation'" from this world of self, time, and suffering. Before Will is allowed to sample "'the reality-revealer, the truth-and-beauty pill'" (138) at the climax of his cure, he must pass his thanatology exam.

Mary Sarojini brings Susila, her mother, news that Lakshmi is "'dying'" (*I*, 245). Will is surprised that on Pala death was not "taboo," i.e., unmentionable before children. For the final step in Will's therapy, Susila invites him to watch Lakshmi die, a most unusual invitation. Susila's special talent, it turns out, is a thanatologist's to "'help people die'" (247). "'She's awfully good at it,'" Mary Sarojini informs Will.[17] "'Going on being aware,'" Susila instructs Will, "'—it's the whole art of dying'" (246). Pala's *ars moriendi* scarcely differs from the "'art of living'" in that Palanese are trained "'to go on practicing the art of living even while they're dying,'" Susila lectures. They are encouraged to remain "'conscious of the universal and impersonal life that lives itself through each of us,'" Susila continues, "'—that's the art of living, and that's what one can help the dying to go on practicing. To the very end. Maybe beyond the end [...] if the universal life goes on, when the separate me-life is over'" (246). One is meant to marvel at the smoothness of Lakshmi's transition from life to death compared to the sudden "'crack!'" that signals "'the end'" for brave new worlders (*BNW*, 91) or to the panic in Linda's eyes.

Actually, Farnaby receives two invitations. Murugan brings one from his mother, the Rani, summoning Will to a meeting of Pala's pro-oil minority. As a "secret agent" for Joe Aldehyde's company, Farnaby has been "'helping'" Murugan, the Rani, and Mr. Bahu, who represents Colonel Dipa of neighboring Rendang, to secure for Southeast Asia Petroleum oil concessions most Palanese oppose granting (*I*, 111, 59). Will declines Murugan's offer, declaring "'I have a prior engagement. With someone who's dying'" (258). The "'someone'" is not only Lakshmi, who dies in chapter XIV, but also Pala, which, with Murugan's contrivance, is invaded by Rendang's Colonel Dipa in the chapter after that.

In accepting an invitation to a death, Will paradoxically chooses life; from now on, he must strive to live the way Dr. MacPhail's wife did if he is to die as peacefully as she does. Susila implies as much when she issues the invitation, calling Will "'someone who needs to know how to live and then how to die'" (*I*, 245–46). Lakshmi's death is another lesson in the value of an ongoing thanatopsis. Huxley patterned her death on Maria's; his first wife died of cancer in February 1955. Throughout her final hours, Aldous "continued to remind her of who she really was—a manifestation in time of the eternal, a part forever unseparated from the whole of the divine reality"; he kept on "urging her to go forward into the light" (Bedford, II, 186).[18] "'Go on, my darling,'" Dr. Robert encourages Lakshmi, "'go into the Light, into the living peace of the Clear Light'" (268).

Will contrasts Lakshmi's with Aunt Mary's pitiful departure. Also, Huxley fashions Lakshmi into a counterpoint for Linda, whose terrible death the former's tranquil expiration redoes (see *I*, 262–64). The latter half of Chapter XIV is a guidebook instructing readers how to make a successful death. The contrapuntal death scenes of the Savage's mother and Susila's mother-in-law are two of the most compelling in modern literature.[19] Lakshmi's beatific end is among the most moving passages that a supposedly cold-blooded satirist ever wrote.

John shakes Linda and brings on her death throes. Aunt Mary was so "bitterly querulous," so full of "self-pity" and "abject despair" (*I*, 262) that Will became impatient for her release. In contrast, Susila and Dr. Robert coordinate their efforts so as to accompany Lakshmi through the final stages of her pain. Linda is drugged senseless with *soma*; Aunt Mary's "artificial sleep" following multiple "injections" was her "only respite from […] brooding fear" (262). Susila refuses to let Lakshmi doze off: "'You mustn't go to sleep,'" she insists; "'[y]ou've got to know you're here. All the time'" (262). Unlike Linda and Aunt Mary, who struggle not to die, Lakshmi willingly contemplates "'the light,'" from which, according to Susila, "'we all came out'" (263). "'The Clear Light of pure Suchness,'" as Susila calls it (265), is another name for the divine Ground. One remains fond of sunshine and sunsets, Susila alleges, because they serve as life-long reminders of the Clear Light that is both origin and goal, the individual soul's alpha and omega.

Huxley makes Lakshmi's death seem benevolent, a boon, despite the ravages of cancer and old age, neither of which can afflict brave new worlders. Viewed objectively, Lakshmi's "dark emaciated face," "parchment-covered bones," and "clawlike hands" (*I*, 261) make her, in extremis, physically as repulsive as Linda. But her smile, when she compliments her daughter-in-law, is "mischievous" (263), not imbecilic, her positive attitude the opposite of Aunt Mary's. When the Clear Light absorbs her attention, Lakshmi whispers with joy: "'The light, […] [o]h, how wonderful!'" (263) Speaking as much for Will's benefit as to remind her mother-in-law, Susila points out that "'no theology'" is involved, no metaphysics, "'[j]ust the fact of dying and the fact of the Clear Light'" (266). Mystics contend that it can only be seen in their final moments by individuals who have lived a good life (see Meckier, "On D. H. Lawrence and Death," 221, note 56). When Will thinks of "poor," disgruntled Aunt Mary, he notices that, by contrast, Lakshmi's "fleshless face on the pillow […] was smiling" (266). Her last breaths are as "stertorous" as Linda's: the latter "could no longer breathe," her face became "horribly distorted, her lips blue" (*BNW*, 169). But when Lakshmi's husband asks her to "'let go,'" to leave behind her "'poor old body'" (268), she complies instantly.[20]

The Will Farnaby who watches Lakshmi die is effectively imbued with Pala's salvationary thanatology. He learns how, in Huxley's opinion, an enlightened person expires. As a reward, he is permitted to go forwards in chapter XV and sample the *moksha*-medicine. As chapter XIV concludes, Susila issues another invitation: "'Would you like to try it?'" she asks (*I*, 270). Will seems prepared for a foretaste of the Beatific Vision. Regrettably, his LSD trip, the novel's climax, is a heaven and hell experience; the brief visionary bliss of being "one with Oneness" (*I*, 271) yields to a painful review of life's manifold "[h]orrors" as countless instances of "vulgarity," "pain," "cruelty," tastelessness," "imbecility," and "deliberate malice" (281) in places such as Korea, Africa, and Algeria flood his consciousness—atrocities of the 1950s as an instance of the "hell beyond hell of utterly pointless suffering" (284) that has always been the case. Against Pala's praiseworthy thanatopsis Huxley pits Will's overpowering awareness of humanity's wearisome condition throughout the ages. Will deplores what he calls "the immortality of suffering," the endless pain and sorrow caused by Crusaders, Nazis, wagers of Holy War, etc. The *moksha*-medicine experience ends abruptly when Rendang's tanks invade and Murugan proclaims "'the United Kingdom of Rendang and Pala'" (293). Dr. MacPhail, the island's Prospero, is summarily shot by the forces of Colonel Dipa, its Caliban.

Dr. MacPhail's is not the final death in the novel; Pala dies along with him. One realizes that Dr. Robert's cancer-stricken wife, who throughout the novel has been "slowly wasting to extinction [...] like a bright fiery flame suddenly snuffed out" (*I*, 25), is a more pervasive *memento mori* than Linda: Lakshmi symbolizes Pala, another bright spot to be suddenly extinguished when, as in a cancerous body, parts of it start to work against the good of the whole. The paradox of "slowly" and "suddenly" fits: the island's pro-oil minority, a cancer within the body politic, springs the surprise coup it has been gradually hatching. Murugan, his mother (the Rani), and Mr. Bahu (Rendang's ambassador) are sure to award oil-drilling concessions to Southeast Asia Petroleum, thereby ruining paradise. The Palanese cure Farnaby of his enervating pessimism compounded of guilt, self-loathing and fear of death, but not before he has assured pro-oilers of the foreign support they will need to seize control and modernize (i.e., industrialize) Pala. In effect, though no longer a sick, demoralized Westerner and despite disassociating himself from Murugan and the Rani, Will has infected Pala; he has been likened to a cancerous cell that behaves contrary to the general welfare. Plentiful oil beneath Pala's edenic surface is itself a sort of "infection," a disease of matter as deadly as an insidious cancer underneath the skin.[21]

The murder of Dr. MacPhail at the novel's conclusion is hardly as ignominious as John's suicide at the close of *Brave New World*, but it strikes the reader as a far greater disaster. Both utopias conclude with a trio of deaths: Linda's, Lenina's and John's in *Brave New World*; Lakshmi's, Dr. Robert's, and Pala's in *Island*. The first set exposes the brave new world's lack of a constructive thanatopsis; in the second, despite Lakshmi's peaceful resolution, her husband's assassination reveals that even Pala's excellent thanatology has limits. Like the World State's policy of concealment and denial, there are some things it cannot prevent.

The World State tries to dispense with a realistic thanatopsis, that is, to do without an honest, uninhibited contemplation of death. This proves more difficult than Mustapha Mond, Eton's Dr. Gaffney, and the callous nurses at the Park Lane Hospital realize. Palanese, on the other hand, do not confuse death with the individual's "*final* end" (*PP*, 38; italics added); it lies beyond the temporal sphere, so that death is ideally the prelude to permanent union with the divine "Ground," the spiritual principle of which everyone, according to the perennial philosophy as taught by Vedanta, is part.[22] From this perspective, death may be seen "as our greatest liberation" from "personal life-time," which can be "mostly destructive" if filled with greed and craving (Rohmann, 101).

Between 1932 and the late 1950s when Huxley was at work on *Island*, he continued to submit utopian proposals through his non-fiction. The essayist remained interested in eugenics and population control, in ecology, education reform, the proper use of language, and in pharmacological pathways to mystical awareness. Nevertheless, he came to suspect that death and utopia might be incompatible ideas, if not a counterpoint like "[p]assion and reason" in the epigraph to *Point Counter Point*. If man's final end lies outside time, even the ideal temporal state can be at best penultimate. Huxley proffers Lakshmi's death scene as a solution, his concept of a utopian death. Witnessing it, Farnaby, unlike John the Savage with Linda, experiences the ideal thanatopsis, proper death-conditioning being a prerequisite for further enlightenment.

Huxley reconfigured the best place as the society with the best thanatology. Only it can develop our latent "human potentialities"[23]—physical, mental, and spiritual—to the fullest. Only it can utilize its knowledge of humankind's goal to discover the best ways of reaching it, the ultimate example of how ends and means should determine each other.[24] If the individual's final end is not bodily death, it is not life's ultimate absurdity, as Huxley once thought. Utopia becomes not just the ideal place to live but also the best place to die. Unfortunately, the socio-political health of the good society, Huxley conceded, is always as fragile as the individual is perishable. Because of death—the insurmountable fact that individuals must pass on, sometimes as violently and unjustly as Dr. MacPhail does, and that admirable societies like Pala are prone to take-over from without and collapse from within—utopia, Huxley concluded, probably can never be.[25]

In sum, thanatopsis in the World State is ludicrous: it amounts to nothing more than rejoining the natural world as fertilizer. But the Palanese, who have raised the art of dying to a science, are encouraged to go back into the Clear Light of Suchness. Pala's emphasis on thanatopsis and the development of a thanatology in support of it distinguish Huxley's island not only from the brave new world but from utopias generally.

---

[1] Aldous Huxley, "Variations on a Baroque Tomb," *TV*, 167.

[2] The author of *Brave New World* described himself as a "Pyrrhonic aesthete" (*Brave New World* [London: Chatto & Windus, 1950], viii [*BNW*]), that is, an artist whose skepticism about life included the value of art itself; see note 2 in Chapter 1 above. In 1962, the author of *Island* was dying from cancer.

[3] Consult B. L. Chakoo's catalogue of the numerous deaths in Huxley's fiction (Chakoo, 45–46). If one were to factor in nineteen thousand Alphas who killed each other during the Cyprus experiment, "'[e]ight hundred Simple Lifers'" machine-gunned at Golders Green, and "'[t]wo thousand culture fans gassed'" during the British Museum Massacre (*BNW*, 183, 41), the death toll in *Brave New World* would skyrocket. According to Janko Andrijašević, Huxley's life and career "can be seen as a series of lessons in the art of dying" (Andrijašević, 195).

[4] Aldous Huxley, *Island* (New York: Bantam, 1963), 144. [*I*] That thanatology has indeed become a full-fledged science can be seen from the wide-ranging essays in Kutscher's *Principles of Thanatology*. Pala's methods for dealing with death and dying compare favorably with ideas and procedures in this volume.

[5] To musicalize fiction, Philip Quarles explains, the contrapuntist shows "several people falling in love, or dying, or praying in different ways—dissimilars solving the same problem" differently provide music-like variations on a theme (*PCP*, 408).

[6] In Bryant's "Thanatopsis," whoever dies supposedly joins thousands who died before: becoming one with the natural world, the deceased "lies down to pleasant dreams" (Pockell, 21).

[7] For Huxley's Vedantic concept of man's "final end," see *PP*, 38.

[8] According to David Moller, thanks to pain-killing drugs, modernized therapies, etc., "we all are very close indeed to the Huxleyan scenario of death-conditioning" because grief, suffering, and mourning have been greatly diminished (Moller, 113).

[9] See Laura Huxley, 238, and Meckier, "The Hippopotamian Question," *MSN*, 305–12.

[10] William Shakespeare, *Macbeth*, V, v, 22–23.

[11] Huxley never names John's victim but the "peach-bright, doll-beautiful face" surely belongs to Lenina. Nor does Huxley call John's assault murder. But as the Savage whips the "plump incarnation of turpitude writhing in the heather at his feet," his shouts of "'Kill it, kill it, kill it'" sound sufficiently murderous (*BNW*, 212).

[12] As Huxley's parody of H. G. Wells's Time Traveller, John is transported to A. F. 632 from primitive Malpais by rocket ship, his time machine.

[13] The argument that Lenina becomes "the Dionysian god figure and, therefore, […] the hero of the tragedy. With the expectation that she will be sacrificed […] so that the community can prosper" (Kirkpatrick, 107) is impossible to credit. Huxley was ridiculing fertility rituals.

[14] For the argument that John and the brave new world turn out to be "equally absurd at dealing with death's sting," see Meckier, "On D. H. Lawrence and Death," 189–90.

[15] Huxley discusses the philosophy of pointlessness in *EM*, 273.

[16] Will is also subjected to contrary views from Murugan, the Rani (his mother), and Mr. Bahu, Rendang's ambassador. In this counterpoint of lectures, Dr. MacPhail and his adherents win out.

[17] A. C. Grayling has called for "a medical sub-division of anesthesiology which might be called 'thanatology.'" Its thanatologists will help people to die (Grayling, 233).

[18] See Aldous's full-length account of Maria's last days and his ministrations in *L*, 734–37. Huxley included a typescript of the account along with a letter to Dr. Humphry Osmond for 21 February 1955. Inasmuch as he wanted the typescript returned, he may already have sensed literary possibilities.

[19] Huxley invites comparisons when Dr. MacPhail discounts "'ponderous, or portentous, or emphatic'" death scenes such as Little Nell's (*I*, 266).

[20] For more on Lakshmi's death scene, see Meckier, "On D. H. Lawrence and Death," 204–7.

[21] See Meckier, "Cancer in Utopia," *MSN*, 298–99.

[22] According to Sebastian Barnack's "minimum working hypothesis," there is a "Godhead or Ground" that human beings can "become actually identified with." Such unitive knowledge is "the final end and purpose of human existence" (*TMHS*, 289).

[23] For Huxley's ideas about developing "Latent Human Potentialities," see the chapter with this title in *HS*, 236–53.

[24] Understanding the appropriate relationship between ends and means, Huxley argued, was essential for behaving well; see *EM*, 9, and throughout.

[25] For the argument that "like Pala, [utopias] may not last, and like Pala they may be partial, but they are none the less real," see MacDonald, 111. In *Ape and Essence*, the post-nuclear dystopia Huxley located in southern California, no one is obsessed with thanatology, the apocalypse having already occurred. An annual slaughter of the innocents rids society of deformed children. Death is thus a gruesome purgative. See *AE*, 86–87.

Chapter Eight

Fabre, Wheeler, and the Mantises in *Island*

In the final chapter of *Island*, Will Farnaby ingests the *moksha*-medicine, "'the truth-and-beauty pill,'" and embarks upon a semi-mystical journey beyond life's counterpoints.[1] Unfortunately, the trip sours when he spies "'*Gongylus gongyloides*,'" the praying mantis. Farnaby observes a "pair of inch-long monsters, exquisitely grisly, in the act of coupling" (*I*, 273): "one of the nightmare machines, the female, had turned the small flat head, all mouth and bulging eyes, at the end of its long neck—had turned it and (dear God!) had begun to devour the head of the male machine" (273–74). After she finishes, a lizard—"a glow of sheer evil radiated from every grey-green scale of the creature's back" (272)—swallows the female mantis.

Having described the perfect place, Aldous Huxley allows the Palanese, an ideal community of enlightened pacifists, to be overrun by neighboring Rendang, a rogue state eager to trade Pala's oil revenues for weapons of mass destruction. Rendang annexes Pala the way the female mantis devours her mate. Just as the lizard feasts on the female mantis, the United Kingdom of Rendang and Pala seems fated to succumb to Western domination, Joe Aldehyde's Southeast Asia Petroleum in particular. Mantises and lizard "enact a play-within-the-play, a mini-drama that summarizes what happens not just in *Island* but throughout history" (Meckier, "Conradian Reminders in Aldous Huxley's *Island*," *MSN*, 277). Farnaby concludes that civilization amounts to cannibalism, "[e]ating and being eaten—forever" (274). *Island* ends with the zoologist contradicting the utopist.

Huxley did not invent his novel's most striking image; an account of a female mantis consuming her edible partner appears as chapter V of J. Henri Fabre's *Social Life in the Insect World* (1912). Illustrations of this grim spectacle stuck in Huxley's mind: the frontis-piece showing "The Mantis Devouring Her Mate" (No. 3 of five drawings on the page) and the first of three drawings on the page inserted between pages 90 and 91, "The Mantis Devouring the Male in the Act of Mating." Huxley knew Fabre's work. In *Point Counter Point*, Philip Quarles observes his wife interviewing the Vicar and Mrs. Truby and feels "like Fabre among the coleoptera" (*PCP*, 343).

After introducing a male into a female mantis's cage, Fabre writes:

> We are near the end of August. The male Mantis, a slender and elegant lover, judges the time to be propitious. He makes eyes at his powerful companion; he turns his head towards her; he bows his neck and raises his thorax. His little pointed face almost seems to wear an expression. For a long time he stands thus motionless,

> in contemplation of the desired one. The latter, as though indifferent, does not stir. Yet the lover has seized upon a sign of consent: a sign of which I do not know the secret. He approaches: suddenly he erects his wings, which are shaken with a convulsive tremor.
>
> This is his declaration. He throws himself timidly on the back of his corpulent companion; he clings to her desperately, and steadies himself. The prelude to the embrace is generally lengthy, and the embrace will sometimes last for five or six hours.
>
> Nothing worthy of note occurs during this time. Finally the two separate, but they are soon to be made one flesh in a much more intimate fashion. If the poor lover is loved by his mistress as the giver of fertility, she also loves him as the choicest game. During the day, or at the latest on the morrow, he is seized by his companion, who first gnaws through the back of his neck, according to use and wont, and then methodically devours him, mouthful by mouthful, leaving only the wings. Here we have no case of jealousy, but simply a depraved taste.
>
> I had the curiosity to wonder how a second male would be received by a newly fecundated female. The result of my inquiry was scandalous. The Mantis in only too many cases is never sated with embraces and conjugal feasts. After a rest, of variable duration, whether the eggs have been laid or not, a second male is welcomed and devoured like the first. A third succeeds him, does his duty, and affords yet another meal. A fourth suffers a like fate. In the course of two weeks I have seen the same Mantis treat seven husbands in this fashion. She admitted all to her embraces, and all paid for the nuptial ecstasy with their lives. (F, 82–3)

One marvels at Huxley's improvements. A female bluebeard whose appetite seems almost comic, Fabre's mantis consumes no fewer than seven males. Huxley settles for a single instance that is horrible without extenuation, as is Farnaby's revulsion. Fabre's mantis "gnaws through" her paramour's neck, "then methodically devours him, mouthful by mouthful, leaving only the wings." In Farnaby's graphic, step-by-step retelling, the mantis eats "methodically," echoing Fabre's passage, but "a purple eye" is chewed out "[f]irst," "then half the bluish face" (273). When the remainder of the head falls to the ground, the "female machine" snaps at her lover's "severed neck" and catches "the oozing stump."

Calling the mantises "a parody of Ares in the arms of Aphrodite" amounts to a mock-heroic classical allusion. It renders Huxley's pair more grotesque than Fabre's implicit reference to fairytale can make them. Nor does horror preclude poetic beauty, which, in fact, augments it. In an amoral world, Farnaby realizes, terrible events can acquire an aesthetic dimension: "[F]rom between the [lizard's] champing jaws, the edge of [the female mantis's] violet-tinted wing […] fluttered, like an orchid petal in the breeze."

But unlike the left-over wings of Fabre's male, the female's legs "waved wildly for a moment, then disappeared from view" in the lizard's "slitlike mouth" (*I*, 274), a thorough consummation.

Huxley telescopes Fabre's account. In the latter, the male's "embrace" of the female can last "five or six hours." The unlucky male "is seized by his companion" later in the day "or at the latest on the morrow." In *Island*, copulation and cannibalism occur simultaneously. Huxley accelerates as he sensationalizes: the female mantis dines while copulating and the male continues to copulate despite being dined upon. Cannibalism during copulation seems more "depraved," to use Fabre's word. Huxley fashions a truly horrific image for a marriage of heaven and hell in which the counterpoint of good versus evil, light against darkness, Pala and Rendang, is resolved in favour of the latter half of each opposition.

If one assumes Huxley read Fabre, he surely remembered the French entomologist's discovery that the grim scenario he had witnessed in his lab also plays out "in the thickets," only faster. "I once surprised a male, apparently in the performance of his vital functions, holding the female tightly embraced—but," Fabre exclaims, "he had no head, no neck, scarcely any thorax! The female, her head turned over her shoulder, was peacefully browsing on the remains of her lover! And the masculine remnant, firmly anchored, continued its duty!" (F, 84) Conceivably, Huxley created his powerful image by conflating this paragraph with those quoted above.

William Morton Wheeler published *Foibles of Insects and Men* the same year that Huxley's *Point Counter Point* appeared.[2] In a chapter devoted to interrelated food and sex interests on the part of ants, crickets, and spiders, the Harvard professor reprinted Fabre's four paragraphs on the copulating mantises as one long paragraph (see W, 160–61). If Huxley read Wheeler's book in 1928 or referred to it any time prior to 1962, he profited from its summary of L. O. Howard's account of the "even more ravenous gluttony" of the American mantis. When the female is confronted with a "male of Mantis carolina," she grasps him, bites off his left front tarsus, tibia, and femur. "Next she gnawed out his left eye," an ugly detail that Huxley incorporates. Only then does the male attempt to mate. By the time he enters her, the female has devoured his right front leg, his head, and most of his thorax. Although "the remnant of the male" continues to mate "for three hours," by "the next morning" the female has "entirely rid herself of her spouse, and nothing but his wings remained" (W, 161).

Huxley was familiar with Wheeler's writings. *Point Counter Point* is a modern satirical novel in which a cynical novelist like himself is composing a modern satirical novel into which he resolves to insert a zoologist. "Since reading Alverdes and Wheeler,"[3] Philip Quarles observes in his Notebook, "I have quite decided that my novelist must be an amateur zoologist. Or, better still, a professional zoologist who is writing a novel in his spare time. His approach will be strictly biological. He will be constantly passing from the termitary to the drawing room" (*PCP*, 438), disclosing parallels uncomplimentary to the latter. *Point Counter Point* is already as zoological as the novel Quarles contemplates. Lady Tantamount's party is presented as a "jungle of innumerable trees and dangling creepers"; her guests are "parrots" and "chattering monkeys" (69).[4] When her daughter, Lucy, opens her mouth to laugh, the novel's man-eating *femme fatale* reminds Quarles of the "sacred crocodiles" he saw "in the palace gardens at Jaipur" (22).[5]

Thirty-four years later, the utopist resurrected the stance he took in *Point Counter Point* in order to explain why utopia must always mean "no place"—not because mantises illustrate human foibles, the modern satirical zoologist tells the professional entomologists, but because entire societies behave no better than male-eating mantises and mantis-eating bloodsuckers. As Rendang devours Pala, one witnesses a startling eruption of the "amused, Pyrrhonic aesthete"[6] from within the Vedantic sage. The negative proposition that the strong eat the weak only to be consumed by the even stronger is on a par with the early Huxley's suspicion that humans have "free will in order to choose between insanity on the one hand and lunacy on the other" (*BNW*, viii), the only options John Savage has. Issued thirty years apart, comparably satiric statements lie at the heart of both *Brave New World* (1932) and *Island* (1962): one must choose insanity or lunacy, to eat or be eaten.

Huxley goes Fabre and Wheeler one better by introducing the lizard. With "tiny claws" that tickle Farnaby's instep as it darts across the floor after the mantises, the bloodsucker is more terrifying than Fabre's report of a second male being devoured, then a third and a fourth. When the eater is eaten, a cruel irony, Huxley establishes life's basic pattern, which is undiscoverable in Fabre and Wheeler. The "gay little dance of death" goes "on and on" beyond their ken (*I*, 274), with increases of magnitude, not just simple repetition. For Farnaby past, present, and future amount to "*Gongylus gongyloides* by millions and, in the midst of them, innumerable bloodsuckers" (*I*, 274).

Fabre often sounds like a modern Aesop.[7] He anthropomorphizes the male mantis into a cautious suitor—"slender," "elegant," awaiting the "propitious" moment; the polygamous female takes "husbands" (F, 82, 83). The Frenchman is scandalized to find her practising cannibalism, a failing supposedly peculiar to humans. "I have not yet recovered from my surprise," he confesses (84). For Fabre, the mantises' conjugal atrocities give "striking confirmation" to the aphorism that "Love [...] is stronger than death" (84). How much irony is intended? Similarly, Wheeler claims to "find increasing resemblance" between insects and his fellow men—"some insects seeming almost human and some humans behaving much like insects" (W, 3). Huxley's zoology is almost always ruthlessly satirical. The threat to civilization, he counters, lies in humankind's perennially insect-like behavior. Fabre admits that the female mantis's penchant for devouring her lover "during the act surpasses anything that the most morbid mind could imagine" (F, 84), but Huxley adds the lizard to worsen the situation.

Thanks to the mynah birds that patrol Pala like itinerant preachers, *Island* begins and ends with an attempt at positive zoology. In the opening chapter, one of the mynahs rouses the shipwrecked Farnaby with its cries of "'Attention'" and "'Here and now, boys'" (*I*, 7, 12), reminders that enlightenment is attainable at any given moment. In chapter XV, after Colonel Dipa's invading armored cars roar by, the birds come out again. Neither predators nor prey, they challenge Farnaby's pronouncement about eating lest one be eaten yet cannot annul it. The Huxley who posited participatory union with the Divine Ground as man's Final End could never forget what he learned from Fabre and Wheeler. Safe and solvent in sunny California, the utopist set up Pala in the tropics half a world away. Then the abiding zoological novelist in his artistic personality reached back to *Social Life in the Insect World* for a ghoulish image that portends the inevitable demise of the ideal society.

---

[1] Aldous Huxley, *Island* (London, 1962), 138. [*I*]

[2] *Point Counter Point* appeared in October 1928. Huxley mentions Wheeler in Chapter XXVI of thirty-seven chapters.

[3] In *Point Counter Point*, Philip Quarles reads several zoologists: the works of Charles Tate Regan, Wolfgang Köhler's *The Mentality of Apes* (1925), Friedrich Alverdes's *Social Life in the Animal World* (1927), and Wheeler's *Social Life Among the Insects* (1923).

[4] Sanford E. Marovitz considers Huxley's novels collectively an intellectual zoo. See Marovitz, "Aldous Huxley's Intellectual Zoo," 33–45. For Quarles's plight as an intellectual in a simian society, see Jerome Meckier, "Quarles Among the Monkeys," *MSN*, 71–87.

[5] Perhaps Huxley refrained from using the female mantis in *Point Counter Point* because he preferred depicting Lucy as a crocodile, a funnier, less ghastly comparison. On the other hand, Walter Bidlake is a "'rabbit'" to Lucy's "'cobra'" and the dung-beetle Spandrell clubs to death Webley the "'lion'" (*PCP*, 11, 32).

[6] Aldous Huxley, "Foreword," *Brave New World* (London, 1950), viii. [*BNW*] This is Huxley's description of the persona he adopted to write *Brave New World*. See "*Erewhon* to *Island*," chapter 1, note 2 above.

[7] Dr. C. V. Legros, Fabre's biographer, asserts that his "lucid, limpid, and captivating essays" resemble "the most delightful of fairytales" (Legros, 156). Admittedly, the brutal manners of some insects, "their cannibalism, and [...] amorality" by human standards were "a source of dismay" (Legros, 218, 230). In God's master plan, Fabre wondered, why did every species have "its appointed enemy, which lives upon it" only to become in turn "the prey" of another creature (Legros, 222)? But "'the Homer of the insects'" came to believe it was all for the best; he touted "the intimate connection of things, the universal harmony which so intimately allies all creatures"; in short, he sang of Nature's marvelous and incomprehensible wisdom, life's "poetry" (Legros, 281).

Works Consulted:

Adorno, Theodor W. "Aldous Huxley and Utopia." *Prisms*. Samuel and Sherry Weber, trans. London: Neville Spearman, n. d. Pp. 97–118. [Adorno]

Akkad, Omar El. *American War*. New York: Knopf, 2017.

Aldous Huxley Annual. Bernfried Nugel and Jerome Meckier, eds. Volumes 1–19. Münster: Lit Verlag, 2001–2019. [*AHA*]

Andrijašević, Janko. "Ars Moriendi: Huxley's Final Exam." Bernfried Nugel, Uwe Rasch, and Gerhard Wagner, eds. *Aldous Huxley, Man of Letters: Thinker, Critic and Artist*. Münster: Lit Verlag, 2007. Pp. 195–98. [Andrijašević]

Atwood, Margaret. *The Handmaid's Tale*. New York: Fawcet Crest, 1985. [*Handmaid*]

—. *The Testaments*. New York: Doubleday, 2019.

Baker, Robert S. *'Brave New World': History, Science, and Dystopia*. Boston: Twayne, 1990. [*BNWHSD*]

—. *The Dark Historic Page: Social Satire and Historicism in the Novels of Aldous Huxley, 1921–1939*. Madison: Univ. of Wisconsin Press, 1982. [*Dark Historic Page*]

—, and James Sexton, eds. *Aldous Huxley: Complete Essays*. Volume I*: 1920–1925*. Chicago: Ivan R. Dee, 2000. [*Complete Essays*, I]

—, and James Sexton, eds. *Aldous Huxley: Complete Essays*. Volume II: *1926–1929*. Chicago: Ivan R. Dee, 2000. [*Complete Essays*, II]

Baker-Smith, Dominic. "The World to Come: Aldous Huxley and the Utopian Parable." C. C. Barfoot, ed. *Aldous Huxley Between East and West*. Amsterdam: Rodopi, 2001. Pp. 101–12. [Baker-Smith]

Bedford, Sybille. *Aldous Huxley: A Biography*. Volume I: *1894–1939*. London: Chatto & Windus, 1973. [Bedford, I]

—. *Aldous Huxley: A Biography*. Volume II: *1939–1963*. London: Chatto & Windus, 1974. [Bedford, II]

Bellamy, Edward. *Looking Backward*. New York: Signet, 1960. [*LB*]

—. *The Religion of Solidarity*. Yellow Springs, OH: Antioch, 1940.

Berdiaeff, Nicolas. *The End of Our Time*. London: Sheed and Ward, 1933.

Bergonzi, Bernard. *The Early H. G. Wells: A Story of the Scientific Romances*. Toronto: Univ. of Toronto Press, 1961. [Bergonzi]

Booker, M. Keith, ed. *Dystopia*. Ipswich, MA: Salem Press, 2013. [*Dystopia*]

—. *The Dystopian Impulse in Modern Literature*. Westport, CT: Greenwood Press, 1994.

Boulle, Pierre. *La planète des singes* (*Planet of the Apes*). Paris: Juillard, 1963.

Bradbury, Ray. *Fahrenheit 451*. New York: Simon & Schuster, 2013. [Bradbury]

Bradshaw, David, ed. *Aldous Huxley Between the Wars: Essays and Letters.* Chicago: Ivan R. Dee, 1994.

—, ed. Aldous Huxley. *Brave New World.* London: Flamingo, 1994.

—, ed. *The Hidden Huxley.* London: Faber and Faber, 1994. [*The Hidden Huxley*]

—. "Huxley's Slump: Planning, Eugenics, and the 'Ultimate Need' of Stability." John Batchelor, ed. *The Art of Literary Biography.* Oxford: OUP, 1995. Pp. 151–72.

Breton, Rob. "Work Perfect: William Morris and the Gospel of Work." *Utopian Studies*, 13 (2002), 43–56. [Breton]

Breuer, Hans-Peter, and Daniel F. Howard, eds. Samuel Butler. *Erewhon.* Newark: Univ. of Delaware Press, 1981. [Breuer/Howard]

Broun, Bill. *Night of the Animals.* New York: Harper and Collins, 2016.

Bryant, William Cullen. "Thanatopsis." Leslie M. Pockell, ed. *100 Essential American Poems.* New York: St. Martin's Press, 2009. Pp. 18–21. ["Thanatopsis"]

Bulwer Lytton, Sir Edward. *Vril: The Power of the Coming Race.* Blauvelt, NY: Rudolf Steiner Publications, 1972.

Bunting, Charles T. "An Interview in New York With Anthony Burgess." *Studies in the Novel*, 5 (Winter, 1973), 504–29. [Bunting]

Burdekin, Katharine. *Swastika Night.* Introduction by Daphne Patai. New York: Feminist Press, 1985. [*Swastika Night*]

Burgess, Anthony. *A Clockwork Orange.* New York: Ballantine Books, 1963. [*CO*]

—. *Honey for the Bears.* New York: Ballantine Books, 1963. [*HB*]

—. *The Long Day Wanes.* New York: Ballantine Books, 1964.

—. *The Wanting Seed.* London: Heinemann, 1962.

Butler, Octavia B. *Parable of the Sower.* New York: Seven Stories Press, 1993.

Butler, Samuel. *Erewhon.* New York: Signet, 1961. [*E*]

Callenbach, Ernest. *Ecotopia.* New York: Bantam, 1975.

Campbell, Bruce F. *Ancient Wisdom Revived: A History of the Coming of the Theosophical Movement.* Berkeley: Univ. of California Press, 1980. [Campbell]

Chakoo, B. L. *Aldous Huxley and Eastern Wisdom.* Atlantic Highlands, NJ: Humanities Press, 1983. [Chakoo]

Claeys, Gregory. *Dystopia: A Natural History.* Oxford: OUP, 2017. [Claeys]

—. "The Origins of Dystopia: Wells, Huxley and Orwell." Gregory Claeys, ed. *Cambridge Companion to Utopian Literature.* Cambridge: CUP, 2010. Pp. 107–34.

Clark, Walter Houston. *Chemical Ecstasy: Psychedelic Drugs and Religion*. New York: Sheed and Ward, 1969.

Cline, Ernest. *Ready Player One*. New York: Broadway Books, 2011.

Combs, Robert. "The Eternal Now of *Brave New World*: Huxley, Joseph Campbell, and *The Perennial Philosophy*." David Garrett Izzo and Kim Kirkpatrick, eds. *Huxley's 'Brave New World': Essays*. Jefferson, NC: McFarland, 2008. Pp. 161–71. [Combs]

Cooke, Beth. *Human Nature in Utopia: Zamyatin's 'We.'* Evanston, IL: Northwestern UP, 2002. [*Human Nature in Utopia*]

Coverley, Merlin. *Utopia*. Harpenden, Herts: Oldcastle Books, 2010. [Coverley]

Cranston, Sylvia. *HPB: The Extraordinary Life and Influence of Helena Blavatsky, Founder of the Modern Theosophical Movement*. New York: G. P. Putnam's Sons, 1993. [Cranston]

Dalcher, Christina. *Vox*. New York: Berkley, 2018.

Dardis, Tom. *Some Time in the Sun*. New York: Charles Scribner's Sons, 1976. [Dardis]

Deery, June. *Aldous Huxley and the Mysticism of Science*. New York: St. Martin's Press, 1996. [Deery]

Deese, R. S. "Agnostic Gospels: Divining Nature in the Works of Julian and Aldous Huxley." *AHA*, 12/13 (2012/2013), 105–19. ["Agnostic Gospels"]

—. *We Are Amphibians: Julian and Aldous Huxley on the Future of Our Species*. Oakland, CA: Univ. of California Press, 2015. [Deese]

Dickens, Charles. *Bleak House*. Duane DeVries, ed. New York: Crowell Critical Library, 1971. [*BH*]

Dyson, George B. *Darwin Among the Machines*. Cambridge, MA: Perseus Books, 1997. [*Darwin Among the Machines*]

Eggers, Dave. *The Circle*. New York: Vintage, 2013.

Eliot, George. *Middlemarch*. Boston: Houghton Mifflin, 1956. [*Mm*]

Eliot, T. S. *The Sacred Wood*. New York: Barnes and Noble, 1960. First published 1920. [*The Sacred Wood*]

Elliot, Robert C. *The Shape of Utopia: Studies in a Literary Genre*. Chicago: Univ. of Chicago Press, 1970.

Fabre, J. Henri. *Social Life in the Insect World*. Bernard Miall, trans. New York: The Century Co., 1912. [F]

Fietz, Lothar. "Myth, History and Utopianism." *AHA*, 6 (2006), 135–47.

Firchow, Peter E. "Brave at Last: Huxley's Western and Eastern Utopias." *AHA*, 1 (2001), 157–74. ["Brave at Last"]

—. *The End of Utopia*. Lewisburg: Bucknell UP, 1984. [*End*]

—. *Modern Utopian Fictions.* Washington: Catholic Univ. of America Press, 2007. [*MUF*]

—. *Aldous Huxley: Satirist and Novelist.* Minneapolis: Univ. of Minnesota Press, 1972.

Ford, Henry. *My Life and Work.* New York: Garden City Publishing Co., 1923. [Ford]

Forster, E. M. *Howards End.* London: Edward Arnold, 1910.

—. *A Room with a View.* London: Penguin, 1958. First published 1908. [*Room*]

Fowler, Alastair. *Literary Names.* Oxford: OUP, 2012. [*Literary Names*]

Frost, Laura. *The Problem with Pleasure.* New York: Columbia UP, 2013.

Frye, Northrop. "Varieties of Literary Utopia." *Dedalus*, 94 (Spring, 1965), 323–47. ["Varieties of Literary Utopia"]

Fukuyama, Francis. *Our Posthuman Future.* New York: Farrar, Straus and Giroux, 2002. [Fukuyama]

Fussell, Paul. "E. M. Forster's Mrs. Moore: Some Suggestions." *Philological Quarterly*, 32 (October 1953), 388–95. [Fussell]

Gaynor, Frank, ed. *Dictionary of Mysticism.* London: Wildwood House, 1974. [Gaynor]

Gilman, Charlotte Perkins. *Herland.* Introduction by Anne J. Lane. New York: Pantheon Books, 1979. [Gilman]

Golding, William. *Lord of the Flies.* London: Faber & Faber, 1954.

Gomes, Michael. *Theosophy in the Nineteenth Century.* New York: Garland, 1994. [Gomes]

Gray, John. *Black Mass: Apocalyptic Religion and the Death of Utopia.* New York: Farrar, Straus and Giroux, 2007. [*Black Mass*]

Grayling, A. C. *The God Argument: The Case Against Religion and for Humanism.* New York: Bloomsbury, 2013. [Grayling]

Greenberg, Jonathan. *Modernism, Satire and the Novel.* Cambridge: Cambridge UP, 2011. [Greenberg]

—, and Nathan Waddell, eds. *'Brave New World': Contexts and Legacies.* London: Palgrave Macmillan, 2016.

Hall, Calvin S. *A Primer of Freudian Psychology.* New York: New American Library, 1954. [Hall]

Hammond, J. R. *H. G. Wells and Rebecca West.* New York: St. Martin's Press, 1991. [Hammond]

Harari, Yuval Noah. *Homo Deus: A Brief History of Tomorrow.* London: Harvill Secker, 2015.

Harrison, Vernon. *H. P. Blavatsky and the SPR.* Pasadena, CA: Theosophical UP, 1997. [Harrison]

Haynes, Roslynn D. *H. G. Wells: Discoverer of the Future*. New York: NYU Press, 1980. [Haynes]

Heard, Gerald. "The Poignant Prophet." *The Kenyon Review*, 27 (Winter 1965), 49–79. [Heard]

Higdon, David Leon. *Wandering Into 'Brave New World'*. Amsterdam: Rodopi, 2013. [Higdon]

Hillegas, Mark. *The Future as Nightmare: H. G. Wells and the Anti-Utopians*. New York: OUP, 1967. [Hillegas]

Hine, Robert V. *California Utopianism*. San Francisco: Boyd & Fraser, 1981. [Hine]

Hood, Bruce. *The Self-Illusion*. Oxford: OUP, 2012.

Horowitz, Michael, and Cynthia Palmer, eds. Aldous Huxley, *Moksha: Writings on Psychedelics and the Visionary Experience (1931–1963)*. New York: Stonehill Pub. Co., 1977.

Hutchings, William. "Structure & Design in a Soviet Dystopia: H. G. Wells, Constructivism, and Yevgeny Zamyatin's *We*." *Journal of Modern Literature*, 9 (1981/82), 81–102. [Hutchings]

Huxley, Aldous. *After Many a Summer*. London: Chatto & Windus, 1939. [*AMS*]

—. *America and the Future*. Austin, TX: Jenkins, 1970. [*America and the Future*]

—. *Ape and Essence*. London: Chatto & Windus, 1949. [*AE*]

—. *Beyond the Mexique Bay*. New York: Vintage, 1960. [*BMB*]

—. *Brave New World*. London: Chatto & Windus, 1950. With Huxley's 1946 "Foreword." [*BNW*] This is the text cited in Chapters 1, 2, 4, 5, 7 and 8.

—. *Brave New World*. London: Chatto & Windus, 1932. [*BNW*] This text is cited in Chapters 3 and 6.

—. *Brave New World & Brave New World Revisited*. Introduction by Martin Green. New York: Harper, 1965. [*BNWR*]

—. "Butler's *Erewhon*." *AHA*, 2 (2002), 49–54. ["Butler's *Erewhon*"]

—. *Crome Yellow*. London: Chatto & Windus, 1921. [*CY*]

—. *Do What You Will*. London: Chatto & Windus, 1929. [*DWW*]

—. *Ends and Means*. London: Chatto & Windus, 1937. [*EM*]

—. *The Human Situation*. London: Chatto & Windus, 1978. [*HS*]

—. *Island*. London: Chatto & Windus, 1962. [*I*] This is the text cited in Chapters 5, 6, 8.

—. *Island*. New York: Bantam, 1963. [*I*] This is the text for Chapters 1, 2, and 7.

—. *Music at Night*. London: Chatto & Windus, 1931. [*MN*]

—. *The Perennial Philosophy*. London: Chatto & Windus, 1946. [*PP*]

—. *Point Counter Point*. London: Chatto & Windus, 1928. [*PCP*]

—. *Proper Studies*. London: Chatto & Windus, 1927. [*PS*]
—. "A Second Visit to a Future World." *AHA*, 12/13 (2012/2013), 23–30. A lecture originally delivered in Italian and translated by Alessandro Maurini. ["Second"]
—. *Themes and Variations*. London: Chatto & Windus, 1950. [*TV*]
—. *Time Must Have a Stop*. London: Chatto & Windus, 1945. [*TMHS*]
—. "Utopias, Positive and Negative." James Sexton, ed. *AHA*, 1 (2001), 1–5. ["Utopias"]
Huxley, Julian. "Evolutionary Humanism as a Developed Religion." *Religion Without Revelation*. New York: Mentor, 1957. Pp. 181–212. ["EH"]
—. "Life Can Be Worth Living." *Man in the Modern World*. New York: Mentor, 1964. 145–51. ["Life"]
—. *Memories II*. London: Allen and Unwin, 1973. [*Memories II*]
—. "Philosophy in a World at War." *Man in the Modern World*. New York: Mentor, 1964. 152–68. ["PWW"]
—. "Religion as an Objective Problem." *Man in the Modern World*. New York: Mentor, 1964. Pp. 135–44. ["ROP"]
—. "Science, Natural and Social." *Man in the Modern World*. New York: Mentor, 1964. Pp. 117–34. ["SNS"]
Huxley, Laura. *This Timeless Moment*. New York: Farrar, Straus & Giroux, 1968. [Laura Huxley]
Izzo, David Garrett. "Introduction." David Garrett Izzo and Kim Kirkpatrick, eds. *Huxley's 'Brave New World': Essays*. Jefferson, NC: McFarland & Company, 2008. Pp. 1–9. [Izzo]
Jacobs, Naomi. "*Islandia:* Plotting Utopian Desire." *Utopian Studies*, 6 (1995), 75–89. [Jacobs]
Jacoby, Russell. *The End of Utopia: Politics and Culture in an Age of Apathy*. New York: Basic Books, 1999. [*The End of Utopia*]
James, P. D. *The Children of Men*. New York: Vintage, 2006.
James, Simon J. *Maps of Utopia: H. G. Wells, Modernity, and the End of Culture*. Oxford: OUP, 2012. [James]
Jayakar, Pupul. *Krishnamurti: A Biography*. London: Penguin, 1986. [Jayakar]
Jemisin, N. K. *The Obelisk Gate*. New York: Orbit, 2016.
Johnson, J. W., ed. *Utopian Literature: A Selection*. New York: Modern Library, 1968. [Johnson]
Kaku, Michio. *The Future of Humanity*. New York: Anchor Books, 2019.
Kateb, George. *Utopia and Its Enemies*. New York: Free Press, 1963. [Kateb]
Kermode, Frank. [Review of *Island*.] *Partisan Review*, 29 (Summer 1962), 472–73. [Kermode]
Kingsnorth, Paul. *Alexandria*. Minneapolis: Graywolf, 2020.

Kirkpatrick, Kim. "The Birth of Tragedy and the Dionysian Principle in *Brave New World*." David Garrett Izzo and Kim Kirkpatrick, eds. *Huxley's 'Brave New World': Essays*. Jefferson, NC: McFarland & Company, 2008. Pp. 107–16. [Kirkpatrick]

Knickerbocker, Kenneth L., ed. *The Selected Poetry of Robert Browning*. New York: Modern Library, 1951. [*The Selected Poetry of Robert Browning*]

Krishnamurti, Jiddu. *The First and Last Freedom*. Foreword by Aldous Huxley. London: Gollancz, 1954.

Kumar, Krishan, "Apocalypse, Millennium and Utopia Today." Malcolm Bull, ed. *Apocalypse Theory and the Ends of the World*. Oxford: Blackwell, 1995. Pp. 200–26. ["Apocalypse"]

—. *Utopia and Anti-Utopia in Modern Times*. Oxford: Basil Blackwell, 1987. [Kumar]

Kutscher, Austin H., Arthur C. Carr, and Lillian G. Kutscher, eds. *Principles of Thanatology*. New York: Columbia UP, 1987. [*Principles of Thanatology*]

Lawrence, D. H. *Lady Chatterley's Lover*. New York: Signet, 1959. [*LCL*]

—. *The Plumed Serpent*. New York: Vintage, 1954. [*Plumed*]

Legros, Dr. C. V. *Fabre, Poet of Science*. Bernard Miall, trans. New York: The Century Co., 1913. [Legros]

Leonard, Maurice. *Madame Blavatsky: Medium, Mystic and Magician*. London: Regency Press, 1976. [Leonard]

Levin, Ira. *This Perfect Day*. New York: Pegasus, 2010. First published 1970. [*Perfect Day*]

Levitas, Ruth. *Utopia as Method: The Imaginary Reconstitution of Society*. New York: Palgrave Macmillan, 2013. [Levitas]

Lewis, Sinclair. *Arrowsmith*. New York: Signet, 1998. [Lewis]

Little, Robert. "Daydream." *Time* (18 May 1942), 86. [Little]

Lorenzo, David. *Cities at the End of the World*. London: Bloomsbury, 2014. [Lorenzo]

Lukacs, Georg. "The Ideology of Modernism." John Oliver Perry, ed. *Realism in Our Time: Backgrounds to Modern Literature*. San Francisco: Chandler Publishing Co., 1968. Pp. 248–71. [Lukacs]

Lutyens, Mary. *Krishnamurti: The Open Door*. London: John Murray, 1988. [*The Open Door*]

—. *The Life and Death of Krishnamurti*. London: Brockwood Park, 2003. [*The Life and Death of Krishnamurti*]

MacDonald, Alex. "Choosing Utopia: An Existential Reading of Aldous Huxley's *Island*." *Utopian Studies*, 12 (2001), 103–13. [MacDonald]

Maddox, Brenda. *D. H. Lawrence: The Story of a Marriage*. New York: Simon & Schuster, 1994. [Maddox]

Mandel, Emily St. John. *Station Eleven*. New York: Vintage, 2015.

Marovitz, Sanford E. "Aldous Huxley's Intellectual Zoo." Robert E. Kuehn, ed. *Aldous Huxley: A Collection of Critical Essays*. Englewood Cliffs, NJ: Prentice Hall, 1974. Pp. 33–45. ["Aldous Huxley's Intellectual Zoo"]

—. "Aldous Huxley and the Nuclear Age: *Ape and Essence* in Context." Jerome Meckier, ed. *Critical Essays on Aldous Huxley*. New York: G. K. Hall, 1996. Pp. 195–207. ["Aldous Huxley and the Nuclear Age"]

—. "*Ape and Essence:* Fright or Fantasy?" Bernfried Nugel, ed. *Now More Than Ever: Proceedings of the Aldous Huxley Centenary Symposium Münster 1994*. Frankfurt am Main: Peter Lang, 1995. Pp. 159–73. ["*Ape and Essence*: Fright or Fantasy?"]

Maskelyne, John N. *The Fraud of Modern "Theosophy" Exposed: A Brief History of the Greatest Imposture Ever Perpetuated Under the Cloak of Religion*. London: Routledge & Sons, 1913. [Maskelyne]

Mathisen, Werner Christie. "The Underestimated Politics in Green Utopias: The Description of Politics in Huxley's *Island*, Le Guin's *The Dispossessed*, and Callenbach's *Ecotopia*." *Utopian Studies*, 12 (2001), 56–78. [Mathisen]

Matter, William W. "The Utopian Tradition and Aldous Huxley." *Science Fiction Studies*, 2.2 (July 1975), 146–51.

McGiveron, Rafeeq O. "'They Got Me a Long Time Ago': The Sympathetic Villain in *Nineteen Eighty-Four*, *Brave New World*, and *Fahrenheit 451*." M. Keith Booker, ed. *Dystopia*. Ipswich, MA: Salem Press, 2013. Pp. 125–41. [McGiveron]

Mead, Margaret. *Coming of Age in Samoa*. New York: Dell, 1970. [Mead]

Meade, Marion. *Madame Blavatsky: The Woman Behind the Myth*. New York: G. P. Putnam's Sons, 1980. [Meade]

Means, David. *Hystopia*. New York: Farrar, Straus and Giroux, 2016.

Meckier, Jerome. "Afterword" to "Brave New World: A Musical Comedy (1956)." *AHA*, 3 (2003), 105–28. ["Afterword"]

—. "Aldous Huxley and Utopia: Five Assertions." A. K. Tripathy, ed. *Aldous Huxley: East-West Centenary Essays*. New Delhi: Creative Books, 2008. Pp. 193–200.

—. *Aldous Huxley, from Poet to Mystic*. Berlin: Lit Verlag, 2011. [*PM*]

—. *Aldous Huxley: Modern Satirical Novelist of Ideas*. Peter E. Firchow and Bernfried Nugel, eds. Münster: Lit Verlag, 2006. [*MSN*]

—. *Aldous Huxley: Satire and Structure*. London: Chatto & Windus, 1969. [*SS*]

—. "Aldous Huxley's Americanization of the *Brave New World* Typescript." *Twentieth-Century Literature*, 48 (Winter 2002), 427–60. Repr. in Jerome Meckier. *Aldous Huxley: Modern Satirical Novelist of Ideas*. Peter E. Firchow and Bernfried Nugel, eds. Münster: Lit Verlag, 2006. Pp. 165–84. ["Americanization"]

—. "*Brave New World* and the Anthropologists: Primitivism in A. F. 632." *Alternative Futures*, 1 (Spring 1978), 51–69. Repr. in Jerome Meckier. *Aldous Huxley: Modern Satirical Novelist of Ideas*. Peter E. Firchow and Bernfried Nugel, eds. Münster: Lit Verlag, 2006. Pp. 225–40. ["*Brave New World* and the Anthropologists"]

—. "Cancer in Utopia: Positive and Negative Elements in Aldous Huxley's *Island*." *Dalhousie Review*, 54 (Winter 1974–75), 619–33. Repr. in Jerome Meckier. *Aldous Huxley: Modern Satirical Novelist of Ideas*. Peter E. Firchow and Bernfried Nugel, eds. Münster: Lit Verlag, 2006. Pp. 293–304. ["Cancer in Utopia"]

—. "Coming of Age in Pala: The Primitivism of *Brave New World* Reconsidered in Huxley's *Island*." *Alternative Futures*, 1 (Summer 1978), 68–90. Repr. in Jerome Meckier. *Aldous Huxley: Modern Satirical Novelist of Ideas*. Peter E. Firchow and Bernfried Nugel, eds. Münster: Lit Verlag, 2006. Pp. 259–73. ["Coming of Age in Pala"]

—. "Conradian Reminders in Aldous Huxley's *Island*: Will Farnaby's *Moksha*-Medicine Experience and 'The Essential Horror.'" *Studies in the Novel*, 35 (Spring 2003), 44–67. Repr. in Jerome Meckier. *Aldous Huxley: Modern Satirical Novelist of Ideas*. Peter E. Firchow and Bernfried Nugel, eds. Münster: Lit Verlag, 2006. Pp. 274–92. ["Conradian Reminders in Aldous Huxley's *Island*"]

—, ed. *Critical Essays on Aldous Huxley*. New York: G. K. Hall, 1996. [*Critical Essays*]

—. "Debunking Our Ford: *My Life and Work* and *Brave New World*." *South Atlantic Quarterly*, 78.4 (Autumn 1979), 448–59. Repr. in Jerome Meckier. *Aldous Huxley: Modern Satirical Novelist of Ideas*. Peter E. Firchow and Bernfried Nugel, eds. Münster: Lit Verlag, 2006. Pp. 121–30. ["Debunking Our Ford"]

—. "Dickens and the Dystopian Novel: From *Hard Times* to *Lady Chatterley*." R. G. Collins, ed. *The Novel and Its Changing Form*. Manitoba: Univ. of Manitoba Press, 1972. Pp. 51–58. ["Dickens and the Dystopian Novel"]

—. "Enemies of Utopia: Young Krishnamurti and Madame Blavatsky in Aldous Huxley's *Island*." *AHA*, 10/11 (2010/2011), 299–315.

—. "Fabre, Wheeler, and the Mantises in Aldous Huxley's *Island*." *Notes and Queries*, 55 (December 2008), 515–18.

—. "Four Notes on Huxley's *Brave New World*." *AHA*, 17/18 (2017/2018), 209–24.

—. "Golf in *Brave New World*." Hermann J. Real and Peter E. Firchow, eds. *The Perennial Satirist: Essays in Honour of Bernfried Nugel*. Münster: Lit Verlag, 2005. Pp. 235–43.

—. *Hidden Rivalries in Victorian Fiction: Dickens, Realism, and Revaluation*. Lexington: UP of Kentucky, 1987. [*Hidden Rivalries*]

—. "The Hippopotomian Question: A Note on Huxley's Unfinished Novel." *Modern Fiction Studies*, 16 (Winter 1970–71), 505–14. Repr. in Jerome Meckier. *Aldous Huxley: Modern Satirical Novelist of Ideas*. Peter E. Firchow and Bernfried Nugel, eds. Münster: Lit Verlag, 2006. Pp. 305–12. ["The Hippopotamian Question"]

—. "'My Hypothetical Islanders': The Role of Islands in *Brave New World* and *Island*." *AHA*, 12/13 (2012/2013), 319–40.

—. "On D. H. Lawrence and Death, Especially Matricide: *Sons and Lovers*, *Brave New World*, and Aldous Huxley's Later Novels." *AHA*, 7 (2007), 185–221. ["On D. H. Lawrence and Death"]

—. "Onomastic Satire: Names and Naming in *Brave New World*." *AHA*, 3 (2003), 155–203. Repr. in Jerome Meckier. *Aldous Huxley: Modern Satirical Novelist of Ideas*. Peter E. Firchow and Bernfried Nugel, eds. Münster: Lit Verlag, 2006. Pp. 185–224. ["Onomastic Satire"]

—. "Our Ford, Our Freud and the Behaviorist Conspiracy in Huxley's *Brave New World*." *Thalia*, 1 (Spring 1978), 35–59. Repr. in Jerome Meckier. *Aldous Huxley: Modern Satirical Novelist of Ideas*. Peter E. Firchow and Bernfried Nugel, eds. Münster: Lit Verlag, 2006. Pp. 131–64. ["Our Ford, Our Freud"]

—. "Poetry in the Future, the Future of Poetry: *Brave New World*." *Aldous Huxley, from Poet to Mystic*. Berlin: Lit Verlag, 2011. Pp. 229–290. ["Poetry in the Future"]

—. "Quarles Among the Monkeys: Huxley's Zoological Novels." *Modern Language Review*, 68 (1973), 268–82. Repr. in Jerome Meckier. *Aldous Huxley: Modern Satirical Novelist of Ideas*. Peter E. Firchow and Bernfried Nugel, eds. Münster: Lit Verlag, 2006. Pp. 71–87. ["Quarles Among the Monkeys"]

—. "Satire as 'Discriminative Sympathy': Form and Format in *Lady Chatterley's Lover*." *AHA*, 6 (2006), 104–34. ["Satire as 'Discriminative Sympathy'"]

—. "Thanatopsis/Thanatology in Aldous Huxley's *Brave New World* and *Island*." *AHA*, 16 (2016), 237–50.

—. "What the Books Were Always Saying." *ANQ*, 9 (Spring 1996), 39–48. ["What the Books Were Always Saying"]

Milner, Andrew, "Need It All End in Tears? The Problem of Ending in Four Classic Dystopias." M. Keith Booker, ed. *Dystopia*. Ipswich, MA: Salem Press, 2013. Pp. 109–24. [Milner]

Moller, David Wendell. *Confronting Death*. New York: OUP, 1996. [Moller]

More, Sir Thomas. *Utopia*. Introduction by Richard Marius. London: Dent, 1994. [*U*].

Morris, Robert K. *The Consolations of Ambiguity*. Columbia, MO: Univ. of Missouri Press, 1971. [Morris]

Morris, William. *News from Nowhere and Other Writings*. Clive Wilmer, ed. London: Penguin, 1993. [*NN*]

Mumford, Lewis. *The Story of Utopias*. New York, 1962. [Mumford]

Murray, Nicholas. *Aldous Huxley: A Biography*. New York: St. Martin's Press, 2002. [Murray]

Nethercot, Arthur H. *The Last Four Lives of Annie Besant*. Chicago: Univ. of Chicago Press, 1963. [Nethercot]

Nozick, Robert. "A Framework for Utopia." *Anarchy, State, and Utopia*. Oxford: Basil Blackwell, 1974. Pp. 297–334.

Nugel, Bernfried. "Aldous Huxley's 'Introduction of a Brand New Personage' in *Island:* Abdul Pierre Bahu, Ambassador of Rendang." C. C. Barfoot, ed. *Aldous Huxley Between East and West*. Amsterdam: Rodopi, 2001. Pp. 131–50. ["Aldous Huxley's 'Introduction of a Brand New Personage'"]

—. "Aldous Huxley's Revisions of the Old Raja's *Notes on What's What* in His Final Typescript of *Island*." *AHA*, 9 (2009), 69–90. ["Huxley's Revisions"]

—. "The Anti-Utopian Drift in Aldous Huxley's Literary Utopias." *AHA*, 19 (2019), 267–80.

—. "How Reliable Are the Current Huxley Texts?" *AHA*, 1 (2001), 211–25.

—, ed. *Now More Than Ever: Proceedings of the Aldous Huxley Centenary Symposium Münster 1994*. Frankfurt am Main: Peter Lang, 1995. [*NMTE*]

Orwell, George. *Animal Farm*. New York: Signet, 1961. [*AF*]

—. *In Front of Your Nose 1945–1950*. Volume Four of *The Collected Essays, Journalism and Letters*. S. Orwell and I. Angus, eds. London: Penguin, 1970. [*In Front of Your Nose*]

—. *1984*. New York: Signet, 1951. [O]

Parkes, Adam. "'A Small Caste of Experts': Aristocracy, Intelligence, and Stupidity in Huxley's Interwar Fiction." *AHA*, 16 (2016), 173–90. [Parkes]

Parrinder, Patrick. "Utopia and Meta-Utopia." *Shadows of the Future: H. G. Wells, Science Fiction, and Prophecy*. Syracuse, NY: Syracuse UP, 1995. Pp. 96–112.

—. *Utopian Literature and Science*. New York: Palgrave Macmillan, 2015.

Pepper, George, ed. *Golf in America: The First One Hundred Years*. New York: Abrams, 1988. [Pepper]

Pockell, Leslie M., ed. *100 Essential American Poems*. New York: St. Martin's Press, 2009. [Pockell]

Poller, Jake. "'God-Intoxicated': An Essay on Jiddu Krishnamurti and His Relationship with Aldous Huxley." *AHA*, 9 (2009), 115–32. [Poller]

Postman, Neil. *Amusing Ourselves to Death*. New York: Penguin, 1985. [Postman]

Powell, Lawrence C. "'All That Is Poetic in Life': Austin Wright's *Islandia*." *Wilson Library Bulletin*, 31 (1957), 701–5. [Powell]

Raby, Peter. *Samuel Butler: A Biography*. Iowa City: Univ. of Iowa Press, 1991. [Raby]

Rand, Ayn. *Atlas Shrugged*. New York: Random House, 1957.

Real, Hermann J., and Peter E. Firchow, eds. *The Perennial Satirist: Essays in Honour of Bernfried Nugel*. Münster: Lit Verlag, 2005. [*The Perennial Satirist*]

Reece, Erik. *Utopia Drive*. New York: Farrar, Straus and Giroux, 2016. [Reece]

Rees, Martin. *On the Future Prospects for Humanity*. Princeton: Princeton UP, 2018. [*On the Future Prospects for Humanity*]

Ricks, Thomas E. *Churchill and Orwell: The Fight for Freedom*. New York: Penguin Press, 2017. [Ricks]

Rimmer, Robert H. *The Harrad Experiment*. Los Angeles: Sherbourne Press, 1966.

Robertson, Michael. *The Last Utopians: Four Late Nineteenth-Century Visionaries and Their Legacy*. Princeton: Princeton UP, 2018. [Robertson]

Robinson, Kim Stanley. *The Ministry for the Future*. New York: Orbit, 2020.

Rohmann, Gerd. "Matters of Life and Death: Montaigne and Buddhist Philosophy in Huxley's Analysis of the American Dream and His Personal Experience." *AHA*, 9 (2009), 91–102. [Rohmann]

Rolph, C. H., ed. *The Trial of Lady Chatterley*. Harmondsworth, Middlesex: Penguin, 1961. [Rolph]

Ruse, Michael. *Darwinism as Religion*. New York: OUP, 2017. [*Darwinism as Religion*]

Sansal, Boualem. *2084: The End of the World*. Alison Anderson, trans. New York: Europa Editions, 2015. [*2084*]

Sawyer, Dana. *Aldous Huxley: A Biography*. New York: Crossroad Publishing Co., 2002. [Sawyer]

—. "What Kind of Mystic Was Aldous Huxley Anyway?" *AHA*, 2 (2002), 207–18.

Schmidt, Michael. *The Novel: A Biography*. Cambridge: Harvard UP, 2014. [Schmidt]

Sexton, James. "Aldous Huxley's Bokanovsky." *Science Fiction Studies*, 16 (1989), 85–89. ["Aldous Huxley's Bokanovsky"]

—. "*Brave New World* and the Rationalization of Industry." Jerome Meckier, ed. *Critical Essays on Aldous Huxley*. New York: G. K. Hall, 1996. Pp. 88–102. ["*Brave New World* and the Rationalization of Industry"]

Shadurski, Maxim. "'Flowers and Landscapes Were the Only Attractions Here': The England of Wells and Morris in Aldous Huxley's Interpretation." Emelyne Godfrey, ed. *Utopias and Dystopias in the Fiction of H. G. Wells and William Morris*. London: Palgrave Macmillan, 2016. Pp. 223–40.

Shakespeare, William. *Julius Caesar*. T. S. Dorsch, ed. The Arden Shakespeare. London: Methuen, 1955. [*Julius Caesar*]

—. *Macbeth*. Kenneth Muir, ed. The Arden Shakespeare. London: Methuen, 1951. [*Macbeth*]

—. *The Tempest*. Frank Kermode, ed. The Arden Shakespeare. London: Methuen, 1954. [*The Tempest*]

Shelley, Mary. *The Last Man*. Peterborough, Ont.: Broadview, 1996.

Shklar, Judith. *After Utopia: The Decline of Political Faith*. Princeton: Princeton UP, 1957. [Shklar]

Sieger, Heike. "Traces of *Erewhon* in *Brave New World*: Samuel Butler's and Aldous Huxley's Utopias and Their Sequels." *AHA*, 15 (2015), 243–72. [Sieger]

Skinner, B. F. *Walden Two*. New York: Macmillan, 1948.

Smil, Vaclav. *Creating the Twentieth Century: Technical Innovations of 1867–1914 and Their Lasting Impact*. Oxford: OUP, 2005. [Smil]

Smith, Grover, ed. *Letters of Aldous Huxley*. London: Chatto & Windus, 1969. [*L*]

Smith, Huston. *Cleansing the Doors of Perception*. New York: Penguin Putman, 2000.

Smith, Marcus. "The Wall of Blackness: A Psychological Approach to *1984*." *Modern Fiction Studies*, 14 (Winter 1968–69), 423–33. ["The Wall of Blackness"]

Stapledon, Olaf. *Last and First Men*. London: Methuen, 1930.

Strauss, Harold. "A Novel That Casts a Spell." *New York Times Book Review* (12 April 1942), 1, 22. [Strauss]

Swift, Jonathan. *Gulliver's Travels*. Robert A. Greenberg, ed. New York: Norton, 1961. [*GT*]

Szczekalla, Michael. "The Scottish Enlightenment and Buddhism: Huxley's Vision of Hybridity in *Island*." Bernfried Nugel, Uwe Rasch, and Gerhard Wagner, eds. *Aldous Huxley, Man of Letters: Thinker, Critic and Artist*. Münster: Lit Verlag, 2007. Pp. 153–66. [Szczekalla]

Tally, Robert T. Jr. *Utopia in the Age of Globalization*. New York: Palgrave Macmillan, 2013. [Tally]

Taylor, Anne. *Annie Besant: A Biography*. Oxford: OUP, 1992. [*Annie Besant*]

Taylor, Frederick Winslow. *The Principles of Scientific Management*. Mineola, NY: Dover, 1998. First published 1911. [Taylor]

Teilhard de Chardin, Pierre. *The Phenomenon of Man*. Introduction by Julian Huxley. New York: Harper and Brothers, 1959. [*Phenomenon*]

Thompson, F. M. L. *The Rise of Respectable Society: A Social History of Victorian Britain 1830–1900*. Cambridge: Harvard UP, 1988. [Thompson]

Tolkin, Michael. *NK3*. New York: Atlantic Monthly Press, 2017.

Tripathy, A. K., ed. *Aldous Huxley: East-West Centenary Essays*. New Delhi: Creative Books, 2008. [*Aldous Huxley: East-West Centenary Essays*]

Vonnegut, Kurt. *Player Piano*. New York: Avon Library, 1967. [V]

Vyleta, Dan. *Smoke*. New York: Anchor Books, 2017.

Waddell, Nathan. *Modernist Nowheres: Politics and Utopia in Early Modernist Writing*. New York: Palgrave Macmillan, 2012. [Waddell]

Washington, Peter. *Madame Blavatsky's Baboon: Theosophy and the Emergence of the Western Guru*. London: Secker and Warburg, 1993. [Washington]

Watt, Donald. "Vision and Symbol in Aldous Huxley's *Island*." *Twentieth-Century Literature*, 14 (October 1968), 149–60. [Watt]

Waugh, Evelyn. *Love Among the Ruins*. London: Chapman and Hall, 1953.

Webster's College Dictionary. New York: Random House, 1992. [*Webster's College Dictionary*]

Wells, H. G. *A Modern Utopia*. Introduction by Mark R. Hillegas. Lincoln: Univ. of Nebraska Press, 1967. [*AMU*]

—. *Anticipations of the Reaction of Mechanical and Scientific Progress Upon Human Life and Thought*. Mineola, NY: Dover, 1999. First published 1902. [*Anticipations*]

—. *The First Men in the Moon*. New York: Airmont, 1965. [*FMM*]

—. *Men Like Gods*. New York: Macmillan, 1923.

—. *The Time Machine*. New York: Airmont, 1964. [*TM*]

Wheeler, William Morton. *Foibles of Insects and Men*. New York: Knopf, 1928. [W]

Wickes, George, and Ray Frazer. "Aldous Huxley." *Writers at Work, Second Series: The Paris Review Interviews.* New York: Viking, 1965. Pp. 193–214. [W/F]

Wind, Herbert Warren. *The Story of American Golf.* New York, 1975. [Wind]

Winters, Ben H. *Underground Airlines.* New York: Mulholland Books, 2017.

Wittbecker, Alan. *Eutopian Essays: Towards the Creation of Good Places through Thought Experiments and Ecological Designs.* Sarasota, FL: SynGeo, 2004; [1]1970.

Woodcock, George. *The Crystal Spirit: A Study of George Orwell.* New York: Minerva Press, 1966. [Woodcock]

Worthen, John. *D. H. Lawrence: The Life of an Outsider.* London: Allen Lane, 2005. [Worthen]

Wright, Austin Tappan. *Islandia.* New York: Signet, 1958. [Wright]

Yucknavitch, Linda. *The Book of Joan.* New York: Harper Collins, 2017.

Zamiatin, Yevgeny. *We.* Mira Ginsburg, trans. New York: Bantam, 1972. [Z]

Index of Names, Titles and Terms

actualization 30, 33, 52, 91, 144
Adorno, Theodor W. 90, 207
Aesop 204
Alverdes, Friedrich 204
ambiguity 18, 38, 217
anti-utopia, see utopia
apocalyptic 7, 31, 33, 84, 88, 92, 180, 182, 199, 210, 213
art of dying, see thanatology
Atwood, Margaret
  The Handmaid's Tale 85, 207
  The Testaments 85, 207
awareness 3, 46, 53, 70, 74, 77, 89, 91, 99, 103, 106, 143–44, 176–77, 191, 193–94, 196–97
Beatific Vision 49, 60, 63, 116, 193, 195–96
beauty 36, 57, 88, 115, 126, 174, 176, 193, 201–2
Beethoven, Ludwig van 114
behaviorism 20, 22, 37, 86, 136, 147, 189, 216
Belief 70
Bellamy, Edward 92, 165, 187
  Looking Backward 31, 34, 44, 66, 86, 93, 95, 121, 130, 207
Benoit, Hubert (psychiatrist) 185
Berdiaeff, Nicolas 118
  The End of Our Time 24, 207
Besant, Annie 171–86, 217, 220
Bible, The 58, 64, 137, 140, 146
bildungsroman 23, 121
biology 2, 7, 11, 16–19, 24, 37, 46, 49–51, 65, 88–91, 95, 127, 133, 141–56, 171, 173, 188, 204
Biran, Maine de 88, 95, 137, 141
birth control 42, 123, 136, 139, 157, 167
Blavatsky, Helena Petrovna 3, 171–86, 209–16
bokanovskification 43, 126–27
Boulle, Pierre
  Planet of the Apes 207
Bradbury, Ray 92, 207
Broun, Bill 208
Browning, Robert 136, 147, 213
Bryant, William Cullen 187, 208
Buddhism 9, 69, 74, 115, 138, 167–86, 191, 218
Bulwer Lytton, Edward 185
  The Power of the Coming Race 32, 208
Burdekin, Katherine 208
Burgess, Anthony 81
  A Clockwork Orange 64, 67–71, 97, 110–14, 208
  Honey for the Bears 90
  The Long Day Wanes 120, 208
  The Wanting Seed 121, 208
Butler, Octavia B. 86, 208
Butler, Samuel 1, 5, 13, 35, 89, 99, 168, 208, 218, 219
  Erewhon 1–2, 5, 13–23, 28, 33–38, 45–55, 62–64, 68–71, 75, 81–99, 107, 117–18, 165, 168, 205, 208, 211, 219
  Erewhon Revisited 13, 91
Cabet, Etienne 86, 91
Callenbach, Ernest
  Ecotopia 208
Campanella, Tommaso 86
cancer 60, 71, 102, 115–17, 121, 163, 192–99, 215
caste (system) 9, 10–11, 19, 32, 39, 42–44, 49, 53, 66, 72, 76, 79, 123, 127, 140, 142, 153, 188, 218

Chaplin, Charles 120, 128
Chardin, Pierre Teilhard de 183, 220
Chopin, Frédéric 152–53
Christ 68, 74, 106, 113, 138, 169, 185–86
Christianity 64, 79, 113, 138
Clear Light 17, 60, 194–95, 198
Cline, Ernest
Ready Player One 209
cloning 73, 127–28
Cloud of Unknowing, The 85
Cobb, Ty (Tyrus Raymond) 128
collectivism 64–69, 74, 108
communism 35, 90, 166
compassion 17, 49, 78
conditioning 3, 6, 9–11, 19, 22, 32, 37–40, 43, 49, 53–54, 59, 64, 68, 77–78, 91, 94–96, 101, 110–11, 123–26, 129, 133, 136, 138–39, 142, 145–46, 149, 154, 189–93, 197–98
consciousness (mind) 16, 45–51, 57, 99, 102, 104, 128–29, 142–44, 147, 151, 156–57, 182, 184, 192, 196
consumerism 19, 36, 41, 64, 73, 80, 97, 125–26, 129, 140, 162, 171, 188
control, see totalitarianism
cure (cure scene, healing) 2, 60–63, 71, 81, 99–121, 163, 176, 192–93, 196
Dao, see Tao
Darwin, Charles 5, 13, 15, 17–19, 34–37, 54, 69, 75, 86–87, 91, 95, 136, 144, 146, 148, 165, 209, 219
The Origin of Species 34, 95
Dickens, Charles 94, 119, 209, 215–16
dictatorship, see totalitarianism
dissident 52, 58, 60, 67–68, 71, 98, 108, 113, 118, 168
distractions, diversions 3, 41–43, 93, 123–30, 154, 188, 190, 193
Divine Ground 46–47, 171, 181, 195, 205
dogma 70, 108
dystopia, see utopia
ecology 49, 59, 85, 174, 197, 221
Eden 30, 61–62, 75, 82, 84, 196
education 9, 39, 43–44, 53, 69, 91, 115, 149, 153, 175, 197
efficiency 11, 39, 54–57, 64–65, 71, 80, 94, 95
Eggers, Dave
The Circle 209
Einstein, Albert 7
Eliot, George
Middlemarch 94
Eliot, T. S. 107, 120, 138
enlightenment (spiritual/mystical) 2, 9, 16–17, 21–23, 30, 46–47, 52–53, 59–61, 70, 77–78, 82, 88–89, 104, 106, 108, 115–16, 128, 136, 143–44, 156–57, 163, 166, 174–91, 196–97, 201, 205
Enlightenment, The 87, 220
entropy 46, 61, 76, 96
escapism 6, 20, 55, 165
eugenics 10, 37, 51, 76, 152–53, 167, 197, 208
Eve figure 62, 63
evolution 6, 13–24, 31, 35–37, 45–48, 54, 86, 91, 93, 102, 119, 142–44, 147–48, 165, 212
Fabre, J. Henri 3, 201–16
Fairbanks, Douglas 128
faith 3, 28, 51, 64, 70, 86, 94, 142, 219
film script 28–29
Ford, Henry
My Life and Work 64–70, 140, 191, 210, 215

Forster, E. M. 129, 184, 210
Howards End 134, 210
Fourier, Joseph 91
freedom 20, 41, 55, 79–84, 97–103, 108, 111, 117, 121, 138, 158, 162
Freud, Sigmund 6, 20, 72–73, 78–79, 90, 135–36, 138, 140, 147, 149–50, 155, 157, 168, 179, 186, 210, 216
Fukuyama, Francis 87, 210
Fulke Greville, 1st Baron Brooke 101, 196
Gibson, William 86
Gilman, Charlotte Perkins
Herland 81, 97, 210
Godhead 8, 46, 52, 60, 89, 144, 181, 199
Golding, William
Lord of the Flies 210
Good Being 70
good doing 70
Gray, John
Black Mass 88, 210
happiness 6, 16, 20, 32, 39, 41, 46, 51, 55, 57–58, 75, 81–86, 97–101, 108, 117, 121, 125, 130, 138, 142, 146, 158, 164, 176, 189, 190
Heard, Gerald 92, 178, 185–86, 211
Helmholtz, Hermann von 47, 136
heresy 46, 52, 60–62, 67, 71, 76, 78, 81, 83, 98, 104–9, 118, 124, 141, 151
Hinduism, see also Vedanta 180
Atman 8, 9, 180–81, 186, 191
Brahman 8, 9, 52, 144, 180–81, 186, 191
Brahmin 177
Hitler, Adolf 21, 24–26, 76, 96, 109
Hollywood 28–29, 92, 177, 179
Homer 206
Howard, Leonard Ossian (entomologist) 203
human nature 6–7, 37, 54, 69–70, 86, 88, 97, 102, 111, 166–67, 209
human potentialities 78, 87, 143
Huxley, Aldous
"A Second Visit to a Future World" 5, 25–26, 32, 88, 212
After Many a Summer 98, 184, 211
Antic Hay 184
Ape and Essence 2, 5, 7–8, 11, 21, 23, 26, 28–34, 53, 58, 60, 62–63, 71–72, 84, 90, 94, 104–7, 118, 120, 182, 199, 211, 214
Beyond the Mexique Bay 157, 211
Brave New World 1–105, 113–68, 178, 180, 182, 184, 187–91, 194–99, 204–19
Brave New World Revisited 10, 12, 21, 25–26, 32, 39, 50, 57, 89–92, 95, 98, 166, 211
Crome Yellow 53, 183, 211
Do What You Will 211
Ends and Means 94, 199, 211
Eyeless in Gaza 184
"Foreword" to *Brave New World* 8–13, 32, 52, 56, 76, 83–84, 89, 120, 131, 134, 144, 167, 178, 205, 211
Island 1–34, 46–55, 59–64, 69–96, 101, 115–21, 130, 149–205, 211–220
"Latent Human Potentialities" 52, 77, 94, 144, 199
Letters of Aldous Huxley 11–12, 48, 88, 94, 160, 166–68, 179–80, 185–86, 199, 219
Music at Night 45, 54, 74, 94, 212
Paris Review interview 6, 9, 162, 168, 221

Point Counter Point 9, 95, 119, 184–85, 197–98, 201, 203–5, 212
Proper Studies 6, 152–53, 186, 212
The Human Situation 52, 77–78, 144, 186, 199, 211
The Perennial Philosophy 9, 63, 89, 115, 144, 167, 171, 180–81, 186, 197–98, 209, 212
Themes and Variations 131, 188, 198, 212
Those Barren Leaves 95, 186
Time Must Have a Stop 23, 181, 199, 212
Huxley, Julian 141–44, 147–48, 220
Man in the Modern World 148, 212
Memories II 147, 212
Religion Without Revelation 147, 212
Huxley, Laura 212
Huxley, T. H. 91, 144
Huxley, Trevenen 184
hypnopaedia 11, 25, 40, 43, 83, 91, 114, 135, 140, 189
industrialism 14, 18, 31, 33, 37, 45, 48–51, 65–66, 71, 79, 86, 90, 94, 102–5, 117, 121, 130, 136, 138, 152, 155, 160–63, 171, 183, 196, 219
Industrial Revolution 37, 45
irony 30, 36, 39–41, 64, 71, 81–82, 89, 91, 99, 101–6, 109–19, 128–37, 146, 168, 204–5
Isherwood, Christopher 173, 179, 185
islands (utopian, exile) 2, 10, 14, 27–30, 35, 54, 61, 75, 84, 86, 89, 100–1, 116–19, 145–72, 191, 198, 216
James, William 58, 137
Joyce, James 51–52, 94, 146, 210
Jung, C. G. 183
Keynes, John Maynard 129
kinetic, see also utopia 16, 19, 22, 44, 47
kingdom of God 63
knowledge 16, 46, 51, 142
unitive knowledge 8, 52, 60, 89, 144, 171, 181, 199
Koot Hoomi 33, 172, 175–77, 180, 182, 185
Krishnamurti, Jiddu 3, 69, 171–86, 212–18
Landor, Walter Savage 147
Laozi (Lao-tze) 186
Lawrence, D. H. 8, 23, 31, 34, 47, 62, 94, 102–7, 119, 155, 157, 160, 166, 178, 180, 184–85, 191, 195, 199, 213–21
Lady Chatterley's Lover 31, 62–63, 71, 102–12, 119–21, 134, 213, 215, 217, 219
The Plumed Serpent 77, 213
Le Guin, Ursula 86, 214
Leadbeater, Charles Webster 171–84
leisure 12, 35, 40, 79, 123, 127–30
Lenin, Vladimir 37, 56, 95, 134
Levin, Ira 213
liberation 41, 80, 89, 110, 193, 197
life sciences 7, 11, 17, 24, 37, 88
love
attachment 9, 35, 41, 63, 77, 106–8, 110, 126, 134, 146, 149, 184, 190, 201–5
promiscuity 42, 47, 50, 62, 76–79, 94, 136, 145–46
romantic love 63
sex 6–9, 12, 22, 37, 41–44, 47, 50, 54, 62–63, 76, 79–80, 90, 94, 103, 105–7, 110, 112, 123–24, 127, 130, 136, 143, 162, 167, 173, 183, 203

yoga of love 9, 115
Lukacs, Georg 51–52, 213
Maine de Biran, François-Pierre-Gonthier 88, 95, 137, 141
malcontent 60–61, 71, 75, 84, 103, 108, 118, 124, 145, 151, 156, 167
man's Final End (unitive know–ledge) 8, 22–23, 47, 52, 78, 89, 144, 171, 181, 205
Manicheism 70, 163
Marx, Karl 34, 72, 80, 182
Capital 95
The Communist Manifesto 34
mass production 17, 19, 54, 65, 96–97, 127, 149–50
Mead, Margaret 167, 182, 214
Milton, John 162
misfit 60–61, 101, 124, 134, 136, 144, 151–54
moksha 9, 49, 53, 63, 115, 117, 157, 174, 184, 193, 196, 201, 211, 215
Mond, Sir Alfred 6–7, 23, 136, 155
More, Sir Thomas 1, 6, 10, 14–18, 22, 26–27, 30, 33, 86, 88–91, 113, 121, 139, 149, 157, 159, 164–169, 181, 214, 217
Morrell, Lady Ottoline 183
Morris, William
News from Nowhere 32–37, 44, 93, 95, 121, 217
The Earthly Paradise 96
motherhood 19, 42, 44, 110, 135, 140
Mowat, C. L. 66
Mussolini, Benito 21, 24, 136
Myers, F.W.H. 179, 186
mysticism 45, 72, 143, 169, 182–83, 209–10
mystic 3, 16, 42, 46–47, 61, 89, 101–2, 120, 156, 163, 177, 181, 195, 213–16, 219
mystical 42, 106, 143–44, 177, 180, 193, 197, 201
proto-mystical 16
Nabokov, Vladimir 146
Newman, Cardinal John Henry 88, 95, 137, 141
no place 3, 17–18, 22, 24, 37, 73, 87, 91, 158, 165–68, 204
novel of ideas 6, 23, 53, 115, 149, 156, 193
nowhere 5–6, 10, 13, 17, 33, 86, 95, 165–66, 220
Oneida Community 91, 167, 182
oneness 43, 53, 116, 196
Orwell, George 1, 10–13, 21, 24–26, 31, 34, 47–55, 61–71, 74, 76–86, 90, 92, 96–97, 106–10, 114, 118, 121, 131, 166, 209, 217–18, 221
Animal Farm 31, 71, 76, 217
Nineteen Eighty-Four 7, 10–13, 25–26, 31, 44, 47, 50–52, 62, 65–67, 71, 74, 76, 79–87, 95–96, 106–13, 119–20, 166, 214
over-organization 25, 44, 56, 57
over-population 57, 139
pacifism 172, 185, 201
parody 5–6, 10–12, 16, 20, 24, 27–28, 32, 35–36, 38, 41, 56–57, 62–65, 96, 100, 107, 119, 121, 123, 128, 130, 135, 139, 155, 157–159, 163, 165–66, 199, 202
Pavlov, Ivan Petrovich 6, 20, 40, 49, 72, 78, 113, 135, 138, 155, 189, 191
Peacock, Thomas Love 168
perennial philosophy 9, 63, 89, 115, 144, 167, 171, 180–81, 186, 197, 209, 212
perfect place 1, 3, 6, 9, 10, 17, 22, 26, 29–30, 52, 60, 63, 78, 88–89, 149, 167, 172, 201
perfect society 53, 70, 75, 165–66, 193

perfection 1, 6, 20, 22, 24, 34, 40, 47, 68–71, 88–91, 97, 111–12, 157, 187
physiology 7, 11–12, 17, 24, 37, 49–50, 58, 76, 105, 135, 149, 188–89
Plato 1, 15, 27, 86
  The Republic 23, 27, 56, 130, 165
posthuman 87, 210
prediction 6, 10, 11, 14–21, 24–27, 30–33, 36–37, 41, 44–45, 48, 51, 55, 64, 74, 87–88, 92, 103, 128, 152, 159, 164, 166
pre-Raphaelite 35–36
progress 9, 18, 28, 32, 45, 49, 56–57, 66, 80, 115, 129, 142, 148, 162, 166, 174
promiscuity, see love
Pyrrho of Elis (Pyrrhonism) 5, 8, 10, 21, 49, 67, 89, 141, 198, 204
Rand, Ayn 85
rational state 53
rationalization 44–45, 94, 127
Regan, Charles Tate 205
religion 19, 24, 41, 45, 54, 75, 85, 97–98, 124, 128–31, 141–42, 147–48, 167, 171–83, 207, 209–14, 219
reproduction 19, 45, 48, 64, 96
revaluation 1, 5–6, 33, 38, 50, 55, 81, 85, 97
revolution 7, 12, 18, 24, 33, 35, 47, 71, 75–76, 86, 96
Rimmer, Robert 218
roman à clef 171, 183
ruler, ruling class 11, 44, 47, 55–62, 74, 116, 147, 152, 171
Russian Revolution 31, 76
Ruth, Babe 128
samurai 6, 8, 23, 31, 42, 44, 56–66, 96, 157, 167
Sansal, Boualem 219
satire 1, 3, 5–8, 13, 20, 23, 31, 38–39, 43, 58, 69, 81, 90–98, 111, 120, 128, 133–36, 140–49, 153, 166, 171–73, 177–82, 203–7, 210, 215–217
scepticism 21, 51, 67, 74, 89, 198
science 3, 6–8, 11, 13, 16, 19, 21, 24–25, 31, 35–38, 42, 44–50, 54–60, 65–66, 72, 76, 81, 86, 94, 112, 119, 130, 135, 142, 144, 148, 157, 165–68, 174, 179–83, 187, 198, 207–14, 218–20
sex, see love
sexuality 6, 8, 9, 12, 22, 37, 42–44, 47, 50, 62–63, 71, 76, 79–80, 90, 94, 103–7, 110, 112, 123–24, 127, 130, 136, 143, 162, 173, 183, 203
Shakespeare, William 85, 93, 100, 119, 137, 149, 199, 219
  Hamlet 149
  Macbeth 199, 219
  Romeo and Juliet 47, 136–37, 141
  The Tempest 59, 129, 137, 147, 162, 168, 196, 219
Shaw, George Bernard 135, 147
Sheldon, William 49, 182
  The Varieties of Temperament 49
Shelley, Mary 121
Shelley, Percy Bysshe
  Adonais 106
  Epipsychidion 106
Skinner, B. F. 86, 219
socialism 34–35, 45, 96
soma 9, 11, 34, 40, 42, 49, 53, 79, 100, 113, 121–24, 131, 140, 145, 147, 149, 154, 190, 195
Spanish Civil War 76
spirituality 9, 16–17, 21–24, 30, 33, 46–47, 52–54, 63, 69, 72, 74, 77–78, 84, 88, 103, 106, 115–16, 137, 143–44, 155–57, 162, 164, 171–178, 180, 183, 191, 197